Principles of Buddhist Tantra

This work is a textual based discourse on the *Cittaviśuddhi-prakaraṇa* of Āryadeva, a seminal text which describes the principle and philosophy of Buddhist Tantra. The dispute on the question of Tāntric meditative practices having any philosophical foundation or whether those practices have been introduced into the ethico-religious praxis of various religious traditions as a later introduction is a continuing discussion. In this work, it is trying to prove that the introduction of Tantra into Mādhyamika philosophy is a natural development and it is proved beyond doubt by reviewing an important work in the Buddhist tradition written by Āryadeva, the *Cittaviśuddhi-prakaraṇa*. The unique dialectical method introduced and used by the Mādhyamikas to interpret their philosophy and the conception of *śūnyatā* is the guiding principle in this regard. Mādhyamika envisages that the conception of *śūnyatā* can be interpreted as the proper understanding of the insubstantial nature of object of the world (*dharma-nairātmya*) and the insubstantial nature of the subjective self which perceives such objects of the world (*pudgala-nairātmya*). The dialectics advanced by the Mādhyamika is efficient in deconstructing the substantiality of the phenomenal world of objects, but that is effectively possible only after reconstructing the notion of a substantive self using Tāntric spiritual practices. The *śūnyatā* as the conception of *dharma-nairātmya* is achieved through reconstructing the substantive notion of the phenomenal world using dialectics, while it as the conception of *pudgala-nairātmya* is achieved using Tāntric spiritual practices.

Mathew Varghese is a scholar of the early Mādhyamika philosophy of Nāgārjuna and Āryadeva, and shows a keen interest in researching their philosophical method and interpreting it in contemporary perspective. He received his PhD from the University of Madras. He has published a number of articles on Buddhist philosophy and now working on a book about the scope and conception of negative arguments in Philosophy based on pre-Buddhistic and Hellenic thought which would be published soon. He is now teaching at Aoyama Gakuin University, Tokyo, Japan.

Principles of Buddhist Tantra

A Discourse on Cittaviśuddhi-prakaraṇa of Āryadeva

Mathew Varghese

Munshiram Manoharlal Publishers Pvt. Ltd..

ISBN 978–81–215–1190–2
First published 2008

Published by
Munshiram Manoharlal Publishers Pvt. Ltd.
Post Box 5715, 54 Rani Jhansi Road, New Delhi 110 055, India

www.mrmlbooks.com

To the memory of my mother
Thrisiamma Varghese
who taught me to see with
an equanimous vision

Contents

Foreword

THIS BOOK is based on a textual study of a Buddhist treatise entitled *Cittaviśuddhi-prakaraṇa* of Āryadeva probably in the third century AD. It is not a direct commentary on the text but it tries to find the philosophical foundations of the discussion of the text based on the position of the early Mādhyamika philosophy of Nāgārjuna and his disciple Āryadeva.

In this book, Dr Varghese gives an excellent insight into the principle of Buddhist Tantra on the basis of Mādhyamika philosophy. I find that the arguments given here are worth noticing as it tries to discern the conception of *śūnyatā* from the perspective of Mādhyamika philosophy and connect it with the conception of Tāntric meditative practices.

Āryadeva's *Cittaviśuddhi-prakaraṇa* is very specific in saying that the conception of *śūnyatā* is complete only with a proper understanding of the inessentialness of the phenomenal world and possible only by the deconstruction of the notion of a self that eternally exists as the basis of human experience. This deconstruction is effectively possible only through Tāntric form of meditation.

It is both, an honour and a pleasure for me to introduce this revised version of Dr Varghese's Doctoral dissertation to the world of specialists in Buddhism, especially the Mādhyamika philosophy, and to the larger world of students of philosophy.

SENGAKU MAYEDA

The Eastern Institute, Tokyo
August 17, 2004

Preface

A STUDY OF THIS KIND on the text of *Cittaviśuddhi-prakraṇa* by Āryadeva might confuse many scholars as the historicity of Āryadeva—the Mādhyamika and Āryadeva—the Tāntric, is an unsettled dispute yet. However, here the attempt is not to settle this dispute on the historicity of these personalities, but to review the principles of Buddhist Tantra from the perspective of early Mādhyamika philosophy of Nāgārjuna and Āryadeva. Another aspect taken here for serious consideration is a proper understanding of the conception of *śūnyatā*, introduced and interpreted by the early Mādhyamika and its innate relationship with the Tāntric spiritual practices. It is argued that a proper understanding of the conception of *śūnyatā* is possible only with the proper conception of *pudgala-nairātmya*, and that is possible only with a proper appreciation of Tāntric systems. The Tāntric spiritual practices are the only structure that provides a foundation to deconstruct the conception of an eternal self-existing as a foundation of human personality. The psycho-experiential method of the Tāntric is the only method that can restructure the human mind from all its conceptual formulations; in that respect it is one of the most efficient spiritual techniques evolved. In essence, the discussion is based on remaking of man without losing his fundamental nature and it is possible only by reconstructing the psycho-physical personality. Man confronts challenges always as a part of his life and he should find suitable philosophical and spiritual methods to redress his worries and concerns. There is nothing called an idealistic situation where man lives without any worries. In this work, we see the methods that can be used to make possible the life bearable for man, where he should be ready to remake himself by appeasing his own dispositions (*upāya*) using his natural wisdom (*prajñā*).

The discussions here are following the method of reviewing the discussions of the text based on various aspects of Mādhyamika philosophy on the basis of a contemporary understanding of it. In some places, the discussion may be repetitive but it is to understand the same discussion of the text from different perspectives. The primary aim is to supplement ideas to support the concept of the remaking of man without losing his fundamental values.

The main purpose of this work is to understand and interpret the philosophical content of the text and put it in perspective with the philosophical position of the early Mādhyamikas. An English translation of the Sanskrit original edited from the Tibetan text is given in the appendix. I must admit that the translation is deficient in many respects, though care is taken to find the most appropriate meaning by taking into account the variant reading, etc. The emphasis of discussion is to get a rational understanding of the notion of *dharma-nairātmya* elucidated in the canonical texts and the explanation given by early Mādhyamikas. The explanations relating to *pudgala-nairātmya* is basically from the *Cittaviśuddhi-prakaraṇa,* together with the Tāntric spiritual practices.

I wish to take the opportunity to acknowledge the help and support I had received during the research and preparation of the manuscript, without which I would not be in a position to complete this work. In the course of my research by the way of identifying the text, translating it, reading, and correcting the manuscript, this work is immensely indebted to Prof. Godabarisha Mishra of the Department of Philosophy, Madras University. I also wish to express my gratitude to the Department of Philosophy, Madras University where I completed my PhD: the head of the Department Prof. R. Gopalakrishnan, Prof. S. Paneerselvam, and the staff and fellow scholars for having given me valuable support and assistance. I am also thankful to the staff members and authorities of the Adyar Library and Research Centre for extending necessary help to find the published original manuscript and the edited version of the text *Cittaviśuddhi-prakaraṇa*, and also for finding me many other books.

I express my sincere gratitude to Prof. M. Narasimhachary, who went through the text and gave valuable suggestions. I am extremely grateful to Dr K. Sasidhar for his friendship together with supports such as, patiently reading through the manuscript, giving valuable suggestions, and supporting me with his insightful discussion; to Prof. N.S. Sadagopan, for correcting the translation of the text; to Dr R. Narasimhan, Lecturer in Sanskrit, University of Madras, for helping me prepare the first translation of the text; to Mr R. Mukundan for typing the Sanskrit manuscript.

I wish to acknowledge and extend special thanks to Mr Noriyasu Kaitoku for his generous financial support and special interest shown to this work. My grateful thanks is due to Prof. Frank J. Hoffman, West Chester University, USA, for the financial support in offering the "Hoffman Shield" and the interest he has shown in the progress of this work.

I am extremely thankful to my wife Dr Yuko Fukuroi, for actively involving with this work and for extending unstinting encouragement and support all throughout the research. To my parents, Mrs Thrisiamma and Mr Varghese Mittathani for allowing me to live the way I preferred, teaching me to appreciate human values and companionship, and inculcating the basics of free thinking, I am deeply indebted. I wish to extend a word of thanks to Prof. Koichi Furusaka of Osaka, Prof. Kazushige Sagawa, Mrs Sachiko, and Mr Mizugu Fukuroi of Tokyo for all the help and support they have given me.

My extreme gratitude to Prof. Sengaku Mayeda, Prof. Emeritus, University of Tokyo, and Executive Director of Eastern Institute, Tokyo, for all his encouragement and support to me and also for writing an appropriate Foreword.

I am grateful to Ashok Jain and the late Devendra Jain of Munshiram Manoharlal Publishers, for showing interest in this work and publishing it.

MATHEW VARGHESE

Tokyo
December 2007

Chapter One

Introduction

The philosophical significance of Tāntric meditative practices is an unsettled intellectual dispute in modern times, particularly with academic thinkers. A large section of these thinkers consider that these methods of practices have no philosophical basis and condemn them as congested with dogmatic beliefs, uncharacteristic techniques and practices without any logical basis; as a result, these systems suffered serious negligence from the academic community, resulting to lack of research and study. A small section of scholars, who supported the importance of these systems, did so because of the revolutionary ideas associated with it and they used those arguments as a contradiction to conventional viewpoints. Another curious section of people, not a part of the academics, who support the Tāntric tradition and literature, are drawn towards it because of its association with sexo-yogic practices as a part of its spiritual discipline. This enthusiasm is due to various socio-cultural developments taking place in the recent times in particular from the western civilisations where there is a new quest for finding innovative connotations to life.

In the eastern civilisations, the Tāntric systems formulate a part of their religious tradition and the interests to these systems are based on religiosity rather than intellectual interest. We can see that in the religio-ethical practices of almost all the countries where Hinduism or Buddhism is in practice, the effective application of Tāntric spiritual practices is a part of their religion. Such religious enthusiasm, mostly, would not encourage intellectual enquiry into the fundamentals of such practices because, in religious beliefs, the fundamentals are accepted as unquestionable principles. My interest in this subject is basically instigated by intellectual curiosity based on academic concern: Why such practices which are considered as dogmatic and uncharacteristic are part of great religious tradition for centuries? What is the fundamental logic and epistemic foundations of such systems? And also the revolutionary ideas connected with those practices which are meant for redeeming a human being from the sufferings and perils of life. Tantra may be an aspect of philosophy that calls for the remaking of man as a constant and continuing process and not an end of a process. It can be argued that human existence in this world has a predistinct beginning or a predistinct end, however, a continuing process and remaking of man is absolutely necessary to make one's life bearable from such extents of confusions and sufferings that one confronts in life in this world.

This study is based on a treatise (*prakaraṇa*) by a Mādhyamika philosopher, Āryadeva whose works follow academic form of writing, and he is a direct student of Nāgārjuna, the founder of the Mādhyamika school of Buddhism. The text *Cittaviśuddhi-prakaraṇa* of Āryadeva is an influential work about the principles of Buddhist Tantra presented with convincing evidences and acceptable reasoning.

The divergent curiosity and enthusiasm to this rather controversial aspect of classical Indian philosophy, because of various reasons, has encouraged a lot of published works to support and criticise it on the basis of personal preference and choices. The lack of dependable information on this system is a very severe problem. As a result, the real problems a modern scholar faces in researching on this subject are quite a few: These systems are out of active practice today and their application in the religious practices is evident only extraneously or in the form of symbolic rituals; secondly, majority of the available texts on Tantra were written centuries ago and the subjects of discussions are dependent on various aspects relating to the time of their narration; thirdly, the texts which were written at the time when these practices were a part of religious trainings mainly described the methods of practices and various such aspects relating to that effect. Another important problem with regard to research is that most of the Tāntric texts are congested with such descriptions of practical application, such as descriptions of Mantras, various methods of propitiating deities, nature of *yantras,* and types of *maṇḍala* employed for ritualistic practices. There are not many authentic texts which describe the principles and the philosophy supporting those practices. In this context where modern studies are inconclusive, and traditional works are deficient in expression, this study reviews a text which is authentic and exclusively describes the principles and philosophy of Tantra.

The principal discussion of the text is about the methods to achieve the important spiritual purpose of cleansing the mind (*cittaviśuddhi*) from all misconceptions that have deluded and would have the potential to delude the mind. The text explains the reasons and the ways through which the human mind get deluded with the phenomenal world. It explains the existence and nature of duality in all forms and envisages that the conception of duality is the working of a deluded mind that can be discerned only at a stage of delusion. The conception of duality is essential for us to understand the phenomenal world. The idea of reality and unreality, existence and non-existence, truth and falsity, originates out of these delusions and when these delusions are removed the causes of confusion also become extinct. In order to understand this unique phenomenon about the world, Mādhyamika introduces the conception of *śūnyatā*. The Mādhyamika method of understanding the meaning of *śūnyatā* is different, in many ways, compared to the conception of the term in other schools of thought or even its etymological meaning.

The Mādhyamika understanding of this unique concept of *śūnyatā* is based on two important aspects. One is on the rejection of the essence of the objective phenomenal world (*dharma-nairātmya*) that has the capacity to form a foundation for discerning apparent world on the basis of objective realities. The second position of the Mādhyamikas in understanding the phenomenal world is the rejection of the substantiation of the subjective entity as the substratum of the existent world, which is called *pudgala-nairātmya*, the essencelessness of the self. Mādhyamika does not accept *śūnyatā* as theory but uses this conception to reveal the essencelessness of both subjective and objective entities. The substitutability of the objective world is a question of philosophical dispute. Most of the philosophical systems across the world agree to this fact that the phenomenal world is not ultimately real, but a few schools allude that the apparent world is a representation of a more certain and deterministic world, and the idea of such a world is permanent and eternal. The phenomena are susceptible for change but the ideas about the objects of phenomena are eternal. In the same manner, a few of systems of philosophy accept the eternal existence of a subjective entity as the substratum and conclude that it exists eternally irrespective of the changes in the phenomenal world such as birth and death. With regard to the existence in this world, both subjective state and objective world should exist, as both are mutually dependent and the rejection of either of the entity creates severe epistemological problems. It is only through the subjective self that the objective world can be understood, and the objective world is the necessary adjunct for the subjective self to realise itself. The mutual dependence of both the entities can be found in the development of views originating with the substantiation of the formulation of theories based on either of these entities. Mādhyamika does not decline the existence of both the entities as far as the conventional life in the world is concerned, but declines to accept the eternal existence of both the entities and discards the authority of information from both the entities as suitable for formulating any theory. This aspect is expressed otherwise by the Mādhyamikas with the conception of *śūnyatā*. Mādhyamikas' conception of *śūnyatā* should not be confused with the conception of *śūnyatā* of other schools of philosophy, where, in some cases, perfect voidness as a theory is introduced.

Another way of introducing the discussion in the text is that one can understand through various methods the insubstantiality of the existent world, but such understandings presuppose the existence of a substantive subjective entity. This creates the problem of theorisations. To avoid this problem, which is one of the greatest problems of philosophy, Mādhyamikas introduce the conception of *pudgala-nairātmya* and suggests that through the Tāntric spiritual practices one is able to deconstruct the notion of substantive self that is experiencing the phenomenal world.

In the Indian context, the Vedic systems formulated theories substantiating the eternal existence of Brahman, which can be defined as the subjective stage and a transformed subjective objectivity. On the contrary, the theories formulated by the Ucchedavādins (nihilists) refuted the existence of such eternal entity as the substratum of the phenomenal world and envisaged emptiness (*śūnyatā*) as a theoretical position; thus they rejected the authority of the Vedas. Buddhist philosophy categorically rejects these two views and introduces a conception of the world in the perspective of *śūnyatā,* which according to the Mādhyamikas is the perfect understanding of the essencelessness of objective phenomenal world and the essencelessness of the subjective self that perceives the phenomenal world.

The basic philosophical tenets of the Mādhyamika School can be traced to two discourses of the Buddha, the *Kātyāyanāvadānasūtra* and the *Dharmacakrapravartanasūtra*.[1] The *Kātyāyanāvadānasūtra*, discusses the philosophical aspect of the Buddha's teaching, which essentially attempts to find the middle path between the absolutistic position of Indian philosophy, the eternity propounded in the Upaniṣads, and the dialectically opposite, extreme nihilism proposed by the Ucchedavādins (materialists). On the other hand, the *Dharmacakrapravartanasūtra* describes the practical interpretation of the middle position, as it seeks to find the middle of the extremes of self-indulgence and self-mortification, and it enunciates the noble Eightfold path that leads to emancipation.[2] Though the teachings of both the texts are accepted by most of the schools of Buddhism irrespective of their rivalries, the Mādhyamika school of Mahāyāna Buddhism accepted the teachings of these discourses in its entirety. Following the dialectics of the *Kātyāyanāvadānasūtra*, Mādhyamikas refuse to accept the extremes of views with regard to the experienced phenomenal world and observe that the phenomena are dependent and, thus, insubstantial.

The Mādhyamika not only accepts the real nature of phenomena as insubstantial, dependent and void, but also rejects the substantialists' position of either eternity or nihilism. Instead of taking a stand on extreme positions in explaining the apparent phenomenal world, the Mādhyamika school seeks to find a middle position in understanding them. It does not seek to find a theory to substantiate them. Furthermore, the middle position rejects both the views with regard to substantiation of the phenomena (*dharma*) of the experiential world and of the experiencing self (*pudgala*), because any position on either of the entities leads to extreme viewpoints. In other words, this school tries to prove the essencelessness of apparent phenomena (*dharma-nairātmya*) and the essencelessness of the experiencing self (*pudgala-nairātmya*). But it does not reject the ontological entity, the experienced objects, the *dharmadhātu*.

The dialectical understanding about the cognised objects is considered as conventionally true and theoretically insubstantial, yet the experiential understanding is possible only with the attainment of *cittaviśuddhi*. A mind, which is deluded by misconception, is not able to experience both the insubstantial nature of the phenomena (*dharma-nairātmya*) and the insubstantial nature of the self (*pudgala-nairātmya*).

Here, it is argued that there is a need to find a middle position in spiritual practices for achieving purification of mind (*cittaviśuddhi*). The text *Cittaviśuddhi-prakaraṇa* takes us to various methods of practices employed for this purpose and a rational understanding of methods adopted based on the position of Mādhyamika philosophy.

The philosophical school founded by Nāgārjuna and Āryadeva can be termed as the early Mādhyamika school.[3] This is because there is a qualitative difference between the discourses of philosophical problems introduced by them and the interpretation given by the latter commentators to those discourses.[4] The *Cittaviśuddhi-prakaraṇa* follows the philosophical tradition of early Mādhyamikas. The text conducts the analysis in two ways, first by describing the doctrinal position of the Mādhyamika philosophy and, secondly, by dealing with the issue of indoctrination of the philosophy into well-defined spiritual techniques. The text also employs a systematic way of discussing the philosophical position of the Mādhyamika. It proves the *dharma-nairātmya* of the experienced objects and the *pudgala-nairātmya* of the knowing self, which is a very important feature of this text. Unlike other works of the Mādhyamikas, *Cittavśuddhi-prakaraṇa* focuses on the effect of the experienced phenomena on the mind and suggests means of redemption from the effects of the dichotomous conceptualisations (*vikalpas*) arising from the objects of experience. To find the real meaning of the subject of discussion in the text, we should look into the concept of *pudgala-nairātmya* and *dharma-nairātmya* from Buddhist perspective. The thesis tries to critically expound the philosophical and practical implications of the early Mādhyamika thinking in the backdrop of Buddhism as a whole. It also tries to analyse the spiritual practices presented in the text to attain enlightenment as a state of mind, which Buddhist terminology describes as *Bodhicitta*.

1.1 The Knowing-Subject and the Objects Known

The Mādhyamika tradition declines to accept an eternally existing subjective entity or a substantive objective entity as the substratum of the existent world of phenomena. The notion of eternity with regard to subjective and objective realities originates from the misconception of a substantive substratum in human personality that transmigrates.[5] In the tradition of Buddhism, human personality is represented by five aggregates (*pañca-skandha*) which are imper-manent, non-eternal, and liable to change. Apart from the conception of aggregates, there is no conceivable self that exists in human personality. In brief, the aggregates are impermanent and dependent, and, thus, there is no permanent self that can transmigrate.[6] Regarding the objects of experience,[7] Buddhism, in general, is concerned about the object conceived and the object cognised as the important aspects of the experience with the objective world. It is least concerned with object *per se* or the things in themselves.[8] In short, Buddhist philosophy is not concerned about the subjective subject or the objective object; instead, it accepts the five aggregates and the conceived and cognised objects as important aspects of human experience of the phenomenal world.

The Buddhist method of understanding the psycho-physical personality, which experiences the phenomenal world does not entail the acceptance of a mysterious self, operating with human personality. However, the explanation given to such an experience of the notion of an eternal entity is the individuating activity, which is due to the dispositional tendencies of the psycho-physical personality. According to Kalupahana,

> Dispositions can function in an extreme way in creating an excessively egoistic tendency culminating in the belief in a permanently existing eternal self (*Ātman*). This may be one reason the Buddha considered the self as a mere 'lump of dispositions.'[9]

The ignorance of an unenlightened person, working together with strong feeling and dispositions, can develop cravings for the conceived objects of experience and configure them as real and eternal.[10] But the cognised objects, verifiable with the help of six senses, are less problematic than the conceived objects of experience. We will see later that the objections of the Mādhyamikas are against the extremes of positions regarding the psycho-physical personality and the object of experience as the substratum of the apparent phenomena. Both the essentialist's notion of permanent *Ātman* and the substantialist's notion of the intrinsic nature of elements of the experienced objective world are rejected. We shall also see that the Mādhyamika rejects not only these two positions but also all the four positions that substantiate the verifiability. However, the middle philosophical position of Mādhyamikas accepts the dependent origination; the analysis of which shows that we need to develop a different understanding of the experienced world of objects.[11] In the *Cittaviśuddhi-prakaraṇa*, it has been said that

> the *cittamātra*[12] (the conceived phenomenon) is constituted of *pudgala-nairātmya* and *dharma-nairātmya*; everything originated from that, for this is elaborately described in the *Bauddhāgamas*.[13]

1.2 The Mādhyamika View—Its Origin and Development

Though the Mādhayamika view owes its origin to various discourses of the Buddha, the most important discussion that inspired the Mādhyamikas is the one that had taken place between Kātyāyana and the Buddha. On a question by the venerable Kātyāyana on "right view," the Buddha replied that generally the world is inclined towards two extremes: existence and non-existence. He said

> to him who perceives with right wisdom the uprising of the world as it has come to be, the notion of non-existence does not occur; to him who perceives with the right wisdom the ceasing of the world as it has come to be, the notion of existence in the world doesn't occur. The world, for the most part, *Kātyāyana*, is bound by approach grasping and inclination. And he who does not follow that approach and grasping, that determination of mind, that inclination and disposition, who does not cling to or adhere to a view; this is my self, "who thinks": suffering that is subject of arising arises; suffering that is subject to ceasing, ceases, such a person does not doubt, is not perplexed. Herein, his knowledge is not other dependent. Thus far *Kātyāyana*, there is right view.[14]

The concept of "right view" is elaborated in the context of the process of knowing about the perceived objective world. In other words, the realm of the right view is purely epistemological. Perceptions provide the details of the phenomena and the process, but the nature of phenomena is simply arising and ceasing and not permanent. Such perceptions are coloured by one's prejudices, because of the clinging and grasping nature of the mind to objects of the world. If grasping and inclination are avoided, then one never takes a determined stand with regard to the objects perceived; on the other hand, one could see that the phenomena are arising and ceasing. In this regard, Nāgārjuna clarifies:

> But ordinary sentient ones are not completely freed from the grab of prejudices, the enlightened ones are completely freed from the notion of any permanent thing. Behind every phenomenon, Buddha proposes to assail all doubts

> about the phenomena by understanding it with the help of causal dependence, rather than trying to look at it as something mysterious, thus the all powerful notion of a creator, who willingly controls the world, could be removed. The significance of bringing up the causal relation is that instead of looking at a mysterious cause for the phenomena one could find a natural causal relation behind every phenomenon depending upon the situation.[15]

According to the *Kātyāyanāvadānasūtra*, if Man doesn't make up his mind regarding the existence of the permanent soul he continues to look for it, but if he understands the nature of phenomena as coming and going, he could transcend the notion of permanent existence.[16]

When we discuss the right view, it is also necessary to specify the wrong view. There are two views which have to be taken into account. One is that "everything exists" and what exists is true; the other is that "everything does not exist" and what exists is void. According to the eternalists' view, every phenomenon is controlled by the existing reality, it is true and existing forever; the apparent world is a mere illusion and everything is supported by an underlying truth, which is permanent and unchanging. This notion of everything existing is wrong, because it doesn't explain the arising and ceasing nature of phenomena, and it leads the mind to total confusion and suffering. The opposite view also does not do any good. It denies not only the view of a permanently existing thing, but also the arising and continuity of all phenomena and their cessation; this view is also wrong and can cause suffering.[17] The philosophy of the middle path assumes significance, as it addresses and explores the nature of all phenomena in the world against this background. All other views have their own inner contradictions. This, in fact, is the philosophy of Nāgārjuna and the early Mādhyamikas, who explore into the inner contradictions of different theories.

1.2.1 *Early Mādhyamikas and Their Contribution*

Scholars like David J. Kalupahana are of the view that Nāgārjuna has reinstated the importance of canonical texts by introducing the philosophy of Mādhyamika; especially, the arguments advanced in the text of *Kātyāyanāvadānasūtra* in construing the Mādhyamika philosophy.[18] Kalupahana places Nāgārjuna as a reformer of the Buddhist tradition who introduced the original teachings of the Buddha to a group of Theravādins and Mahāyānists, who caught on to theoretical postulations of philosophising.[19] Some other commentators opine that the philosophical system introduced by Nāgārjuna is original and consider him as the second Buddha who propounded the philosophy of Mādhyamika which is different from the original teachings of the Śākyamuni Buddha. Prominent among them is T.R.V. Murti, who is of the opinion that Nāgārjuna rejected a "theory of elements" (*dharma*), accepted by the Buddha and instead presented a theory of "emptiness" (*śūnyatā*).[20] These two views might be partially and contextually true. As part of reviewing the Mādhyamika view in a different context, I wish to argue that Nāgārjuna's view is the continuance of a long philosophical tradition advanced by the Buddha as well as many philosophers contemporary or prior to him like Sañjaya Belaṭṭhiputta and the sceptics, the nihilists and other materialist schools of Indian philosophy. The conception of *śūnyatā* is a major contribution of pre-buddhist non-Brāḥmanical schools. The discussion here is made on this background; nevertheless, it must be admitted that this theme requires a separate study.

The most important work of Nāgārjuna, *Mūlamādhyamakakārikā* displays strong allegiance to the *Kātyāyanāvadānasūtra*, in content and spirit. This work paved the way to clear the water muddied by the speculations of the metaphysicians of Buddhist tradition. Most of the works of Nāgārjuna represent a criticism of the Abhidharma philosophy,[21] which was exalted by the Theravādins for many centuries.[22] The Abhidharma literature, especially the commentorial traditions, began to inculcate a sort of sectarian attitude into the Buddhist tradition. The elevation of the Abhidharma to a level of supreme body of literature, more important than the discourses, is the ground on which Nāgārjuna developed his philosophy. The endeavour of Mahāyāna is to overcome the sectarian interpretations of the original text in the Abhidharma literature, and go back to the non-sectarian form of Buddhism as embodied in the early discourses.[23] Analysing Nāgārjuna's philosophy in the light of *Kātyāyanāvadāna-sūtra* and Kāśyapaparivarta of the *Ratnakūḷasūtra*,[24] one can see that Nāgārjuna is not merely an interpreter of the canonical literature of Buddhism, but has looked at Buddhism from the perspective of an original thinker, who provided a new impetus to Buddhist literature in particular and to the philosophical tradition of India and Asia for centuries.

Nāgārjuna's prime concern in his system of philosophising is to save Buddhism from the speculative systems developed by interpreters, like Sarvāstivāda and Sautrāntika and restore the supremacy of the original discourses of the Buddha. These interpreters of original discourses are called Abhidharma schools. Their analysis of the categories that deal with both human personality and human experience into aggregate elements and faculties are called *dharmas* or elements of existence. They (the elements of existence) are subjected to severe exegetic elaboration and are formulated as antithesis to Sāṅkhya and Vaiśeṣika, the two important schools in the orthodox section of classical Indian philosophy. The purpose of such an analysis is to repudiate the existence of self in these phenomena, by rightly understanding the "dependently arising phenomena" and "dependent arising" which leads to the revelation of freedom (*nirvāṇa*).[25] But the Abhidharma schools, the Sarvāstivādins and the Sautrāntikas, involved in the exigencies of Abhidharma and the original discourses, have themselves to accept the antithesis of the opponents. The original teaching of Buddhism does not accept any theoretical postulations, but when these schools have to engage in the dialectics of the opposing Vaiśeṣikas and Sāṅkhyans, they are forced to refute their views. The school of Sarvāstivāda accepts ultimate discrete atomic elements. To put them together in logical format they have to accept the concept of innate-nature (*svabhāva*) of the phenomena, because the explanation of *svabhāva* as everchanging and impermanent is logically inconsistent and self-defeating. Consequently, they have to accept the existence of the self-nature of phenomena in all three periods of time, the past, the present, and the future. These views are heretical to the very teachings of the Buddha that are based on non-substantialism of all phenomena.[26]

The other school, Sautrāntikas criticises the Sarvāstivādins as "disguised Ātmavādins" and dismisses exegetic treatises (*śāstra*) by affirming faith in the original disclosures (*sūtras*) of the Buddha. But it too has failed in its interpretation about the theory of atoms and the conception of moments. These two aspects have led the second to accept the non-identity theory of causation (*asatkāryavāda*) and the task of experienced continuity in the individual person (*pudgala-vāda*).[27]

The Sarvāstivādins and the Sautrāntikas developed complicated theories; the former accepted self-nature and the identity of cause and effect, while the other school accepted other-nature, insisted upon difference between cause and effect (*nānātva*), and introduced the conception of self or person (*pudgala*) in human personality.[28] These two schools have a strong similarity to the Vedic systems of Sāṅkhya and Vaiśeṣika, which are called as Ātmavādins by the Buddhists. The Sarvāstivādins have a strong resemblance to the Sāṅkhya system, in their acceptance of *svabhāva* (self-nature) and *satkāryavāda*. The Sautrāntikas are close to the Vaiśeṣika system, accepting *nānātva*, atomism, and *astkāryavāda*.

Nāgārjuna introduces the original teachings of the Buddha in a language understandable to the Abhidharma schools, for he expounds the philosophy of the middle way in the light of the basic human tendency to seize and to cling, functioning under false imagination and not on right understanding. It is considered as the root of conflict in understanding, and the root of suffering.[29] The tendency to seize the relative as absolute is the root-thirst for reality in man. In *Mahāprajñāpāramitāśāstra*, it is discussed in detail:

> The thirst for the real is indeed the root of all the activities of man, it is under ignorance, not knowing the true nature of things that one seizes hold of everything one comes across, cling to it as a safe refuge, as ultimately and fully satisfying the thirst for the unconditioned, only to meet with disappointment and frustration.[30]

In the case of Buddhist realists, the counter arguments have taken many aspects from the opponent's views. On their interpretation about the Abhidharma, they compromise with the arguments of the Vedic schools of Sāṅkhya and Vaiśeṣika. This frustrated the canonical teaching of Buddhism and brought conflicts in reasoning.

Nāgārjuna's direct disciple Āryadeva was a great exponent of the Mādhyamikas philosophy. He is credited to be a critic of Brāhmanical schools of philosophy like Sāṅkhya, Vaiśeṣika, and Mīmāṁsā. He has introduced the *catuṣkoṭi* mode of negation to existentially qualified statements in all four premises, for perceiving reality. By introducing *catuṣkoṭi* into the Mādhyamika philosophy, Āryadeva provided a new methodology for the dialectical analysis of phenomena.

1.2.2 *Mādhyamika Dialectics—Rejection of the Theoretical Evaluation of Phenomena*

The strength of the Mādhyamika philosophy is its dialectics, the spacious philosophical argument that dressed up the fallacious reasoning and the arguments of the Sarvāstivādins and Sautrāntikas and, consequently, the Sāṅkhyans and the Vaiśeṣikas. The fourteen inexplicable questions (*avyakṛtas*) that the Buddha refused to answer are evident in the dialectical analysis employed by Mādhyamika.[31] The Buddha refused to fall into the trap of absolutistic metaphysics of the Brāhmanical schools (the eternalists), and the antithesis of the materialistic schools (the pre-Buddhistic non-Brāhmanical schools), who engaged in the enterprise of speculative philosophising. According to the Buddha, speculative philosophy leads only to confusion and disharmony, and it is harmful for spiritual life.[32]

The materialist schools introduced a dialectical system in which fourteen questions are formulated to refute the arguments about the absolutistic position of the Brāhmanical schools. The fourteen inconclusive questions (*avyakṛtas*) can be put into four set pattern of questions, three of which have four alternatives each, and the last one concerning the soul has only two alternatives. The questions are:

> Whether the world is eternal, or not eternal, or both, or neither?
> Whether the world is finite (in space), or infinite, or both, or neither?
> Whether the Tathāgata exists after death, or does not exist, or both, or neither? Is the soul identical with the body or different from it?[33]

This type of argument formulation is a part of the speculative philosophy of the materialists and logical sceptics in order to refute the extreme eternalist position of the Brāhmanical schools. One of the prominent philosophers in this category is Sañjaya Belaṭṭhiputta, known as the profound scholar of Amaravikṣepa (or Vācavikṣepa) School which was one of the prominent schools of thought at the time of the Buddha. The method of philosophical argument introduced by him is an important contribution of this school to classical Indian philosophy.

The skill of this school of thinkers always confused the opponents. The name *vācāvikkhepas*, meaning who can propitiate "verbal jugglery," is more appropriate for them.[34] The encounter with Ajātaśatru and Sañjaya Bellaṭṭhiputta is the best example of this verbal arguing skill of these thinkers. To the questions of fruits of homeless life; he answers: 'If you ask me: "Is there another world?" If I thought so, I would say so. But I don't think so. I don't say it is so, and I don't say otherwise. I don't say it is not, and I don't not say it is not. If you ask: "Isn't there another world?..." "Both?..." "Neither?..." "is there fruit and result of good and bad deeds?" "Isn't there?..." "Both?..." "Neither?" "Does the Thatagata exist after death?" "Does he not?..." "Both?..." "Neither?..." "I don't say it is not."[35]

The pattern of dialectics is as follows:

Evamapi me ni—I do not say so
Tathā pi me no—I do not say thus
Aññathā pi me no—I do not say otherwise
No ti pi me no—I do not say no
No no ti pi me no—I do not say "no, no."[36]

By maintaining silence to these ambiguous questions and answers, the Buddha refused to fall into the trap set by such dialectical arguments. Though these arguments are set to refute the absolutistic viewpoints of the Brāhmanical schools, according to the Buddha, such extreme form of dialectics, would lead to severe moral danger.

Similarly, to the questions of the wanderer Vacchagotta regarding the eternity of self, the Buddha kept silent. He later clarified to the Śrāvaka Ānanda on the meaning of his profound silence:

> If the answer was that there is a self then it is equivalent to supporting the arguments of recluses and Brāhmins who are eternalists; and if answer was that there is no self, then I would be siding the arguments of the recluses and Brāhmins who are annihilationists.[37]

Both would leave the listener to the fallacy of accepting some sort of theoretical postulation. Again the Buddha has said,

> To hold that the world is eternal or to hold that it is not, or to agree to any other of the proposition you adduce, Vaccha, is the jungle of theorising, the wilderness of theorising, the tangle of theorising, the bondage and shackle of theorising, attended by the ill, distress, perturbation, and fever; it conduces not to detachment, passionlessness, tranquillity, peace, to knowledge and wisdom of Nirvāṇa.[38]

The Buddha's silence and the explanation to that silence should be taken seriously to understand the philosophy of Buddhism. According to T.R.V. Murti,

> By denying to answer such speculative questions, he was not shying away from his critics, nor was he professing the inadequacy of the available premises to adduce truth and waiting for a more favourable time to publish truth, but by doing so he transcended and annulled the dogmatic procedure of reason.[39]

The silence of the Buddha has paved the way for a spacious argument that could dress up the fallacious reasoning, fallen into the pseudological theoretical grab of the metaphysicians, both eternalists and nihilists. Murti writes,

> The Buddha's silence only can be interpreted as the consciousness of the indescribable nature of unconditioned reality.[40]

The Buddha's silence signifies his refusal to accept any extremes that lead to theoretical postulations and that the conflicts of reason are better solved by the dialectics of silence. The understanding of the world based on metaphysical formulations represents, unfortunately, a partial view of things and does not have a comprehensive understanding of the things.[41]

1.2.2.1 *The Catuṣkoṭi*: In order to argue the Buddhist position with regard to the phenomenal world of things, Āryadeva introduces tetralemmas or *catuṣkoṭi*[42] from the Buddhistic point of view in the *Catuḥśataka*, the conjunction of four negations of the existentially qualified statements to solve the problem of conflict in reasoning. Human reasoning can go only in the four positions of perceiving reality. According to Murti:

> Mādhyamika dialectic tries to remove the conflict inherent in reason by rejecting both the opposites taken singularly or in combination. Mādhyamikas are convinced that the conjunctive or disjunctive synthesis of the opposites is but another view and it labours under the same difficulties. Rejection of all views is the rejection of the competence of the reason to comprehend reality.[43]

The problem confronted by the Sarvāstivādins and Sautrāntikas is that they have to take some form of position in countering the arguments of the rival schools. In effect, they accepted the positions held by the opponents. Mādhyamikas never took position in a dichotomous argument and held that a problem of opposites would lead to the problem's conjunctive and disjunctive synthesis.[44]

We can see that fourfold negation pattern set in the fourteen *avyakṛtas*, is the basis for *catuṣkoṭi*. It is true that Buddhists have adopted the fourfold negation method of argument from the pre-Buddhistic non-Vedic schools especially from the sceptics like Sañjaya Belaṭṭhiputta. The ambiguous answers given by Sañjaya make his system different to that of the Mādhyamikas.[45] The fourteen *avyakṛtas* are used to prove the nihilistic view about the world. On the other hand, it is interesting to note that the Buddha's silence finds a new formulation in the fourfold negation of the Mādhyamikas.

The discussions in the next chapter are about various dialectical analyses employed by the Mādhyamikas to refute the truth-value of the perceived phenomena. It will be clear from the discussions that the realm of *catuṣkoṭi* is not to prove the perfect voidness of the phenomena, as interpreted by many critics; but it is meant to direct the human mind to view the phenomena in a different perspective. The perceived phenomena are true only conventionally, not ultimately. It can be stated that every true proposition, interpreted referentially, will be false for a Mādhyamika philosopher, because he finds inner contradictions in existentially true statements. The fourfold negation is the only way to annul the effect of such propositions. Accordingly, the analysis is directed to the text *Cittaviśuddhi-prakaraṇa* in the light of the philosophical positions of the early Mādhyamikas and other works of Āryadeva, in order that the text is properly read with all philosophical ramifications.

1.3 *Pudgala-nairātmya* through Tantrism

The Mādhyamikas' view that for explaining the essence of phenomena (*dharmadhātu*) and essencelessness of phenomena (*dharma-nairātmya*), is possible only by removing ignorance, appeasing the dispositions and changing the clinging nature that is produced from strong feelings. The objective world and the subjective self appear as real because ignorance, dispositions, and strong feelings influence the mind's activity. So, to understand the insubstantial nature of the phenomenal world, one needs to acquire wisdom (*prajñā*) and a carefully devised practical methodology (*upāya*) for the inculcation of spiritual merit to remove the notion of self. The commingled *prajñā* and *upāya* liberate the mind from the notion of permanence. Hence, one may notice that the introduction of Tāntric systems into the ethico-religious practice of Buddhism is a natural development, which enunciates the purification of the mind (*cittaviśuddhi*) naturally and effectively. The purification is complete with the realisation of *pudgala-nairātmya*, as a result of which the ignorance gets removed, the dispositions appeased, and the feelings changed. Thus, purification of mind through spiritual practices (*cittaviśuddhi*) is necessary for experiencing *nairātmya*.

Mādhyamika view and Tāntric spiritual practices are similar in that they avoid the extreme views and practices. As H.V. Guenther says:

> It is at this point that the Buddhist Tantras, particularly because of their unbiasedness and their going in a middle path avoiding the extremes, come as a valuable guide to new orientation of man's outlook.[46]

Mādhyamika's philosophical position and Tantra's message on spiritual development are the same, avoiding the easy and facile extremes, though it may involve many difficulties. The canonical traditions set by two discourses of Buddha the *Kātyāyanāvadānasūtra* and the *Dharmacakrapravartanasūtra* also endorse this position. The introduction of Tantrism into Mādhyamika tradition paved the way for an ethical system that is grounded on the Mādhyamika tenets. This ethical system is a way of life, and not a set of moral codes and principles. The Tāntric practices cultivates the mind of the practitioner and nurtures his behaviour to achieve Bodhisattvahood; he in turn, helps the sentient beings with suitable ethical means (*upāyas*) for attaining release from the dichotomous conceptualisations (*vikalpas*) of *saṁsāra*.

The dialectics introduced by Mādhyamika is effective in identifying the essencelessness of the existent phenomenal world together with its criticism of the positions held by the substantialists and essentialists; however, it is not able to establish the consequent essencelessness of the psychophysical world. Here, the Tantrism finds its natural space, as it assails the extremes of self-mortification and self-indulgence. Thus, the philosophical position envisaged by the Mādhyamikas finds its logical maturation with the introduction of Tāntric spiritual practices, which are effective in releasing the mind from all afflictions and manifestations. The result of such a spiritual practice is the realisation of enlightened mind, the *Bodhicitta* and the experience of essencelessness *nairātmya*.

The Mādhyamika method of purification of mind, *cittaviśuddhi* is distinctly different from the other systems, and this uniqueness is the main concern of discussion here. The text addresses a yogic aspirant who wishes to practise spiritual discipline in order to achieve *cittaviśuddhi* or cleansing of the mind from the dichotomous conceptualisations (*vikalpas*). Because the mind latches and clings to the apparent phenomena, the existent world appears as real, even though we understand that they are comparatively unreal and insubstantial (*śūnya*) ultimately. The practices enunciated in the text would enable the aspirant to free himself from the influence of the illusory nature, or the illusions that originate together with the perception of the phenomena. In other words, he will be able to perceive the essence of the phenomena (*dharmadhātu*), which is devoid of illusions. Knowing the *dharmadhātu* helps the aspirant to free himself from the clutches of the dichotomous misconceptions (*vikalpas*) arising from perception. The essencelessness (*nairātmya*) is established reciprocally, in order that with the achievement of *cittaviśuddhi* or cleansing of the mind, essencelessness of self (*pudgala-nairātmya*) is realised; this enables one to understand the insubstantial nature (*śūnyatā*) of phenomena or the *dharma-nairātmya*. The concept of *dharmadhātu*, thus, can be explained as the cognition of the objects the way they appear. The *śūnyatā* is discernible through dialectical analysis, but the *cittaviśuddhi* is achievable only through disciplined spiritual practices.

1.4 Āryadeva—the Person and the Philosopher

Nāgārjuna and Āryadeva are the two most important thinkers of Mādhyamika tradition. It is believed that Āryadeva hailed from a princely family of Sri Lanka, came to the mainland for furthering his studies in Buddhism, and became a disciple of Ācārya Nāgārjuna.[47] According to Tārānātha, the renowned fourteenth century Buddhist historian, Āryadeva was the son of the king Pañcaśṛṅga of the Island of *Siṁhala*.[48] He relinquished his royal life and pursued the path of religion and spirituality and received initiation to monastic order from Ācārya Hemadeva, under whom he completed all the Tripiṭikas. He then travelled to India and visited many holy places. At a place called Śrīparvata, he met Nāgārjuna and studied under him.[49] Another traditional Buddhist historian Bu-stön says that Āryadeva became proficient in both orthodox and heterodox Indian philosophical systems, after mastering all branches of Śāstras.[50] Tārānātha's account says that after the death of Nāgārjuna, Āryadeva took up the responsibility of furthering the doctrine of Mādhyamika.[51]

Scholars like E. Lamotte suggest that Āryadeva is associated with the Vetullavāda heresy, the Sinhalese name for Mahāyāna Buddhism. After coming to India, he studied under Ārya Nāgārjuna's tutelage and authored many works.[52] Some of the other Buddhist historians identify Āryadeva as a south Indian Brāhman, who studied under Nāgārjuna and became particularly proficient in arguing against non-Buddhist schools.[53] According to Tārānātha, Āryadeva defeated a learned Brāhman, Durdharṣakāla, at a public contest, consequently, the Brāhman became a disciple of Āryadeva and later taught Buddhism.[54] After staying in Nalanda for a considerable period of time, Āryadeva returned to Kāñcī, and he took up the responsibility of teaching prince Rāhulabhadra. At Kāñcī, he passed away.[55]

There are various views regarding the time of Āryadeva's life and works. Karen Lang, who made an extensive study, shows that Āryadeva was the student of Nāgārjuna, a contemporary of Sātavāhana dynasty, whose reign, according to historical records, ended in the middle of the third century. With reference and support of such evidences, she places Āryadeva's main literary work at a time between AD 225 and 250.[56] The relationship between Nāgārjuna and the Sātavāhana King Goutamiputra can be seen in the famous Mādhyamika work called *Suhṛtlekha* which is a collection of communications between the King Yajñaśrī Gautamīputra and Nāgārjuna. This is one of the persuasive evidences to show the time of Early Mādhyamikas.[57] According to Karen Lang:

> The theory that Āryadeva and Theradeva, a *Vetullavādin* thinker from Srilanka, is one and the same person, citing from the Siṁhalese sources, should be dismissed for not having enough substantiating evidence to prove that these two thinkers are the same person. The theory that Theradeva left Siṁhala, when the King Voharikatissa suppressed the Vetullavāda, is giving an impression that Mahāyāna heresy is originated in Siṁhala and migrated to India.[58]

Karen Lang's observation of the year between AD 225 and AD 250 as the time of Āryadeva's literary works is more authentic than the conflicting and insubstantial views of other scholars.

Karen Lang further clarifies that south India, being the centre of Mahāsaṅghikas, was visited by monks from all over India and Sri Lanka to learn here the revolutionary and innovative ideas of the Mahāyāna Śāstras. Nāgārjuna and Āryadeva organised various Mahāsaṅghika groups.[59] Āryadeva was known to be proficient in refuting the views of the adversaries of scholars such as the Abhidhārmikas, the Vaiśeṣikas, the Sāṅkhyans, and the Jainas.[60] The texts of *Cittaviśuddhi-prakaraṇa* and *Catuḥśataka* provide enough evidence to support this argument. In the *Catuḥśataka*, Ārydeva expounds the insubstantiality (*niḥsvabhāvatā*) against the orthodox schools who put emphasis on the doctrine of substantiality of the phenomenal world and the eternity of the self.[61] In the *Cittaviśuddhi-prakaraṇa*, he focuses more on refuting various religio-ethical practices based on dogmatic ritualism and theoretical assumptions. Such ritualistic based practices, according to Āryadeva, do not lead to liberation; on the contrary, the people who have purity of mind and complete awareness of the truth of things would be liberated.[62] He vehemently criticises the arguments of the realists who claim that the apparent world is the representation of a permanently existing reality, and the dogmatic rituals reveal the truth of that reality and liberate the individual self. The Mādhyamika rejects the belief that the self attains liberation and merges into an eternal reality.

The main works of Āryadeva are the *Catuḥśataka*, commented and interpreted by Candrakīrti and the *Śataśāstra*, commented, interpreted, and translated into Chinese by Kumārajīva.[63] Apart from these two well-known works, the other noteworthy works, according to Bu-stön, are *Catuḥśataka*, *Hastavāla-prakaraṇa*, *Skhalita-pramathana-yuktihetusiddhi*, *Jñānasāra-samuccaya*, *Śataśāstra*, etc.[64]

From the Tibetan canon, we find the following works attributed to Āryadeva:[65] *Catuḥśataka*, *kārikā* with Candrakīrti's commentary; *Akṣaraśataka*, Tibetan canon attributes it to Nāgārjuna but Chinese canon and the Tibetan *Dunhaung* translation attribute it to Āryadeva; *Hastavāla-prakaraṇa* with the commentary; *Skhalita-pramathana-yuktihetusiddhi* (Āryadeva II); *Mādhyamaka-brahmagāthā* (Āryadeva II); *Jñānasāra-samuccaya* (Āryadeva II).[66]

The Tohoku Catalogue of the bisTan' gyur attributes the following works to Āryadeva:[67] *Hastavāla-prakaraṇa*, *Hastavāla-prakaraṇa-vṛtti*, *Hastavālavṛtti*, *Catuḥśatakaśāstra-kārikā*, *Skhalita-pramathana-yuktihetusiddhi*, *Mādhyamika-brahmagāthā*, and *Jñānasāra-samuccaya*.

The Taisho contains the following works attributed to Āryadeva:[68] *Catuḥśataka*, *Akṣaraśataka*, *Mahāpuruṣaśāstra*, and *Cittaviśuddhi-prakaraṇa*.

Theodore Stcherbatsky opines that the *Catuḥśataka*, *Akṣara-śatakaṃ*, *Hastavāla-prakaraṇa*, and *Cittaviśuddhi-prakaraṇa* are works of Āryadeva.

1.4.1 *Āryadeva II and the Authorship of the Cittaviśuddhi-prakaraṇa*

The theory of a second Āryadeva as the author of the *Cittaviśuddhi-prakaraṇa* is accepted by many scholars. This is because of the assumption that Tantrism is a later development in the tradition of Mahāyāna Buddhism. The text is considered as a work by a Tāntric

Buddhist who lived in the latter part of eighth century. However, there is no clear evidence to substantiate the existence of a second Āryadeva, who assumed the name from the first Āryadeva, the author of *Catuḥśataka* and the disciple of Nāgārjuna. The popular belief among scholars is that the Āryadeva I focused on discussing philosophical aspects, while the Āryadeva II was a different person, a practising Tāntric, who followed esoteric Buddhism. One of the reasons for such confusion in assessing authorship is the practical nature of philosophising adopted in the *Cittaviśuddhi-prakaraṇa*. We can find that while other texts explain the theoretical aspects, this text follows the canonical tradition set by *Dharmacakra-pravartanasūtra*,[69] which explains the development of spiritual virtue. Especially in our discussions of *Cittaviśuddhi-prakaraṇa*, the practical exegesis of the philosophy of Mādhyamikas forms the main subject of discussion.[70] Āryadeva is known for his criticism on the Brāhmanical schools of Indian philosophy. In *Catuḥśataka* and *Akṣaraśataka,* he attacks the Sāṅkhya and Vaiśeṣika schools' doctrinal positions. The same tradition is continued in the *Cittaviśuddhi-prakaraṇa* with the criticism of validity of Mīmāṁsaka views on conducting rituals and following Vedic way of conducting *dharma* and *karma*. He places the Buddhist view on enlightenment through purification of the mind above all other spiritual practices for getting redemption from the dichotomies of the phenomenal world. Moreover, his use of Sūtra tradition of explaining philosophical questions and the use of philosophical language is very similar to the methods of the early Mādhyamikas, of Nāgārjuna and Āryadeva.

Prabhubhai Patel, who edited the *Cittaviśuddhi-prakaraṇa*, after studying the original Sanskrit version and other Tibetan translations, introduced the theory of a second Āryadeva. One of the reasons for the theory of a second Tāntric Āryadeva is accentuated because the concept of *Cittaviśuddhi* is considered as one of the *Pañcakramas* of the Tāntric practices; and hence, it is concluded that the author is probably a Tāntric. Another reason is based on the common belief that the system of Tantrism became popular in the socio-religious tradition of Buddhism only after the sixth century and most of the literature developed after that period. These two arguments are not substantiated with proper evidence.

The name of the text, *Cittaviśuddhi-prakaraṇa,* actually was not given by Āryadeva, but after studying the Tibetan version,[71] the *Cittavāraṇa-viśodhana-prakaraṇa* and another translation named *Cittaratna-viśodhana* and from the last verse of the text, Prabhubhai Patel has named the text as *Cittaviśuddhi-prakaraṇa*.[72] The contextual reasoning adopted by Prabhubhai Patel for naming the *Cittaviśuddhi-prakaraṇa*, is based on the assumption that *Cittaviśuddhi* is the main theme of the text and the category in which text could be placed is a *prakaraṇa*. This is not an exhaustive prescription and its validity can be questioned.[73]

A careful reading of the text would reveal that even though one of the main themes of discussion is *Cittaviśuddhi*, it is clear that the text attempts to set an agenda, in detail, for the Bodhisattvas (Yogis) to follow in order to attain spiritual perfection of mind, the *Bodhicitta*. Certainly, *Cittaviśuddhi* is the path to attain *Bodhicitta*, the perfection of mental faculties by changing the influence of disposition and feelings on psychophysical personality. However, it is difficult to accept the idea that the text belongs to the Tāntric of the eighth century, which is based on such exiguous evidences. It is quite possible that the concept of *Cittaviśuddhi*[74] introduced by Āryadeva, might have been taken up by the later Tāntric writers, but to make a conclusion about the authorship of the text with such evidence is untenable.

Another scholar, Tom J.F. Tillemans, contends that being a disciple of Nāgārjunapāda, who is considered as Nāgārjuna II, the Tāntric Āryadava II assumed his name after Āryadeva I, the Mādhyamika.[75] Also, according to him, the *Cittaviśuddhi-prakaraṇa*, is a commentarial interpretation of the *Guhyasamājatantra* of Nāgārjunapāda. However, there are no textual or historical evidences to substantiate this viewpoint. Not much substantiating evidence to validate the historicity of Āryadeva II is available, though he might have lived much later than Āryadeva I. Nevertheless, the evidences put forward by Prabhubhai Patel are silent on the historicity of Āryadeva II. Patel writes:

> As regards with the date of this, Āryadeva (read Āryadeva II) there is very little evidence. Some of the verses of the work occur in other works of settled dates; but that too, does not throw any light on the point, as these verses occur in the texts themselves without any indication that they are quoted from some other works. When the tenets of *Vajrayāna* were current in Bengal there was a writer of this name. He is supposed to have been known under two or three other names.[76]

We are not able to discern anything conclusively from these arguments about the existence of another person, Āryadeva II. The claim about the existence of Āryadeva II is not conceptually proven, historically established, or referred to in any other authentic sources. Based on these positions, the claim about the existence of Āryadeva II is fictitious, unfounded, unclear, and liable to be dismissed, especially for the authorship of *Cittaviśuddhi-prakaraṇa.*

The *Cittaviśuddhi-prakaraṇa* contains enough evidence to show that it has authorial allegiance to Āryadeva, the Mādhyamika. A very careful study is required in the case of such an important text for distinguishing its central theme or the authenticity of the author. Unfortunately, most of the scholars who commented or quoted it in their works, have never given any serious thought to these aspects. According to Sasibhushan Dasgupta, the *Cittaviśuddhi-prakaraṇa* is very important in the Mādhyamika tradition:

> Tāntric Buddhists were sometimes over conscious about the justifiability of their practices and advanced various arguments in defence of these practices. These arguments, as in the case with their arguments are not found in the texts in a systematic form, they are rather being culled from the texts. But two works are found mainly devoted to something like a philosophical explanation to these practices; the first is the *Cittaviśuddhi-prakaraṇa* of Āryadeva and the second is the *Tattva-siddhi* of Śāntarakṣita.[77]

The normal Tāntric texts, developed later as a part of the Tāntric tradition in Buddhism, contain mostly descriptions of Mantras and descriptions of the nature of *yantras* for a particular deity, or of names of particular deities and the mode of Tāntric practices attributed to them. On the contrary, the *Cittaviśuddhi-prakaraṇa* describes the Mādhyamika philosophy and various spiritual practices based on the Tāntric tradition, because the text pioneered the introduction of Tāntric spiritual practices into the Mādhyamika school of Buddhism. It is clear from reading the text that it follows the canonical tradition of *Dharmacakrapravartanasūtra*, where the practical application of the philosophical explication is taken as the methodology. Also, the pedagogical nature of description in the text shows that it was written by a mature philosopher and not by an impostor who wants to extrapolate certain ideology using a famous name. As we can see, his criticisms are against the spiritual practices of the Brāhmanical schools such as Mīmāṁsakas, who encourage ritualistic practices to emancipate the soul. This is an area pioneered by Āryadeva. Furthermore, Āryadeva has pinpointed *vikalpas* or mental thought constructs as the real obstacles for spiritual development, and he introduces suitable means, Tāntric psycho-experimental techniques, to remove such *vikalpas*.[78] The text explains the ways and means for cleansing the mind *cittaviśuddhi*. The *Bodhicitta* should not be misunderstood as the substratum of the phenomenal world, but it should be understood as the original stage (*pudgala-nairātmya*) of mind, not tainted by the thought modes.[79] It should not also be misunderstood as a spiritual journey to higher levels of consciousness.

A careful review of other works of Āryadeva would reveal that the real nature of the philosophical methodology adopted in the *Cittaviśuddhi-prakaraṇa* finds suitable culmination by delineating the *pudgala-nairātmya*. Moreover, it is evident that the discussions advanced by early Mādhyamikas about the nature of phenomena (*dharma*) as *śūnya* has been sufficiently dealt with the *Cittaviśuddhi-prakaraṇa*, as the text is explicit in sketching an agenda for the purification of the *citta* from *vikalpas* (misconceptions). The purification of the *citta* through Tāntric form of spiritual training is instrumental in realising *cittaviśuddhi* and, as a result, *pudgala-nairātmya*, the original stage of mind.

1.5 A Review of Other Works of Āryadeva

1.5.1 *The Catuḥśataka*

One of the well-known works of Āryadeva, discussed in the philosophical community as his most important contribution to philosophy, is the *Catuḥśataka*. This text has been extensively commented by later scholars, especially the later Mādhyamika scholar, Candrakīrti. The main discussion in the text is the disciplined conduct for Bodhisattvas, for acquiring spiritual merit and other virtues. As Karen Lang writes:

> Āryadeva's *Catuḥśataka* shows the worthy student how to acquire the requisite equipment for enlightenment. The first eight chapters discuss the accumulation of merit, the later eight, the accumulation of knowledge. These two accumulations bring about the attainment of Buddhahood.[80]

This text elaborates the importance of self-improvement, for creating the right atmosphere for spiritual practice. As a result, the mind should be at its original stage without thought constructs (*vikalpas*).

The first four chapters of the text deal with the way to abandon the four erroneous conceptions of things as: permanent (*nitya*), pleasant (*sukha*), pure (*śuci*), and Self (*Ātman*).[81] From the perspective of the Mādhyamika philosophy, these are the most important attainments of a Bodhisattva for *nirvāṇa*, redeeming the mind from illusory notions about the world of things. In the first chapter, Āryadeva discusses right mindfulness about death, in order to transcend the fear of death. In the second chapter, he argues against the popular notion of acknowledging human body as a medium of enjoyment and pleasure. In fact, it is a source of sorrow (*duḥkha*). The body experiences ordinary pain of hunger, injury, and also the pain originating from the excessive enjoyment of pleasure, etc. For example, a seemingly enjoyable horse ride would turn out to be a painful experience, if performed excessively. Here, Āryadeva explains the importance of proper meditations on the body, to make one aware, that the body is impermanent and is of painful nature.[82] He cautions against the presumption that the beautiful and sensuous bodies of women are pure and a source of eternal pleasure. Besides, neither bathing nor scented garlands counteract the bodies' inner impurities, but only meditation on the actual inner constitution of the body can eradicate this misconception. In the fourth chapter, he attacks the notion of a permanent self, which transcends the limitations of the experiential world and which sanctions an individual deterministic action. For example, in the process of protecting the subjects, if a king performs wrong actions, it in turn cumulates demerit to him and destroys him. A good king loses all his pride of the sovereign power after he has seen equal or superior power.[83]

Commenting on the career of a Bodhisattva, as the total dedication towards the welfare of all beings and non-beings, Āryadeva suggests control of desire (*kleśa*), kind treatment towards hatred, and elimination of confusion through knowledge.[84] Since confusion sustains the other two afflictions, it is important to eliminate them through correct knowledge, the knowledge of momentariness, and interdependent origination.[85]

Afflictions arising from deceptively attractive sense objects and *karma* work to perpetuate the bondage in a painful cycle of birth and death. Āryadeva also cautions people who acquire merit in anticipation of rewards like wealth, power, and good rebirth, because these things too would create sufferings. Understanding the illusory nature of the phenomenal world is the only way to redeem oneself from the world of sufferings.[86] The discussion in the eighth chapter relates to the creation of an interface between concentration and knowledge. Through concentration, it is possible to eradicate the afflictions to sense objects and *karma*, which cause involuntary rebirth. Through the knowledge of dependent origination and insubstantial nature of the phenomenal world, it is possible to redeem oneself from the ill-effects of *karma*.

The existence of permanent things and the belief of a permanent stage of liberation are the main subject of discussion in chapter nine. Āryadeva accepts the self at the mundane level while refusing its existence ultimately. Because of this reason there is no permanent liberation.[87]

In chapter ten, Āryadeva again argues against the impossibility of accepting the existence of a permanent self. The Vaiśeṣika's view is that the unconscious self which is distinct from the body instigates the body's actions and experiences the results. He repudiates this argument that such a self must undergo change and, thus, cannot be permanent. He also rejects the Sāṅkhyan belief in the conscious and potentially conscious permanent self. He counters that the senses are useless, if the self is always conscious. If it is potentially conscious, then it cannot be permanent; a thing undergoes change always, if it is potentially conscious at one time and actually conscious at another time, and that which changes is not permanent. The Vaiśeṣika and Sāṅkhya argument about permanent self is logically inconsistent.

According to Āryadeva, one requires intelligence and impartiality to understand the Buddhist view of *saṁsāra* and *nirvāṇa*, which is discussed in the twelfth chapter. He contends that in order to transcend the notion of *saṁsāra* and *nirvāṇa*, one needs to practice virtuous life (*dharma*) and non-injury (*ahiṁsā*). According to him, the right view understands the non-intrinsic nature of the *saṁsāra* that liberates one from the shackles of recurring birth and death.[88]

In chapter thirteen, the discussion takes another turn. He refutes various views on the sense organs and the perception of respective objects. He contends that since various views on perception fail to establish authenticity, the perceiver and the perceived have no real existence, they resemble mirages and illusions.[89]

Āryadeva uses the strongest possible language to refute the existence of conditioned things and their marks such as, origination, duration, and cessation. These things, according to Āryadeva, do not exist independent of one another; they neither arise simultaneously nor sequentially. Similarly, they do not arise from themselves or from something different.[90] In the final chapter, he refutes the theoretical positions of people who perceive things as empty as if they are not empty. He discusses the problem of philosophy of emptiness wherein the negation of one thesis is not implied as a concomitant establishment of the opposite thesis. He concludes that a person who finds error would find it in all the four possible alternatives (*catuṣkoṭi*) and, thus, no opponent can refute it.[91]

Reading through the sixteen chapters of the text, one can identify that the main concern of the text is the discussion on Bodhisattva's spiritual practices, especially, regarding inculcating spiritual merit and an impartial and independent understanding of the world. The phenomenal world and its deceiving appearances make one to identify with unreal as real and with illusory as actual. The text is very explicit in criticising the Brāhmanical schools like Vaiśeṣika and Sāṅkhya, and their views on eternally existing permanent soul. It also critically examines the Buddhists' Abhidhārmikas on their affinity to interpret the teaching of Buddha with the help of theories.

1.5.2 *The Akṣaraśatakam*

Another important work of Āryadeva is *Akṣaraśatakam*, which is lost in its original, but fortunately preserved in Chinese and Tibetan. The authorship is wrongly ascribed to Nāgārjuna. T.R.V. Murti accorded that the text is a logical evolution of the *Catuḥśataka*. In short and specific arguments, Āryadeva refutes the Sāṅkhyan and Vaiśeṣika philosophy.[92] The arguments, which are to establish the apparent nature of things, are directed against the *satkāryavāda* and *asatkāryavāda*. The text contains twenty verses and is strongly footed in the philosophy of Mādhyamika.[93]

1.5.3 *The Hastavālanāma-prakaraṇavṛtti*

Another very important work of Āryadeva is the *Hastavālanāma-prakaraṇavṛtti*. According to Fernando Tola's opinion, Āryadeva wanted to assert that he can explain the subject as clearly as one sees a hair in the arm of his hand.[94] The work explains the different stages involved in the perception of an object by citing the example of rope and snake: the snake seen on a rope is an apparent erroneous perception and when the rope is realised on veridical perception, the existence of the snake becomes extinct. This is how we experience the conventional world of experience. On a different level of analysis, the veridically perceived rope also becomes extinct in relation to the finer elements (fibre) of the rope. The cognised phenomenal object lose its identifiable nature on progressive analysis, as in the case of the object rope, it turned into unidentifiable sub-atomic particles. Thus, the things we perceive are apparent and relative in nature.[95] According to some schools of Indian philosophy, on the ultimate analysis of an object, one arrives at the most indivisible element of that object called an atom.[96] It is evident that the atom does not have the property of the object (rope) originally perceived. The existence of rope is relatively true when compared with the ultimate sub-atomic particles;[97] the conceived object of snake is also relatively true until verification with other sense faculties. Āryadeva has opined that on close examination the certainty of the rope becomes redundant, existing only contextually and relatively like the snake.[98] In this text, we find a mature epistemologist in Āryadeva. He says in the last verse:

> The man who perceives the things of the world should act as the worldly people in the established way; the one who wishes to eliminate the impurities must investigate according to supreme reality.[99]

Here, Āryadeva emphasises the importance of having a right view regarding the objective world. The right view is to apprehend the *dharmadhātu* (essence of the phenomena), the rope, from the perceived phenomena, the snake. Similarly, one should discard eternity of the rope as the existing entity, by understanding the *dharma-nairātmya*, the essencelessness and relative nature of the existent rope. Āryadeva gives a new statement with regard to the *dharma-nairātmya* of the phenomenal world with this special dialectical system. The main subject of discussion in the *Hastavālanāma-prakaraṇavṛtti* is based on the *dharma-nairātmya* of the existent world and not based on the *pudgala-nairātmya* of the self. The rational deconstruction[100] of *dharma* (snake) to *dharmadhātu* (rope) and then to *dharma-nairātmya* (atomic particles) introduced in the *Hastavālanāma-prakaraṇavṛtti* finds its practical application and logical conclusion in the *Cittaviśuddhi-prakaraṇa*, which focuses on the realisation of the *pudgala-nairātmya*.

1.6 *Cittaviśuddhi-prakaraṇa*—Introducing Tantrism in Mādhyamika

Āryadeva introduces the discussion of the *Cittaviśuddhi-prakaraṇa*, by explaining the inherently pure nature of the mind and the problem created in the mind in the form of conceptualisations (*vikalpas*). Āryadeva again says that the thought constructs retard the mind's natural function and makes it view the unreal as real or the relative as eternal. The mind can cognise the conceived phenomena (*dharma*) only if the speeds of both are equal; consequently, it expresses the existence of unperceivable *dharma*, whose speed varies from the perceivable limit of the mind.[101] The whimsical notion of existence (*saṁsāra*) manifested by the mind through conceptualisation of phenomena is like a crocodile that grabs its prey with a tight grip, dragging him deep down to the water of the illusions of *saṁsāra*. Human actions under this influence are unaccountable for assessing merit or demerit, because actions at this stage are unintentional. Thus, acquiring *Cittaviśuddhi* which removes all affliction of *vikalpas*, is the only way to redeem one from the world of existence (*saṁsāra*).

The apparent objective world of things is like a mirage (*marīcikā*) or an imaginary city (*gāndharva-nagara*), for the ignorant people who get attracted to the spell of such illusory world of things. The deep attachment to the world of things is due to the internal mechanism of the mind created out of ignorance, dispositions, and feelings. Āryadeva suggests that the practice of yoga with the help of the patent deity, is the way to acquire sufficient knowledge to understand the illusory nature of the phenomenal world. And such a person is neither bound nor released, and for him *saṁsāra* and *nirvāṇa* are redundant. The spiritual practices suggested for a yogi are censured for normal human beings, because a yogi is supported by his guru and the patent deity in his spiritual journey; especially, the sexo-yogic practices or martial art practices, which are a part of the Tāntric practices, could generate negative effects on normal people.[102] The justification of such practices is similar to the instance of a *viṣa-vaidya*, eradicating the effect of poison with the help of poison.

A yogi attains purity of *citta* (*cittaviśuddhi*) through spiritual practices that open up the *Bodhicitta*,[103] which is by nature independent, pure throughout its existence, un-originated, and taintless. A yogi, who realises this stage of *citta*, is neither bonded nor liberated. Liberation (*nirvāṇa*) is a reality only to one who is under the influence of existence (*saṁsāra*). The *vikalpas*, dichotomous conceptualisations created from thought constructs, are like the water locked inside the ear, which can be removed only by pouring more water into it. It is like the dusted mirror cleaned using the same type of dust; or it is like the washerman cleaning the cloth using clay (a form of dirt). It means that the removal of the influence of the *vikalpas*, using the method of appeasing the mind's faculties, is like a metallic ball converted into vessel that can float on water. The mental faculties like dispositions, ignorance, and feelings are appeased using various spiritual techniques directly or indirectly to remove the *vikalpas*.

Contrary to the views of many schools of philosophy, Āryadeva reiterates that it is not possible to remove the *vikalpas* by spiritual practices alone, but through knowledge (*prajñā*). Thus, the method to achieve spiritual perfection is by yoking *prajñā* and *upāya*. The desire is like a metallic ball, which has the inherent property to sink into the—*saṁsāra*—of water; however, when it is made into a vessel using the technique of commingling the *prajñā* and *upāya*, the purified mind functions like the vessel, which helps others from the grip of *vikalpas*. The united *prājñopāya*[104] turns the impediment of mind, desiring for things, into an advantage of removing such desires. Ignorant people, resorting to desire, naturally fall into the trap of bondage like milk drunk by a snake, which increases the effect of poison, despite milk having the property to neutralise poison. A Yogi, like a *haṁsa* (swan) drinks the milk from a mixture of milk and water, would be able to enjoy the objects of desire with a sense of detachment. The *prajñā* combined with the *upāya* can be aptly compared to a lamp, which destroys darkness with its thin flame.

According to Āryadeva, the commingled *prajñā* and *upāya* would be able to show the *dharmadhātu*[105] of things. The *dharmadhātu* or the essence of the objective phenomenal world would help the Yogi to protect himself against the illusory nature of such phenomena. A Yogi, without being attached to objects of desire, is allowed to enjoy the same objects of desire.

The criticism against the realists' notion about the permanently existing entity as the substratum of the phenomenal world, is the main thrust area of discussion in the text. Both Buddhist realists and the Brāhmanical schools like Mīmāṁsā are refuted suitably. As the Mahāyāna system never advocates the attainment of *nirvāṇa* as the ultimate spiritual attainment, Āryadeva pointedly says that the Hīnayānists inculcate the fear of death in the process of attainment of *nirvāṇa*, because the fear of death impedes spiritual growth. To the Mīmāṁsakas, who advocate the attainment of *mokṣa* through rituals, Āryadeva questions the validity of dogmatic rituals. He pointedly asks that if the person is under the grip of desire and negative notions such as *rāga*, *dveṣa*, *moha*, and *īrṣyā*, it is logically inconsistent to think that the rituals like bathing in the River Gaṅgā could purify a person from the sins caused by *rāga*, *dveṣa*, *moha*, and *īrṣyā*. The water in the Gaṅgā has no such power to remove negative human notions. The spiritual practice should be aimed at eradicating the attachment to the world of things that create *rāga*, *dveṣa, moha, īrṣyā*, and also relieving one from the fear of death.[106] The negative notions cannot be washed away by taking bath in the Gaṅgā but by the correct spiritual practices.

Delineating the reasons of sufferings and causes for rebirth, Āryadeva opines that *avidyā* or ignorance caused by desire or mistaking the non-self for self is the real reason for rebirth. The *Ātmā*, and those belonging to the self, *Ātmīya*, are causing immense problem to the *citta;* just as the imaginary silver that belongs to the *Ātman* (*Ātmya*) is seen on a shell. The notion of the silver is removed with the realisation of the shell; likewise the notion of *Ātmā* and *Ātmīya* are removed with the realisation of *nairātmya*, the insubstantial nature of the phenomenally existing entities. The fear generated out of perceiving the snake is removed with the realisation of the *nairātmya* of rope-snake. Thus, the realisation of the *nairātmya* of all the phenomenally existing entities would remove the misconception about their eternal existence.

The one who realises the purity of *citta* through the commingling of the *prajñā* and *upāya* would realise that the appearances are mere creations of mind (*vikalpas*), and he is able to interpret everything clearly, because purified *citta* is his wealth. Since the problem of desire would not affect his mind, he is allowed to enjoy everything, because like a swan he could drink the milk even from an admixture of milk and water. Having maintained the equanimity and purity of the mind, the world of a Yogi is different from the world of an ordinary human being, for the Yogi is able to see the world as the way it appears without the influence of *vikalpa*. The Yogi who practices

Mahāyāna is superior to the Yogis of other systems and schools, because Mahāyāna provides liberation in this birth itself; the spiritual merit that one could attain through innumerable births, can be attained in this birth itself. The path of Mahāyāna is followed by a *Mahāsattva*, a person who is endowed with *mahāprajñā*, *mahopāya*, and *mahākaruṇā,* leading to supreme bliss (*mahāsukha*).

The *prajñā* of the Yogi would attain perfection after spiritual practices, and this perfected knowledge is called adamantine knowledge (*vajrājñāna*). The action of *vajrājñāna* on *citta* can be exemplified to the instance of the gem called Sūrya-kāntamaṇi, which catches fire on exposition to sunlight. Similarly, when the *citta* is exposed to *vajrajñāna*, it originates the fire that removes all *vikalpas* about the phenomenal world. A Yogi endeavours to seek the *vajrajñāna* through spiritual practices, which removes all the *vikalpas*; like a fried seed that never germinates, the *citta* never again creates thought constructs. When two pieces of Araṇi wood are rubbed together, fire originates; likewise, when the *prajñā* and *upāya* are yoked properly, the fire of *vajrajñāna* originates which reveals the essence of phenomena (*dharmadhātu*),[107] and dispels the misconceptions that eliminates pain and pleasure. When one can see the *dharmadhātu* of the objects, enlightenment happens instantaneously, like a creeper suddenly blossoms with beautiful flowers.

By practising the Mantras as part of his spiritual practices, a Yogi is able to protect his mind from *vikalpas*, achieving perfection in his vision. He will be able to see the phenomenal world as the way it appears, like one could perceive the objective phenomena as clearly as he could see the bracelet on his hand. The physical body is considered as a beholder of self and the foundation of existence for a normal human being, but for a Mahāyānist Yogi, it is just the conglomeration of the *pañcabhūtas.*[108] For such a Yogi there is no distinction between superior Brāhman and the lowly Caṇḍāla. The subjective stage of the mind, identical with the *pañca-skandhas*,[109] which are interdependent, insubstantial, and the cause of *duḥkha*, are essentially void. Thus, there is no meaning in the assumption of the superiority of a human being because of his human existence.

Through the mastery of Mantra[110] one can change the *svabhāva* of anything. Even elements like *pṛthvī*, *agni*, *jala*, and *vāyu* can be changed by men who have mastered the Mantras. The text focuses mostly on the Māntric aspect of the Tāntric practices and not on the ritualistic side of Tāntric practices. The efficacy of the practice of Mantras is that it helps the mind and protects one from all conceptualisations, configuring the unreal as real, and the process of gestalt. Mantra-vāda is a suggested method for the maintenance of the acquired spiritual perfection. The Yogi should find refuge in the *triratnas* (three gems), as the guiding spiritual constants, which are respectively, the Buddham, the Dharmam, and the Saṅgham.[111] A purified *citta* should be protected against negative notions like doubt, etc., in order that even a minute quantity of poison could cause a lot of trouble to a human being.[112]

In the last part of the discussion, Āryadeva extols various aspects of Tāntric practices: the guru, an embodiment of the God *vajrarāja*[113] whose words are never transgressed;[114] the faith (*śraddhā*), which purifies the *citta* from turbid thought, like the gem Udakamaṇi clears turbid water; the *prajñā*, which is obtained from the Āgamas and Ādhigamas;[115] the *upāya*, which is obtained from understanding the true nature and the behaviour of the phenomena. In conclusion, Āryadeva opines that a Yogi, with the help of meticulous practices (the *upāyas*) and perfected knowledge (the *prajñā*), is able to cleanse his *citta*. As a result, he is able to suggest suitable *upāyas* to those who aspire for the *cittaviśuddhi*.

1.7 About the Text

This text *Cittaviśuddhi-prakaraṇa* was originally collected from the manuscript sources and edited into Devanāgarī script from Newari script by H.H. Hariprasāda Śāstrī for the Asiatic Society of Bengal. It was published by the society for their *Journal of Asiatic Society* (1898), with a small English introduction. A few verses from the text were missing because of damages on the palm leaf manuscripts. Subsequently, Prabhubhai Patel, a Sanskrit scholar from Santiniketan, edited this text. He brought out an edition of the original Sanskrit text by supplementing the lost verses after reading the Tibetan translations namely, the *Cittaratna-viśodhana* and the *Cittāvaraṇa-viśodhana-prakaraṇa*. He too gave a small English introduction and the text rendering as the edited form in Sanskrit. Both these editions were taken as sources for the preparation of the edition used for the present study. In the introduction of the edited version, Prabhubhai Patel points out that the text was written by a Buddhist Tāntric scholar of the eighth century who assumed the name of Āryadeva and contended that the text was written by Āryadeva II. This claim is neither substantiated with historical evidence nor with any internal evidence from the text. The text, at the outset, never offers any evidence to call it an exclusive Tāntric text, or to prove that it had been written by a person other than Āryadeva, the author of the *Catuḥśataka* and the *Akṣaraśataka*. In fact, the *Cittaviśuddhi-prakaraṇa* is a continuation of a certain philosophical discussion initiated by Āryadeva in the *Catuḥśataka*. The purport of Āryadeva's philosophical enterprise is to introduce the philosophy of Mādhyamika to a wider audience and assail the misconceptions relating to it. He begins this endeavour by initiating dialectical arguments against the Sāṅkhya and Vaiśeṣika in *Catuḥśataka*, while in the *Cittaviśuddhi-prakaraṇa* he focuses his criticisms against the tradition of Mīmāṁsaka or the *Karma-kāṇḍa* doctrines. He introduces the efficacy of the Tantra as an enduring spiritual discipline against the highly ritualistic Mīmāṁsā systems.

In an effort to find the philosophical foundations of Buddhist Tāntric practices, I wish to focus on the philosophical positions of the early Mādhyamikas where they have interpreted the conception of *śūnyatā* in a distinctive manner, adhering to the conception of that idea in the original discourses of the Buddha. The idea of *śūnya* is interpreted by various scholars and thinkers of the classical Indian philosophy (both Buddhists and non-Buddhists) in order to highlight their positions. We must be aware that considering the idea of *śūnyatā* as a theory is one such method; the original discourses of the Buddha sternly criticises the view of interpreting *śūnya* as a theory or philosophical position. He, on the other hand, introduces it as a tool to understand the phenomenal world differently, so as to comprehend it effectively, but at the same time the proclamation of the Buddha was not philosophically interpreted to avoid it falling into the control of thinkers who might misinterpret it. In this context, the early Mādhyamikas interpreted the conception of *śūnyatā* as the insubstantial nature essence of the phenomenal world (*dharma-nairātmya*) and the insubstantial nature of substantive human personality apprehending it (*pudgala-nairātmya*). On clear analysis, real and existing nature of the phenomenal world would not withstand, because the human perceptive faculties apprehending them are insubstantial, and, also, an objective analysis of those objects would change its intrinsic nature turning into objects with manifold manifestations. In the original discourses, the Buddha has interpreted the conception of self as the *pañca-skandhas*, and the real nature of self is a lump of dispositions which is one of the adjuncts of the *pañca-skandha*. Here I am reviewing both these aspects, the insubstantial nature of the objective phenomenal world and the influence of dispositions on human mind.

The insubstantial nature of the phenomenal world is accepted as the property of the world even by analytical science, but the human mind's urge to understand the truth about the phenomenal world by analysing the objective world is an unending quest because most of the dispositions are oriented towards the realities of the objective world. The conception of *cittaviśuddhi* is considered a process of the removal of dispositions that tempt the mind to apprehend what is unreal as real. The text *Cittaviśuddhi-prakaraṇa* is a seminal work which teaches how to handle the dispositions that manifest the world as real and eternal. It explains the process of cleansing the mind and reinstating the original nature of the mind, *Bodhicitta*, which is enlightened always.

References

1. David J.Kalupahana, *Mūlamādhyamakakārikā of Nāgārjuna*, 1986, p. 1.
2. Ibid.
3. Theodore Stcherbatsky, *The Conception of Buddhist Nirvāṇa*, 1968, p. 17.
4. "We have Candrakirti's authority of the fact that there exists no difference in the philosophical standpoints of Nāgārjuna and Āryadeva." See Peter Della Santina, *Mādhyamika Schools in India*, 1986, p. 21; see also, T.R.V. Murti, *The Central Philosophy of Buddhism*, 1955, p. 92.
5. David J. Kalupahana, *A History of Buddhist Philosophy*, pp. 165–66.
6. Ibid., p. 69.
7. The object of experience is the object that has become a part of the experience and should be used in past participle. It can be called the objects known, they are, objects conceived, objects cognised, objects seen, objects heard, etc. The other aspect of the objects of the world is objects of knowledge, they are: objects of material form, sound, smell, taste, touch, and concept. (Ibid.)
8. Ibid., p. 79.
9. Ibid., p. 75.
10. Ibid., p. 76.
11. Ibid., p. 74. The middle position is explained as "dependent arising," explained in terms of the twelve factors. In its positive statement, this

twelve-fold formula represents an explanation of a person in bondage, while the negative statement that immediately follows, explains the process of freedom.

12. The conceived objective thing is called *citta-mātra*, the subjective aspect of the object for mind *caitta*, see Thomas A. Kochumuttom, *Buddhist Doctrine of Experience*, 1999, p. 203; see also, David J. Kalupahana, *A History of Buddhist Philosophy*, p. 81.
13. *Cittaviśuddhi-prakaraṇa*, v. 8.
14. As quoted from the translation given in the David J. Kalupahana, "Everything exists,'—this *Kātyāyana*, is one extreme' [...]. Everything does not exist, [...] this, *Kātyāyana* is the second extreme." (*The Philosophy of the Middle Way*, p. 10)
15. Ibid., p. 12.
16. Dependent upon ignorance arise dispositions; dependent upon dispositions arises consciousness; dependent upon consciousness arises the psychological personality: dependent upon the psychological personality arise the six senses; dependent upon the six senses arises contact; dependent upon contact arises feeling; dependent upon feeling arises craving; dependent upon craving arises grasping; dependent upon grasping arises becoming; depend upon becoming arises birth; dependent upon birth arises old age and death, grief, lamentation, suffering, dejection, and despair. Thus arises the entire mass of suffering. (Ibid., p.10)
17. Ibid., p. 13.
18. David J. Kalupahana, *Philosophy of the Middle Way*, 1995, pp. 6, 7.
19. Ibid., p. 7.
20. T.R.V. Murti, *The Central Philosophy of Buddhism*, 1978, pp. 49, 50.
21. The Theravāda and Sarvāstivāda schools held the Abhidharma discourses to very high esteem. The human personality that is discussed in the discourses received discursive treatment. The analysis of human experience into aggregates, elements, and faculties; all of which were considered to be *dharma*, or elements of existence. This was to establish that there is no permanent self-existing eternally or any substance in these phenomena. These two schools Sarvāstivāda and Sautrāntikas, in the job of interpreting the Abhidhārmic literature, diverted from the tenets of the original texts and placed their arguments to counter the onslaught of orthodox schools of Indian philosophy. In that process, Sarvāstivādins were to accept ultimate discrete atomic elements, and that to accommodate this aspect they had to accept some type of *svabhāva* (self-nature) for all the phenomena. They contented that self-nature is impermanent and changing; but this lead to further logical difficulties. In that process, they had to accept the existence of phenomena in all the three periods of time. A sort of deviation from the original teachings of Buddhism had entered into Buddhism. This school of Buddhism almost looked like the Sāṅkhya school in its method of philosophising. While the other school Sautrāntika considered *svabhāva* as

the self in disguise and opposed the theory of *svabhāva*. Sautrāntikas accepted the theory of momentariness and ended up in recognising a sort of non-identity theory of causation. Though they abandoned the substantialist conception of *dharma*, the adherence to the theory of moments made them accept the experienced continuity of the individual person. Schools like *pudgala-vāda* are closely related to Sautrāntikas. See, David J. Kalupahana, *A History of Buddhist Philosophy*, p. 32.

22. Ibid., p. 4.
23. Ibid., p. 6.
24. Ibid., p. 7. This text contains two discourses dealing with the Middle Path.
25. Ibid., p. 21.
26. Ibid., p. 22.
27. Ibid.
28. Ibid., p. 23.
29. K.V. Ramanan, *Nāgārjuna's Philosophy as presented in Māhāprajñāpāramitāśāstra*, 1975, p. 38.
30. As quoted from the author who compiles this conclusion from the *Māhāprajñāpāramitāśāstra,* loc. cit.
31. Peter Della Santina, *Mādhyamika Schools in India*, p. 2.
32. T.R.V. Murti, op. cit., p. 37.
33. Ibid., p. 38.
34. Ibid., p. 122.
35. *Dīghanikāya*, Brahmajālasutta, v. 32.
36. K.N. Jayathilake, *The Early Buddhist Theory of Knowledge*, 1963, p. 135.
37. T.R.V. Murti, op. cit., p. 45.
38. Ibid.
39. Ibid., p. 47.
40. Ibid., p. 48.
41. K. Venkata Ramanan, op. cit., p. 50.
42. *sad asat sadasac ceti sadasan neti ca karmaḥ / eṣa prayojya vidvadhir ekatvādiṣu nityaśaḥ //* (Existent, in-existent, both existent and in-existent, neither existent nor in-existent, that is the method which the learned should always use with regard to oneness and other such (theses). See, Karen Lang, *Aryadeva's Catuḥśataka*,1986, chap. XIV. Differing to Western logic, here excluded middle and double negation is added in the fourfold negation of the Mādhyamikas. See, Tom J.F. Tillemans,*Materials for the Study of Āryadeva, Candrakīrti and Dharmapāla*, 1990, p. 75.
43. T.R.V. Murti., op. cit., p. 148.
44. David Kalupahana, *The Philosophy of the Middle Way*, p. 22.
45. Watanabe Fumimaro, op. cit., p. 91.
46. H V. Guenther, *The Tāntric View of Life*, 1952, p.v.
47. T.R.V. Murti, op. cit., p. 92.
48. Tārānātha, *History of Buddhism*, trans. Lama Gamba, 1970, p. 124.
49. Ibid.
50. Bu-stön, *History of Buddhism*, trans. Obemitten, p. 130.
51. Tārānātha, op. cit., p. 124.

52. Karen Lang, op. cit., p. 7. Cited from Lamotte's paper from the *Ceylon Historical Journal*, VII, 1957–58, p. 123.
53. Tom J.F. Tillemans, op. cit., p. 75.
54. Peter Della Santina, *Mādhyamika Schools in India*, p. 20, quoted from Tārānātha, *The History of Buddhism*, 1970.
55. Tārānātha, op. cit., p. 126.
56. Karen Lang, op. cit., 1986, p. 8.
57. Nāgārjuna, *Suhṛllekha*, summary by Peter Della Santina, *Encyclopaedia of Indian Philosophies*, General editor: Karl H. Potter, vol. VIII, p. 163.
58. Karen Lang, op. cit., p. 8.
59. Ibid., p. 9.
60. Ibid.
61. Ibid, p. 16.
62. *Cittaviśuddhi-prakaraṇa*, v. 19.
63. Peter Della Santina, *Mādhyamika Schools in India*, p. 21. Here, the opinion of T.R.V. Murti is cited that this text of *Śataśāstra* is an abridged rearrangement of the contents of *Catuḥśataka*.
64. Bu-stön, op. cit., p. 136.
65. Tom J.F. Tillemans, op. cit., p. 7.
66. Ibid., The details given are same as that is given in the quote. There is a contention among various scholars that there are two Āryadeva(s), one is the Mādhyamika scholar and disciple of Nāgārjuna and the other is a Tāntric who lived much later in the eighth century, who authored many texts. The *Cittaviśudhi-prakaraṇa* and various other texts mentioned above by Tom J.F. Tillemans as Āryadeva II is the second Āryadeva
67. Karen Lang, op. cit., p. 10. She also comments that the Vajrayāna works attributed to Āryadeva are written by the second Āryadeva.
68. Ibid.
69. The *Dharmacakra-pravartanasūtra*, as the practical interpretation of the middle position, seeks to find the middle of the extremes of self-indulgence and self-mortification, it consisted of the noble eight-fold path that leads to freedom. David J. Kalupahana, *The Philosophy of the Middle Way*, p. 1.
70. The Tāntric tradition is the practical interpretation of Mādhyamika (Mahāyāna) tradition. See, S.B. Dasgupta, *An Introduction to Tāntric Buddhism*, 1974, p. x.
71. Prabhubhai Patel, *Cittaviśuddhi-prakaraṇa of Āryadeva*, p. xiii.
72. *Cittaviśuddhi-prakaraṇa*, v. 134.
73. Prabhubhai Patel, op.cit., p. xiii.
74. Ibid.
75. Tom J.F. Tillemans, op. cit., p. 6.
76. Prabhubhai Patel, op. cit., pp. xv, xvi.
77. Sashibhushan Dasgupta, op. cit., p. 179.
78. *Cittaviśuddhi-prakaraṇa*, 25 and 46.
79. Ibid., v. 1. See also, v. 8.
80. Karen Lang, op. cit., p. 16.

81. Ibid.
82. Ibid., p. 17.
83. The Buddhist philosophy declines the eternity of the self, and that the merit acquired by the self makes a person born in a particular caste. Being born in a caste gives permission for an individual to perform certain action whether it is desirable or not, which in turn leaves him to suffer in the future. Buddhist philosophy, on the other hand, accepts the transferability of *karma*, so *karma* done in the name of duty finally brings suffering for the individual. (Ibid.)
84. Bodhisattva is one who denies *nirvāṇa* and strives for liberating other sentient beings. He can have the freedom to choose his rebirth, because he is not affected by any *karma,* also birth, death, and *nirvāṇa* do not affect him. (Ibid.)
85. Ibid.
86. Āryadeva, indirectly criticises the Brāhmanical schools which profess the benefits of meritorious actions that redeem the soul from lower births to higher births. (Ibid., p. 18)
87. The criticism of Āryadeva goes against the Vaiśeṣikas who advocates the permanence of atom that is partless. In fact, atoms have parts and are impermanent. Modern science also supports this argument of Buddhists that the ultimate particle is inconceivable and impermanent. (Ibid.)
88. Here, the emphasis is on liberation that is more than attaining heaven. Heaven can be depicted as peaceful stage of life, and the liberation from birth and death might be the cessation ot desire and, thus, the craving for more. (Ibid., p. 20)
89. The idea behind such a conclusion is that the objects have no real existence that would help the wise man understand the illusory nature of the *saṁsāra*. (Ibid.)
90. Ibid., p. 21.
91. The bondage produced by conceptual construction is the best way to understand the emptiness of things. (Ibid.)
92. T.R.V. Murti, op. cit., p. 93. During Āryadava's time Sāṅkhya and Vaiśeṣika were two very important opponents of Buddhism. His objections to these Vedic schools is very evident in all his works.
93. Ibid.
94. Fernando Tola and E. Dragonetti, *On Voidness*, 1995, p. 4.
95. Ibid., pp. 9-13.
96. Now we know that the atom is divisible into subatomic particles of indefinable characteristics.
97. The observations of modern science are also similar to that of Āryadeva, the ultimate particle of matter is not perceivable to human cognitive faculties. This substantiates the Buddhists' notion of *dharma-nairātmya*, in Fernando Tola and C. Dragonetti, *On Voidness*, p. 13.

98. The *Hastavālanāma-prakaraṇavṛtti*, vv. 1c-d, in ibid., p. 10, commentary.
99. *Hastavālanāma-prakaraṇavṛtti*, vv. 6a-d. For the Mādhyamikas there is no supreme reality in the sense as an entity existing permanently and etern illy. The *śūnya* of Mādhyamika is inexplicable in any terms, neither it is a position that is based on inexplicability. Mādhymikas refute all theories and doctrines with the inconsistencies prevailing in every thesis that claims to explain the world. Ultimately one discerns the *pudgala-nairātmya* and *dharma-nairātmya*.
100. Also called logical reconstruction, translation of a discourse of a certain conceptual type into a discourse of another conceptual type with the aim of making it possible to say everything that is expressible in the former more clearly in the latter. Quoted from the *Cambridge Dictionary of Philosophy*, p. 676.
101. *Cittaviśuddhi-prakaraṇa*, v. 10.
102. This becomes one of the main practices of the Tāntrics, a system of spiritual practice developed later in this school of Yogis. See Sasibhushan Dasgupta, *An Introduction to Tantric Buddhism*, p. 172.
103. The possible meaning of *Bodhicitta*, in Mādhyamika parlance, is that stage of mind which understands the *śūnyatā* of all phenomena.
104. The term *prajñopāya* is having the widest connotation in the Mahāyānistic Buddhists' terminology. See S.B. Dasgupta, op.cit., p. 120.
105. In the *Aṭṭhasālinī*, Buddhaghoṣa states that a change of attitude is necessary to liberate from the *saṁsāra*. Here, a change of the *dharmadhātu* is possible only by the commingling of *prajñā* and *upāya*. The *dharmadhātu* that leaves phenomenal appearance (*dharma*) as empty or *śūnya*. Herbert V. Guenther, *Philosophy and Psychology of Abhidarma*, 1974, p. 26.
106. In fact, the feeling of purity normally leads one to self-esteem, this, in turn, results in more desire for life.
107. *Dhamadhātu* as per the Abhidharma literature could be explained as the root of all phenomenon elements. See the *Buddhist Hybrid Sanskrit Grammar and Dictionary*, p. 277. See Watanabe Fumimaro, op. cit., pp. 11-13. As far as we can see in the Nikāyas, there are ideas about the nature of all *dharmas*, as impermanent, empty, without soul, being stations, or bases for other *dharmas*, etc.; there are attempts to establish the regularity of *dharmas* as determined by dependent origination; and there are tendencies to consider the *dharmas* as realities under proper conditions; these *dharmas* are not merely elements by principle. In the *Śraddhotpadaśāstra*, Aśvaghoṣa describes the term *dharmadhātu* as the totality of the all things, its essential nature is uncreated and external; the unity of all. Aśvaghoṣa's explanation is more appropriate since he is one of the founders of Mahāyāna thought and had lived in the first century. See, Surendranath Dasgupta, *A History of Indian Philosophy*, vol. 1, 1922, p. 131.
108. A human being is made of the conglomeration of the four elements, space and consciousness, it is the earth makes the body solid; it is due to water there is fat in the body; it is due to fire there is digestion in the body; it is due

to air there is respiration; it is due to *ākāśa* there is porosity; and it is due to *vijñāna* there is *citta*. Only a combination of all these we could call man, not a singular element (Surendranath Dasgupta, op. cit., p. 143.)

109. The word *skandha* means trunk of a tree and is generally used to mean group or aggregates. The *skandhas* are aggregates of bodily and psychic states and are divided into five classes: (1) *rūpa* (four elements, the body, and the senses), sense data, etc., (2) *vedana* (feeling-pleasurable painful and indifferent), (3) *sañña* (conceptual knowledge), *saṅkara* (synthetic mental states and the synthetic functioning of compound sense affections, compound feelings and compound sense concepts), (5) *viññana* (consciousness). (Ibid., p. 94)

110. Meaning of the term *mantra* is instrument of thought, sacred text, song of praise, individual formula addressed to individual deity, etc. As per *Buddhist Hybrid Sanskrit Grammar and Dictionary* the meaning is "formula." The meaning of the word *mantra*, according to Vasubandhu in *Bodhisattvabhūmi* is that the absolute meaninglessness is the real significance of the *mantras*. When a Yogi meditates on the absolute meaninglessness of the *mantras* he will gradually lead to the state of mind, where it will be easy for him to meditate on the ultimate nature of the *dharmas* as absolutely meaningless. This leads the Yogi to realise the *śūnya* of all *dharmas*. (Ibid., p. 59)

111. The given instructions are meant for a serious practitioner who likes to attain Bodhisattvahood; such people should have the internal sincerity to follow the difficult path that leads to the desired availing of *Bodhicitta*; otherwise he should accept defeat and stop his practices and live like a normal human being. Most importantly, one should observe that he wouldn't fail in his endeavours. See Herbert V. Guenther, *The Tāntric View of Life*, 1952, p. 23.

112. The fall of a fly into some food substance can cause a lot of trouble to one who eats that food; poison, however small it is, can create trouble. Thought activities also have this problem and it can create great trouble unless the thinker doesn't understand the nature of *citta*. *Cittaviśuddhi-prakaraṇa*, v. 127.

113. "To you Buddha as *guru* will be revealed, if you rely on *cakrasaṁvara*," Herbert V. Guenther, *The Tantric View of Life*, p. 28.

114. During initiation the student is given a symbol that he should keep with him until the completion of his training. See Herbert V. Guenther, *Life and Teaching of Naropa*, 1963, p. 29.

115. Mahāyāna doesn't accept the supremacy of Āgamas, but in the case of understanding the ways of wisdom, Āgamas are of great help.

Chapter Two

Structure of Mādhyamika Dialectics

2.1 Dialectics as a Method to Discern *Dharma-nairātmya*

The study of the *Cittaviśuddhi-prakaraṇa* requires a clear understanding of the structure of the dialectical system introduced by the early Mādhyamikas. The unique strength of the Mādhyamika philosophy is based on its special dialectics that is aimed at protecting the reasoning process from sliding into pseudo-theorising. Since Mādhyamikas do not seek the support of any theoretical position as a solution to the problem of dialectics, it is inevitable to understand the nature of dialectics and the possibility of solution in the Mādhyamika way. Hence, the attempt here is for defining and demonstrating the philosophising methodology of Nāgārjuna and Āryadeva, and the concept of *śūnyatā* introduced by them. It is not the emptiness as the term means. In fact, the Mādhyamikas consider *śūnyatā* as the most effective analytical tool developed to examine the real nature of the apparent world of phenomena. Therefore, this study tries to understand the structure of Mādhyamika dialectics, by focusing on two of the most important works of the early Mādhyamikas: the *Vigraha-vyāvartinī* of Nāgārjuna and the *Hastavālanāma-prakaraṇavṛtti* of Āryadeva. The *Vigrahavyāvartinī* is considered as the foundation of Mādhyamika dialectics, which assails the authority of epistemological evidences (*pramāṇa*) as the authentic way to understand the phenomenal world; subsequently, the insubstantial nature of the phenomenal world is interpreted in the text *Hastavālanāma-prakaraṇavṛtti*, Āryadeva consolidates these arguments in systematic format and explains the same matter by systematically analysing the objective phenomena. The philosophical foundations of the arguments advanced in the *Cittaviśuddhi-prakaraṇa* follows the *Hastavālanāma-prakaraṇavṛtti*, for interpreting *dharma*,[1] *dharmadhātu* and *dharma-*

nairātmya; and, consequently, with the introduction of Tāntric spiritual practices, for interpreting the conception of *pudgala-nairātmya*.[2]

The question here is how can one position the world of appearance in the realm of actual experience? The concept of *śūnyatā* is an implicit aspect that goes together with every conceived phenomenon of the experienced object of the world. At the same time, the *śūnyatā* of things are not an eternal entity that forms a substratum for the world of appearance, or the *śūnyatā* of things are merging into a transcended *mahā-śūnyatā*. On the other hand, the *śūnyatā* is instrumental in revealing the *dharma-nirātmya* (essencelessness of the phenomena).

Three important ways of analysis are taken into consideration in this discussion to prove the concept of *dharma-nairātmya*. Firstly, the regressive method of analysis is interpreted based on a technique employed by Nāgārjuna in the text *Vigrahavyāvartinī*, to prove the *dharma-nairātmya* of the objects of experience, by critically analysing the epistemic premises, the *pramāṇas*. Secondly, the progressive method of analysis has been introduced based on the discussion of in the text *Hastavālanāma-prakaraṇavṛtti* by Āryadeva, where the discussion is based on the progressive analysis of the objects of experience at its various levels of manifestations, ending in *dharma-nairātmya*. Thirdly, the systematic scientific analysis method is introduced, the mode of analysis employed by the scientists in the modern period. A detailed discussion on various issues involved in understanding the world based on this method has created a lots of misunderstanding and confusion, when the scientific analysis fails to find an ultimate solution in explaining the world with absolute certainty. By focussing on the findings of Werner Heisenberg, it is demonstrated that modern science too agrees with the conception of *dharma-nairātmya*. The presumption of modern analytical science is that by analysing the truth-value of objects of the experienced world, it is possible to arrive at the truth about the phenomenal world; that truth is perfectly understandable and is perfectly deterministic, revealing the identity of the true nature of things. This problem arises because of modern sciences' direct or indirect dependence on classical western philosophy where the conceptions of universals or ideas are accepted as a metaphysical reality. This argument finds disorientation with the introduction of the uncertainty principle introduced by a modern thinker, Werner Heisenberg, who assails the notion of scientific determinism. We know that theoretical science is unable to promulgate another theory to disprove the uncertainty principle and it has almost accepted the uncertainty principle as a property of the world. In other words, modern science accepts *dharma-nairātmya* as a property of the objective world, and Werner Heisenberg joins with Nāgārjuna and Ārydeva in this issue.

The foundation of Mādhyamika dialectics is built on the Buddha's silence to opinion on various metaphysical questions advanced by various schools of philosophy of his time. He refused to answer directly any question substantiating or refuting any theoretical position explaining the phenomenal world. The Buddha's silence can also be interpreted as the inability and limitations of the human faculties to make judgments about the world of experience, or can be stated that the deterministic objective world is apparently real and certain, not ultimate.

2.2 The Buddha's Silence—the Source of Mādhyamika Dialectics

The Buddha refused to answer and remained silent to various contentious questions that were asked to him by both materialists and Brāhmanical thinkers of his time. The Mādhyamika dialectics can be explained as the rationalisation of this silence of the Buddha. To illustrate this, on the question of his silence over the contentious questions relating to eternalism and nihilism, the Buddha answered to the Śrāvaka Ānanda that

> if, Ānanda, when asked: "Is there a self?" I had replied to him: "There is a self," then Ānanda, that would be aiding with the recluses and Brahmins who are eternalists. But if, Ānanda, when asked: "Is there not a self?" I had replied that it does not exist, that, Ānanda, would be aiding with those recluses and Brahmins who are annihilationists.[3]

The Buddha was equally silent to disputatious questions about rebirth or the finiteness of the world, or about the body's identity with the self. On the question of rebirth, the Buddha's answer to the Sage Vacchagotra was that

> Vaccha, it is not true to say that he is reborn. Then Gotama he is not reborn; Vaccha, it is not true to say that, he is not reborn. Then, Gotama, he is both born and not reborn. Vaccha, it is not true to say that, he is both reborn and not reborn. Then, Gotama he is neither reborn nor not reborn. Vaccha, it is not true to say that he is neither reborn nor not reborn.[4]

These words of the Buddha are not aimed at evading the dialectical trap set by the wanderer ascetic Vacchagotra to accept either of the positions, but they highlight the inability of our thinking patterns and analytical faculties to express the truth about such metaphysical questions. Hence, the world of realities should be seen and understood from a different perspective with a new dialectical method. According to T.R.V. Murti:

> He (the Buddha) is conscious of the indeterminable nature of the conflict, and resolves it by rising to the higher standpoint of criticism. Dialectics was born. To Buddha then, belongs the honour of having discovered the dialectics long before anything approximating to it was formulated in the West.[5]

The dialectics is applicable only when there is a conflict in reasoning about the world of appearance and the truth-value of perception. In fact, the development of thought into philosophy is to solve the problem of conflicts in reasoning and to realise the truth. The profound silence of the Buddha indicates that he was not comfortable with the ways in which we understand the world of appearance and with the metaphysical positions formulated to understand it. Therefore, his call was to see the world from different standpoints and perspectives, or to see the world as the way it appears before us, without resorting to any theory. After all, the conceptualisation process is a property of the mind, which tempts us to cling to the perceived, configuring it as real and eternal; or due to the inner contradictions of the perceived, visualising it as empty and void. In short, the theories are partial views formulated out of inner weakness of human mind. The silence of the Buddha calls for the enhancement of the faculties of human reasoning to develop spacious arguments to repudiate the authority of theories and the dependence on them.

2.3 The Development of Mādhyamika Dialectics

The philosophy of Mādhyamika should be understood in the light of the teachings of the Buddha and the meaning of the "Buddha's silence." In this regard, the problem of extremes in the metaphysical positions of eternity and nihilism, the conflict of reason of "is" and "is not," and the logical impossibility of discerning the empirical realities as the reflection of the ultimate reality, are the questions that Mādhyamika attempts to answer. Mādhyamika is conscious of the meaning of the Buddha's silence and their dialectical system rises above all the conflicts of reasoning which calls for answers like "is" and "is not." Thus, the Mādhyamika attempt is to explain the idea of rising and ceasing nature of the world of phenomena, without falling into the fallacy of taking positions in explaining them from either of the extreme positions, but from the middle position.

Describing the middle position, Nāgārjuna says in the *Mūlamādhyamikakārikā*:

> "Exists" implies grasping after eternalism. "Doesn't exist" implies the philosophy of annihilation. Therefore, a discerning person should not rely upon either existence or non-existence.[6]

The middle position here should not be seen as a naïve synthesis of the two extreme standpoints, but it is the most difficult aspect of viewing the phenomenal world from a different standpoint, without relying on either of the alternatives.

The way of Mādhyamika philosophical enterprise, where the arguments are formulated based on negative questioning, is to show the inconsistency in accepting the views of the substantialists' positions of both eternalism or nihilism. The Buddha kept silent to those questions that call for a certain and clear answer, because he understood that affirmation or negation of either of the position would lead to serious problems, of clinging and grasping to either of the extremes. The negation of eternalism is not the celebration of annihilations or vice versa. As T.R.V. Murti aptly commented on this position:

> Rejection of views is not based on any positive grounds or the acceptance of another view; it is solely based on the inner contradiction implicit in each view. The function of the Mādhyamika dialectics, on the logical level, is purely negative, analytic.[7]

This statement of T.R.V. Murti does not explain every aspect of Mādhyamika dialectics, but it can be understood clearly, only when we study the treatise of Nāgārjuna, the *Vigrahavyāvartinī* and the *Hastavālanāma-prakaraṇavṛtti* of Āryadeva, in detail. Mādhyamikas' views on epistemology and logic are well explained in the *Vigrahavyāvartinī*.[8] The subject of discussion of this text is the truth-value of the conceived and cognised objects of the phenomenal world, and the use of epistemic premises, *pramāṇas*[9] as a tool for achieving clear and certain knowledge that could support logical thinking. Mādhyamikas are not against the use of *pramāṇas* as a means of cognition of the phenomena, but according to them, the use of *pramāṇas* as a tool for determining truth-value and for theorising would lead to inconsistent and fragmented results. We can very well see that most of the realists' theories, based on such inconsistent epistemic premises (*pramāṇas*) stand repudiated, revised, or substituted with another theory. The process of theorization and repudiation unceasingly continues. The origin of *Prasaṅga*,[10] which was promoted by later Mādhyamikas, emanated from this fundamental view that the theories can appear to be true in certain contexts, which are based on certain causes and conditions; the certainties of those theories are notwithstanding, when the causes and conditions are removed. The formulation of a perfect theory that is true and usable for future reference is impossible. In other words, the existences of entities are similar to that of the existence of a lamp which depends on wick, oil, etc. The *Majjhimanikāya* says:

> It is not in oil or in wick, or anything in itself, the lamp exists. The phenomena are like the lamp. They are nothing in themselves. All things are unreal; they are deceptions, Nibbāna (Nirvāṇa) is the only truth.[11]

Most of the theories are formulated in the belief that the apparently perceived phenomena are a true and genuine reflection of a permanently existing reality. But, such positions are never self-explanatory or established beyond doubt. Mādhyamika contends that no theory is consistent and unassailable when confronted with the actual nature of the world. In the *Vigrahavyāvartinī*, Nāgārjuna uses a different pattern of arguments to repudiate their substantiating arguments about theories. Those patterns of arguments are same as the arguments used by the realists to substantiate their position about the truth function of *pramāṇas* and the validity of theories.

The questions that Nāgārjuna raises are a continuance of the thinking which was in vogue for centuries before him. Materialists and logical sceptics criticised the Vedic schools of Brāhmans viewpoints based on the Vedas and the Vedic schools of philosophy. The severe criticism on to a metaphysical position implicitly agrees to the contraposition, in this case agreeing with nihilism. Nihilism is the logical conclusion of refusing the authority of eternalism. On the other hand, the prime concern of the Mādhyamikas is different from both these viewpoints; it is to highlight the inconsistency of the *pramāṇas* and their effectiveness as a tool for interpreting the world. Here, it calls for a new logical system in the place of the traditional thinking to discern the real nature of the world of phenomena. The limitations of logical thinking are purely based on two aspects, truth and not truth or existence and non-existence. In other words, the two ways of analysing the phenomena to reveal the truth are inherently insubstantial. It may be suggested that the *Vigrahavyāvartinī* presents a compendium of the current objections, which were advanced by naïve realism in general against the standpoint of the Mādhyamikas.[12]

2.4 *Dharma-nairātmya*—Through the Method of Regressive Analysis

The dialectical methodology adapted in the *Vigrahavyāvartinī* is called regressive method,[13] because Nāgārjuna introduces a very unique way to explain his position. He accepted the epistemological value of *pramāṇas* to assail the notion that he is supporting the nihilistic view. After substantiating his arguments, he introduced the reasons why the *pramāṇas* should not be accepted as valid instruments of knowledge. His introduction of *śūnya* as *dharma-nairātmya* is to settle the inconsistency generated of accepting the epistemological authority of *pramāṇas.*

Notwithstanding the critics' arguments to push the Mādhyamika view as nihilism, Nāgārjuna takes care of the critique's position that may presumably come up against his arguments. He carefully analyses the arguments of the realists advanced against his view on the concept of *śūnyatā* and introduces the dialectics that questions the authenticity of *pramāṇas*. Mādhyamika dialectic is perfectly analytical, accepting the *pramāṇas* in order to discern the world of phenomena, but rejecting their authority in revealing the absolute truth about the world of existence. In other words, the arguments advanced in *Vigraha-vyāvartinī* try to reject the authority of *pramāṇas* to establish truth-value of the objective world of experience by citing the problems that are evident with the realm of those epistemic premises. Though those problems are evident, they are overlooked by the realist schools of philosophy. Elaborating the problem of inconsistency from another perspective, the Mādhyamikas, further, contends that it is not the *dharmas* (phenomena) but the association of the mind with the *dharmas* that creates conceptualisations (*vikalpas*), which in turn bind the mind, creating illusory manifestations about the perceived phenomena.[14]

It is clear that human thought and ideas are based on inconsistent information. Mādhyamika dialectics help to redeem the human thought from all misconceptions and psuedological grab, that haunt his mind. In the first twenty verses of the *Vigrahavyāvartinī*, Nāgārjuna criticises the position that rejects the authority of *pramāṇas*, in order that to account for the conception of the cognised objects. However, in the later discussion, he argues against the authority of *pramāṇas* as a valid means for true cognition and against the validity of theories formulated out of them.

The early Mādhyamika accepts the theories to the extent of discerning the world of things. According to T.R.V. Murti:

> To cover all cases of knowledge and objects, the Mādhyamika accepts the four sources of knowledge—the perception (*pratyakṣa*), inference (*anumāna*), comparison (*upamāna*), and testimony (*śabda*) like the *Nyāya*, as against the (Abhidharma) Buddhist view of two *Pramāṇas*—perception and inference based on two different kinds of objects—the particular and universal.[15]

This is contrary to the popular view that Mādhyamika refuses to accept any source of knowledge to account for the world of phenomena. In fact, they accept all possible sources of knowledge to know the phenomenal world perfectly. Their refutation is not about the phenomenal world as such but against the theorisation based on such sources of knowledge, because, for them, sources of knowledge themselves are insubstantial and dependent.

2.4.1 *Discerning Dharma and Dharmadhātu— On Authority of Pramāṇas*

The first verse of the *Vigrahavyāvartinī* questions the validity of denying the "intrinsic nature" (*svabhāva*) of the phenomena. It is necessary to accept the "intrinsic nature;" otherwise, the very statement (of acceptance or denial) becomes invalid. Negation without acceptance is impossible, and thus the existence of intrinsic nature should be accepted.[16] It seems that here Nāgārjuna looks at the problem from the arguments of the critiques of Mādhyamika.[17] Contextually, this criticism can be interpreted as a critique to the position of the Sautrāntika school of Buddhism, who rejects the *svabhāva* of the elements of things, but accepts the *svalakṣaṇa* of things.

In the second and third verses, he answers the question in a different manner. He points out that if a statement is without intrinsic nature (*svabhāva*), then how can there be its negator? The two things are complementary, such that the perception of intrinsic nature (*svabhāva*) of an object and the negation of the intrinsic nature of that object are mutually dependent. He argues further that if there is no statement to be made then the negation of that statement is impossible. If both the statement and its negation are devoid of intrinsic nature, then it is a matter of serious discordance and it is required to find a special reason for that. The third verse is a clarification to what is stated in the second verse. The statement like "don't make a sound" would not stop any sound that would precede it.[18] Such things never happen in actual practice. It means that a statement, which says that "all things are void," lacks any power to defy the intrinsic nature of things or statements. The prime argument is that how could one make a negative statement without accepting the positive statement? It is not proper to deny the things after they are apprehended.[19] The denial is, in other words, an assertion of the things or statements that are denied.

If the things are denied after apprehending them through perception, then the perception, through which they have been apprehended also, gets denied. Besides, the denial of perception as a *pramāṇa* has consequent cascading effect on other *pramāṇas* such as, inference, comparison and verbal testimony. All the cases of knowledge are supported by perception. This epistemological uncertainty leads to severe logical problems.[20] When the fundamental premise has the problem of authentication, then all the other premises too stand invalid. Here, Nāgārjuna is speaking in support of the *pramāṇas*, as a valid means of apprehending knowledge.

The negation of intrinsic nature without things is also impossible to understand, because a question arises as to "what" the negation belongs. If it is to say that the intrinsic nature *per se* exists, it does not belong to things; then it requires special explanations about such intrinsic nature, because intrinsic nature without things is logically impossible.[21] In other words, if it is held that there is nothing called intrinsic nature (*svabhāva*), which can be established, then there is nothing to be negated, because the non-existent need not be established by words.[22] These two arguments, one about the non-existence of intrinsic nature and the other about existence of intrinsic nature *per se* without things, are logically impossible to accept. For instance, it is not necessary to establish the coolness of fire.

The ignorant person perceives mirages as water, when he is in a desert. It is a wrong perception and it needn't be removed by negation; it is impossible to negate the non-existence of a thing.[23] It is impossible to accept the validity of a mirage as water; similarly, the misconception about the wrongly perceived entities could be removed with the right understanding of its non-existence. Accordingly, the learned people know that the *svabhāva* of all phenomena is discernible through true cognition. Moreover, wrong cognition can be removed by the right understanding of the non-existence of such entities such as mirage. This answers the question of the impossibility in using negation to wrongly cognised things. The *svabhāva* of things is given for our perception and understanding, not non-existent things. The non-existent things such as mirages should be understood in this way, because they are not available for our experience.

In the next few verses, Nāgārjuna brings in certain realistic arguments for careful observation. Whatever it may be, existence of "six things" whose existence should be established for acceptance and rejection of anything: (1) the perception, (2) the object to be perceived, (3) the perceiver of that object, (4) the negation, (5) the object to be negated, and (6) the negator. If the contention is that there is nothing to be perceived, no perceiver and no object to be perceived, then the negation, object to be negated and the negator also become invalid. Thus, if the reasons for the objects to be negated and the negator are invalid, then it is clear that the things are established with their intrinsic natures.[24] If the three aspects of negation are true, then the three aspects of acceptance of perception are also true. On the other hand, if the validity of perception is impossible and denied then the negation of perception is impossible. The intrinsic nature (*svabhāva*) of things is also established beyond doubt, if the negation is impossible.

Also, if the argument is that the negation of intrinsic nature is established "without reason," then the establishment of things having intrinsic nature is also established "without reason."[25] When a proposition is made, one must accept the validity of its intrinsic nature in such a way that it conveys some meaning; otherwise, the proposition will be illogical, conveying nothing. On the other hand, if the contention is that the non-intrinsic nature is a property of the universe, it is beyond reason and established without any doubt, then, using the same logic, intrinsic nature is also established. For that reason, it is the duty of the dialectician to show a thing without "intrinsic nature" in the world and at the same time existent.[26]

If one is to form dialectics using negation, then one has to look into the following things:

> Is it possible to hold that negation comes first and then the thing to be negated; or is it possible to hold that the negation comes after, or are they simultaneous? In all these cases, negation is not possible without accepting the intrinsic nature. Therefore, the intrinsic nature of things is existent.[27]

It is not possible to adduce to negation without accepting the truth-value of the objects to be negated. This means that the dialectician who forms negative argumentation has to accept the existence of those things that are to be negated.

In the first twenty verses, Nāgārjuna tries to explain why it is necessary to accept all possible means of knowledge that could help one understand the true nature of the world of things. He has no hesitation to say that it is impossible to negate the existence of something without accepting the existence of the same thing. This criticism is actually directed against the Sautrāntikas and Satyasiddhi schools of Buddhism, who criticise the Sarvāstivādins' notion of intrinsic nature (*svabhāva*), by accepting the "unique particular" (*svalakṣaṇa*) or qualities as the basis of existence, and rejecting the existence of the substance.[28] This view of the Sautrāntikas is criticised by Nāgārjuna in the first twenty verses. Any criticism against "intrinsic nature" (*svabhāva*) is nothing but the acceptance of the "intrinsic nature" (*svabhāva*) of things, because of the logical impossibility of negating something without accepting its existence (the positive aspect). In the next fifty verses, he criticises the views of Sarvāstivādins about the intrinsic nature of things and the existence of substance. This is the main cause of conflicts in reasoning from the Buddhist perspective.

2.4.2 *Examining Truth Function of the Pramāṇas—the Concept of Dharma-nairātmya*

In order to establish his views by refuting the possible criticism, Nāgārjuna comes up with the argument that, if his statements are not valid in combination of cause and effect or independently of them, then the voidness of things are established.[29] If things are dependent, then they are devoid of intrinsic nature and, thus, the voidness of things is established. The things, dependently originated, do not have any intrinsic nature. It is illogical to counter the existence of an artificially created man to be negated by another artificially created man.[30] The same argument holds well in the case of the question of validity of negation: the intrinsic nature (*svabhāva*) of dependent things cannot be established, so the negation of such things also cannot be ascertained. Both are devoid of intrinsic nature and hence are in agreement with *śūnya*. Nāgārjuna further states that the critique does not hold any good, since the proposition and its negation are intrinsically invalid, and it is needless to elaborate on this aspect.

In the first section, Nāgārjuna argued in support of the intrinsic nature of sound, where the argument was that, "Don't make sound" does not prevent another sound being produced, such that the statement have no effect on the sound that is produced or the one that would be produced. Notwithstanding the negation of intrinsic nature, the realists incessantly argue supporting their position on the existence of the intrinsic nature of things. As a clarification to his position, Nāgārjuna states that both the sound uttered and the sound that has stopped the former sound from being uttered, do not have any intrinsic nature. Thus, a sound cannot prevent another sound from being produced.[31] Neither the statement nor its negation has any essence. The "sound that is to be uttered" and the negative statement "Do not make sound" are equal in nature; both lack intrinsic nature (*svabhāva*). In other words, both the statement "Do not make sound" and the sound that is not stopped from being uttered, behave in the same manner.

Nāgārjuna further clarifies that it is similar to the case of an artificially created man stating the existence of another artificially created man. Both the affirmation and its negation are intrinsically invalid, and, thus, are in agreement with *śūnya*. Further, a statement or sound is an entity dependently originated and, thus, does not have any intrinsic value phenomenally and should be in agreement with *śūnya*. A statement such as "Do not make sound" does not always evoke the same response in practical life and, thus, stopping sound being produced is not the intrinsic nature (*svabhāva*) of the statement. The statement such as "Do not make sound" holds only conventional truth or *saṁvṛti-satya* and depends on a situation, which is of the arising and ceasing nature of the apparent phenomena.[32] Thus, the essential nature of a dependently arisen thing, intrinsically insubstantial, is regarded as *śūnya*.

Nāgārjuna categorically asserts that he does not have any proposition to make and hence, for him the existence of the antinomies regarding the negations of the perception does not arise.[33] In the question of accepting or rejecting the validity of perception or any other *pramāṇa*, Nāgārjuna is clear that he does not have any theory to put forward that needs to be substantiated with arguments for and against.[34] The "no theory" argument of Nāgārjuna is difficult for the normal human mind to identify, since it needs conclusive explanations based on theories and clear statements based on the "instruments of true cognition" to satisfy its internal desires and grasping. Furthermore, the quest for an eternally existing reality is an internal urge of the human mind that is produced out of the urge to cling and grasp,[35] but unfortunately, the world of experience is contradictorily different. As a result, we can see that the apparent phenomenal world is not projecting enough evidence to substantiate the existence of any reality that exists permanently; on the other hand, it is dependent and is insubstantial independently. Analysing this idea in the *Vigrahavyāvartinī*, Peter Della Santana explains:

> The attack made by the realists is conditioned by an initial misunderstanding, which leads him to understand efficiency with ultimate reality. On the contrary, the Mādhyamika holds that efficiency is a property of conditioned phenomena only but in as much as conditioned phenomena are devoid of self-existence, they are ultimately unreal. Their causal efficiency is indeed compatible with their emptiness.[36]

Since the conditioned natures of apparent phenomena are not substantial and independent, the analysis of the phenomenal world would not reflect the ultimate reality.

2.4.2.1 *Arguing Against the Authority of Pramāṇas*: In *Vigrahavyāvartinī*, Nāgārjuna deals with this problem in detail, by criticizing the epistemological validity of *pramāṇas*. He asks, if the objects are established through *pramāṇas*, then how those *pramāṇas* in turn are established. If a *pramāṇa* is established through another *pramāṇa*, then that leads to an infinite series (*ad infinitum*).[37] The realists did not just fail to look into the intricacies that are involved in the perceptual process but considered the perception to be error-free and true always and eventually, completely, substantiating the existence of the ultimate reality.[38] According to Nāgārjuna, this process of configuring truth from the cognition is an internal weakness of human beings, an evolution of the urge to cling and grasp to what is apprehended, and it turns out to be the compendium for false ascription (*vikalpas*). If the *pramāṇas* are established through other *pramāṇas*, then that leads to infinite regress.[39] Nāgārjuna goes on to say that since the independent existence of *pramāṇas* is not established perfectly, the dependence on such *pramāṇas* as revealers of truth cannot be accepted.

If the *pramāṇas* are self-explanatory and do not require another *pramāṇa* to substantiate them, then, Nāgārjuna says, the philosophical position of the realists should be abandoned. Since there is logical discordance in the self-explanatory nature of *pramāṇas*, the realists should state the special reason for that.[40] But the realists' argument to this self-explanatory nature of *pramāṇas* is that it is like the fire, which illuminates itself and illuminates the objects near it, expressing itself and revealing the world of things. However, this position is not valid. Nāgārjuna cites the example of the pot that existing in the darkness is perceived in the presence of the fire; and asks, is it correct to say that the fire also existed in darkness, like the pot (existed) in darkness? It is impossible for fire to exist in darkness. These two entities, the fire and the pot, are not behaving in the same manner in darkness, and hence the comparison is invalid.[41] Let us consider another argument regarding fire, if fire illuminates itself and other objects, then the fire also should burn itself as it burns the objects; or if the fire illuminates both, the other thing and itself, then darkness also will cover both other things and itself.[42] As far as our world of experience is concerned, these contingencies are impossible; we cannot understand the function of darkness in the same way as the fire. Thus, the examples that correlate the *pramāṇas* and fire are not acceptable.

Again with specific arguments, Nāgārjuna substantiates his point more clearly that there is no darkness in fire and there is nothing on which fire stands. Thus, it is also wrong to state that illumination of fire is the destruction of darkness.[43] Nāgārjuna argues that the exemplified fire itself has discordance in ascertaining its independent self-existence; similarly, one cannot resort to *pramāṇas* for the revelation of the ultimate truth about the world. If the realists argue that fire exists in darkness and darkness is the source of fire, then the validity of argument "fire destroys darkness" is not valid. If they argue that fire has independent existence from darkness, then fire doesn't come in contact with the darkness.[44] Nāgārjuna dismisses this argument that, as the fire reveals darkness, the *pramāṇas* reveal the world of things completely. The relationship between fire and darkness is inexplicable; consequently, it is difficult to explain which of them can exist independently of the other, or which of them is the source of the other, or whether these two entities exist to oppose each other. Nāgārjuna puts forward another argument, which clarifies the above dichotomies. If fire destroys darkness even without coming in contact with it, a single speck of fire could destroy the darkness of the whole world.[45]

Nāgārjuna further argues that if *pramāṇa* is self-established, then it doesn't have any relation to objects (*prameyas*) it reveals, for self-establishment never requires another thing. In this case, another problem arises that, if the *pramāṇas* are established without *prameya* then those *pramāṇas* would be of nothing.[46] Another important argument of the realists is that the *pramāṇas* are always established in relation to the *prameyas* and the *prameyas* are not established in relation to the *pramāṇas*. But, if the *prameyas* can be established without *pramāṇas*, then it is nonsensical to establish something (*prameya*), which has already been established. Alternatively, it is to argue that through the establishment of the *prameyas* one has to establish the *pramāṇas*. As a result, there is an interchange of *prameyas* and *pramāṇas*.[47] From the above arguments, Nāgārjuna clarifies his position about the independent existence of the *pramāṇas* and the realists' contentions are untenable logically. Thus, the independent existence of *pramāṇas* should be dismissed. He goes on to say the logical impossibility in accepting the realist argument is that the *pramāṇa* and *prameya* are establishable only in mutual relation. In short, Nāgārjuna concludes his position with this argument:

> If the son is to be produced by the father, and if that father is to be produced by that very son, tell me which of these produces which other.[48]

When there are logical difficulties in accepting the validity of independent existence of *pramāṇa* as an entity or in accepting the validity of *pramāṇa* in dependence with *prameya*, Nāgārjuna cites the problem differently. He says that

> the *pramāṇas* are neither established by themselves nor by one another nor by other *pramāṇas*, and they are not established by the *prameyas*, or accidentally?[49]

The perception is not established by the very perception, the inference is not established by the very inference, or the comparison is not proved by the same comparison. Nor is perception established by inference, or comparison by testimony, or inference by perception; again perception, comparison, inference, and testimony are not established respectively by another perception, another inference, another comparison and, another testimony. At the same time, we cannot also say that they are established accidentally, as it is contrary to the very arguments of the realists.

If both the *pramāṇas* and the *prameyas* depend on each other, or the *pramāṇas* are mutually dependent, or the *pramāṇas* are depending on independent *prameyas*, in all these cases, the independence of *pramāṇas* is not established. If the *pramāṇas* are dependent, then they are not suitable for formulating any theory that can be taken as a premise for any further analysis. The purport of Nāgārjuna to formulate such a procedure of argumentation is to highlight the extraneous dependence on *pramāṇas*, for revealing the intrinsic nature (*svabhāva*) of the world of things by the realists. He, however, is not adverse to the practical utility of *pramāṇas* as for knowing the conventional truth (*saṁvṛti-satya*).

Another prominent argument of the realists is that good things have good intrinsic nature. Nāgārjuna refutes this claim by saying that if good intrinsic nature originates dependently, then it is the extrinsic nature of good things. Since the independent existence of a thing is not established, then how can it be their intrinsic nature?[50] If the argument is that intrinsic nature of good things originates without depending on anything, then there is no meaning for the practice of religious life. Independent origination of things is not accepted in the religio-ethical practice of the Buddhists. Whereas the canonical texts unequivocally states that all phenomena are dependent, causally linked and impermanent, accepting the intrinsic nature of good things originates without depending on anything would be a contradiction to the very teaching of the Buddha. Mādhyamika accepts the theory of dependent origination (*pratītya-samutpāda*) and the existence of the phenomenal world conventionally. There is no existence of *dharma* or *adharma*, or worldly conventions, if all things were endowed with intrinsic nature. It is clear that the thing that is not causally originated is permanent.[51] Articulating on such a permanent entity for explaining the real nature of phenomena is not the right way for the foundations of Buddhist philosophy. According to them the apparent phenomena are of the nature of arising and ceasing, for the existence of which is impermanent. Mādhyamikas have formulated their philosophy not from any articulated metaphysical standpoint, but from the actual experience of the world of phenomena. The experiences are not meant to configure a theory that is outwardly looking; instead, the experiences are set to move inwardly for showing the inconsistencies of the instruments of true cognition and experience.

The Vedic realists contend that the reality is beyond the comprehension of the ordinary mind and hence such reality could only be discerned partially. The experiential world of phenomena is merely an abstraction of the eternally existing reality, which is permanent and has good intrinsic nature; it is unoriginated, unchangeable, and incomprehensible to the ordinary human mind. However, Buddhists differ from this view, as they have identified the inherent difficulties in accepting such views. The permanent substance that would be supporting the phenomena would obstruct understanding the real nature of phenomena. Mādhyamikas assert that the arguments of the realists leading to the realisation of the permanently existing entity or the *svabhāva* of the things are not valid, since what the realists call as the instruments of true cognition (*pramāṇas*) are not substantial and independent, leading their arguments self-contradictory, leaving their views on *svabhāva* eternity baseless, making their theoretical positions suitable only to be abandoned.

Nāgārjuna focuses on that point in the next verses. He contends that if things of good nature lack good intrinsic nature, then the bad things also lack bad intrinsic nature. All those things that are conditioned would become unconditioned if things have intrinsic nature.[52] In the apparent world, such things never happen. There is nothing that is independent but all is dependent and conditioned. If the argument of the realists is that the "name" denotes the intrinsic nature of things or that calls one to say that there is an intrinsic nature, then, knowing the nature of things, one cannot make such a remark.[53] The argument that the dialectically opposite position of "non-existent" denotes something "existent," Nāgārjuna reveals his dialectical position, here, that both the statements and their opposites are good only to be abandoned. The reason for Mādhyamikas to conclude that things are void in nature, is because of the fact that things themselves are insubstantial and intrinsically lacking self-nature (*svabhāva*). Mādhyamikas in fact impel us to change the perspective through which we view the world of phenomena.

2.4.2.2 *The Meaning of Śūnyatā or Dharma-nairātmya*: In the *Vigrahavyāvartinī*, Nāgārjuna exactly clarifies the structure of Mādhyamika philosophy. He does not try to promote nihilism, though his criticisms are against the arguments of the realists; at the same time, Nāgārjuna tries to introduce another method to philosophy based on a new dialectical understanding about the world of phenomena. He again highlights this position about non-existence:

> Does this name "non-existent" designates something existent or non-existent. Be it the name of an existent or of a non-existent; in both ways your position is abandoned.[54]

One of the most important aspects of Mādhyamika philosophy (dialectics) is the correct understanding of the nature of *śūnya*. Nāgārjuna says in the beginning itself that he introduces the essential nature of the world of phenomena as *śūnya*, and that his criticisms against the realists' arguments are not in the form of any proposition.[55] Here comes the real position of the Mādhyamikas in that they object to the realists' view based on the insubstantiality of the *pramāṇas* to prove the self-nature (*svabhāva*) of the world of things. At the same time, Mādhyamika never introduces any negative proposition that would substantiate the opposing view of nihilism. The real existence of the things are not established beyond doubt, because the *pramāṇas* through which they are comprehended are not self-sustaining and the logical arguments that are drawn out of them (from the premises of the *pramāṇas*) are not established with clarity. Hence, one can only say that the essential nature of things is in agreement with the conception of *śūnya*. Again a question can be asked how one could perceive things in worldly conviction,[56] as it can be explained only by understanding the inconsistency that is inherent in the theoretical positions of the realists. For conventional purposes, Mādhyamikas accept the *pramāṇas*, but reject them as a premise for a theory. The most profound argument the realists could pose to counter criticisms is that there is an intrinsic nature existing, but that does not belong to things.[57] To Nāgārjuna, this argument is not acceptable. Most of the schools that propound their philosophy based on the Vedas share this opinion that the apparent reality is only a reflection of a reality that permanently exists. The self-nature of the things is leading one to understand that reality.

Nāgārjuna says that if there is negation of the existent, then *śūnya* is established; again, if you negate *śūnya* and that *śūnya* does not exist then your position of negation of existence should be abandoned.[58] The Mādhyamika here uses the opponent's logic against him that negation is possible only with an established existent thing; then he (the realist) approves the Mādhyamika position, by proving the *śūnyatā* he negates. In other words, if the realists say, like in the case of mirage, that non-existent need not to be established by negation, then the non-existence of *svabhāva* and the authority of *pramāṇas* need not be refuted with negative argumentation. Here, Nāgārjuna solves the problem of negative argumentation that he introduces in the beginning of the text.

Nāgārjuna is very clear when he says that the intrinsic natures of things are not established beyond doubt and hence their independent existence cannot be discerned. This aspect explains the reason why the statement "*śūnyatā* of things" is introduced, and it is not for agreeing with the realists' contraposition of nihilism. The realists alludes that the perception of things like mirage is a clear case of non-existent things; for them such things are examples of *śūnyatā.* Mādhyamika, on the other hand, dismisses the notion of proclaiming *śūnyatā* as a theory, and they take extreme care to avoid this; otherwise, the whole philosophical methods professed by Mādhyamikas turn meaningless. Mādhyamika again says that making a statement like "there is no *śūnyatā*" would only further substantiate the existence of *śūnyatā.*[59] This contention is based on the realists' position that the negation of a thing implies the substantiation of the existence of the same thing. To clarify this point, Nāgārjuna further says that he is not negating anything. He says that negation is not his way of philosophising, and reiterates by saying:

> Leave me on the point when you say that "you negate," there ends the argument.[60]

The concept of *śūnyatā*, which the realists refute as a position unacceptable for them in explaining the true nature of the world of things, is established its existence, beyond doubt, by the realists' refutation.

The existence of mirage is dismissed as a non-entity that can be substantiated; same is the case with perception and the *pramāṇas*, the independent existence of which also is not substantiated; thus, the idea of *pramāṇas* also should be suitable only to be dismissed as entities like mirage.[61] The essential nature of a thing, which is dependent, is *śūnya*.

If the perception of the mirage arises by its own nature then it is independently originated, but here the perception encounters the mirage that is dependently originated. Moreover, the idea of mirage arises through the dependence of certain things like the craving of a person in the desert, his expectation, the visual appeal of the horizon, and the non-existence of expected water and coolness are just other two aspects. Otherwise, the dependently arisen mirage is a thing like any other dependent things in the world of existence. If a perception arises on its own, nobody could remove the perception that exists forever.[62] Perception and cognition are dependent on things which are essentially insubstantial; thus, the perception and the objects of perception are independently non-existent. This can be applicable to all things that are a part of our daily experience. We could experience the realists' explanation to things that exist and have intrinsic nature, which are self-contradictory, and hence one should be in agreement with the *śūnyatā*. Since things are devoid of intrinsic nature, it should be considered as *śūnya*. The insubstantial nature of the object of perception is the subject of discussion of the next session.

One must understand the subtle changes happening with the apparent realities, so that he can understand the phenomenal world properly. As a conclusion, Nāgārjuna says:

> All things prevail for him for whom this voidness (*prabhavati ca śūnyateyaṁ yasya prabhavanti tasya sarvārthaḥ*) prevails. Nothing prevails with him, for whom voidness does not prevail (*prabhavati na tasya kiñcin na prabhavati śūnyatā yasya*).[63]

This clear and strong statement clarifies the real philosophical position of the Mādhyamikas that he is not advocating the philosophy of nihilism after refuting the theoretical positions based on conventional epistemology and logic of the realists. Mādhyamikas' *śūnya* is a window through which one could see the world clearly as the way it appears. The concept of *śūnyatā* is not another theory, but an analytical tool with which one could understand the phenomenal world and the apparent realities better.

2.5 *Dharma-nairātmya*—Through the Method of Progressive Analysis

The *Hastavālanāma-prakaraṇavṛtti* explains the phenomena in all the three stages of its apprehension: (1) the conceived phenomena, the *dharma*; (2) the cognized phenomena, the *dharmadhātu*; and (3) finally, the insubstantial aspect of each phenomena, the *dharma-nairātmya*. When we examine them progressively, each apparent phenomenon in the world passes through these three phases of existence. This work comprises only of six *kārikās*, and it expresses another method to discern the Mādhyamika view.[64]

The meaning of *Hastavālanāma-prakaraṇa* is:

> "Treatise named the hair in the hand." With the title the author wanted to express that he explained the subject of this work as clearly as we can see a hair in the hand.[65]

The text explains another important analytical methodology of the Mādhyamika dialectics, which tries to discern the nature of *śūnyatā* and *dharma-nairātmya*, through a progressive method where the conceived phenomenon (*dharma*) is taken as the basic nature of the object. As can be seen in the previous discussions, Mādhyamikas refute the metaphysical positions of the realistic schools of Indian philosophy with the help of regressive analysis. The regressive analysis proves the inconsistencies of the premises of phenomena, the epistemic premises (*pramāṇas*) or the instruments of true cognition, to find truth-value. On the other hand, using the progressive method, it is possible to analyse the conceived object and its ultimate nature. The conceived object is analysed progressively at its different level of manifestations: from snake to rope and rope to neither snake nor rope, ending in total chaos in ascertaining the truth-value of the object.

As discussed earlier, the psycho-physical personality configures the objects conceived as real, because dispositions, strong feelings, and ignorance are working together in a cyclic manner. The analysis begins from the premise of the most dichotomous conception (*vikalpa*) of snake and rope. According to the first verse of the *Hastavālanāma-prakaraṇavṛtti*:

> In front of the rope the idea of a snake is conceived. When (the rope) is seen as a rope, that idea becomes without (a real corresponding) object.[66]

Certainly the snake seen in a rope is illusory and lacks clarity, and when the rope is seen as the rope the idea of snake remains without a corresponding snake. Similarly, the nature of the perceived apparent world is such that it does not intrinsically hold any certainty or reality. Thus, one must reflect on the ontology of all the perceived objects, to ascertain their certainty or to see whether they exist only as an illusion. The ontological status of the conceived phenomena (the snake) is quite different from the cognised phenomena (the rope) because on verification the object rope is subjected for verification by all the sense faculties. The rope's existence in the empirical world can be ascertained relatively clearer than the existence of the snake. Discerning the essence of phenomena (*dharmadhātu*) from the apprehended phenomena (*dharma*) is one of the purposes of the Mādhyamika dialectics. Though they reject the ultimate existence of both the snake and the rope, Mādhyamikas give importance for the cognition of the essence of phenomena (*dharmadhātu*); as far as the empirical life is concerned, the understanding of the essence of phenomena is absolutely necessary. It is the *saṁvṛti satya*. When one acquires the power to view the *dharmadhātu* of the objects around, he would be in a position to view things without the dichotomous influence of the *vikalpas* and conceptualisations. This ability is the criterion of a wise person.

In the next verse, one gets closer to the result of the dialectical technique explained in the *Vigrahavyāvartinī* where the authority of the *pramāṇas* is dismissed; here, using a different analytical technique, the same aspect is explained by Ārydeva:

> When the parts of that (rope) are seen, also the cognition, concerning that (rope) is erroneous-illusory, as (the cognition of) the snake.[67]

There is no essential difference between the perception of the snake and that of the rope, the first, depending on the clinging and craving nature of the mind that conceptualised the illusory object of snake; the second is the cognised object that is ratified by the senses; but on closer examination the cognised object of rope is seen as a formation of fibre, etc. These perceptions of both the rope and the snake are dependent on various conditions: the snake is perceived because of the clinging and craving nature of the perceiver; on the other hand, the rope is perceived because of the correct perception happened dependent on the sense faculties. Depending on the same sense faculties, on closer verification, the existence of snake and rope become redundant, revealing fibre, etc. on the same object. Thus, the object that revealed as snake, rope, and fibre lacks any intrinsic nature (*svabhāva*). Subsequently, this analysis proves the essencelessness of all objective phenomena (*dharma-nairātmya*). This point is further established by the Mādhyamikas:

> If the existence of the things can only be perceived through dependent things then all those things empirically perceived are depending on something else.[68]

If the things are dependent, it is difficult to establish the ontology of its existence. It is clear that when the dependent conditions are removed, the thing ceases to exist. On the other hand, we are not able to discern a thing, which is independent and existent at the same time. Thus, the actual Mādhyamika position on the *dharma-nairātmya* can be interpreted as:

> Since something without parts cannot be imagined, the (alleged) last part is similar to something non-existent.[69]

Perceiving the rope as the snake is an illusory perception, depending on the rope; the rope at the same time is not the ultimate substratum of the erroneous perception. On close examination, the existence of rope also changes to fibre and minute atomic particles, which do not have the property of the rope or the snake. In short, the conflicts of reasoning in the case of snake or rope are not settled with either the discernment of the two entities or the rejection of the two entities. Here, Mādhyamika dialectics cautions about difficulties in arriving at a conclusion based on the basis of snake or rope, the illusory perception and the veridical perception. Āryadeva further elaborates this problem:

> In such a situation a wise man is sure that everything he perceives in this world is mere erroneous and that it is not substantiated to be any true reality.[70]

Here, the discussion proceeds not by rejecting completely the conceived phenomena of perception, but by identifying the inconsistencies in accepting perception (*pramāṇa*) as the basis of analysis. Thus, a wise man, understanding the problem of the conflicts in reasoning with regard to the perceived objects, should desist from making theoretical conclusion and metaphysical assertions. Again it should not be concluded that there was no perception of any object.

The following verse in the text shows another phase of the argumentation:

> Those (things) also, since they are not real, are not such as they appear in the erroneous-illusory (cognition). As to the representation (in the mind) of an object which does not exist, how can it (the representation) have a real existence?[71]

The perceived snake does not exist at all; it is an illusory cognition. An object, represented only in the mind and whose origination is dependent on certain condition, is not true as an existing object. The representation of the object in the mind is not even certain, and is illusory as in the case of snake and erroneous in the case of rope. So, it is impossible to ascertain the ontology of its real existence. However, what Mādhyamika wants to say, comes in the next verse:

> Whosoever with subtle mind knows that all things are only dependent, that intelligent man easily throws out desire, etc., as (the man who knows that there is no snake but only a rope, throws out) the fear (produced) by the snake.[72]

It is accepted by most of the schools of philosophy that all things of the world are dependent, and they endeavour to find the truth-value of the things of the world by creating theoretical premises. Notwithstanding this view, Mādhyamikas try to understand the retroactive effects such dependent and illusory things can have on the human mind. The illusory snake can create irrational fear in the mind of the human being; the perception of the rope could remove that fear from the mind. But at the same time, if a person is afraid of rope, he needs to have knowledge that would repudiate the effect of the rope on the mind. Mādhyamika finds the solution to this problem in two ways: first, the understanding that on ultimate analysis the existence of rope gets disseminated into finer division that never hold the character either of the snake or of the rope; second, to dissociate oneself from the influence of the objective things, one needs to know that the existent is insubstantial and dependent. The last verse of the text reveals the real wisdom of the Mādhyamikas, that

> the man who perceives the things of the world should act as the worldly people in the established way; the (man) who wishes to eliminate the impurities must investigate according to the supreme reality.[73]

In the case of perception of rope as a snake, it is evident that the illusory notion of snake is removed on veridical perception of the rope; at the same time when the object (rope-snake) is analysed thoroughly, both the snake and the rope cease to exist. To put it in another way, the man who wants to be liberated from the influence of both the entities (rope and snake), should understand that neither rope nor snake is substantial. This is the supreme reality (*pāramārtha-satya*). But, with regard to the apparent world (*samvṛti-satya*), the veridically cognised rope, is neither illusory nor essenceless. It is the essence of phenomena *dharmadhātu*. The spiritual endeavour of a person is to discern the essence of all the *dharmas* that can act as a source of the mind's conceptualisation process and to progress to the essencelessness of phenomena (*dharma-nairātmya*). The *dhama-nairātmya* is a property of the world of existence, or the phenomena are *dharma-śūnya*. The real purport of Mādhyamikas' philosophical position is not just to clear the Buddhist position on this issue, but to highlight the real problem a human being faces with his life in the world. He confronts various types of conceptualisations, yet he is not able to identify the real meaning of those confusions. In other words, one confronts always with the illusory snakes and lives in the feeling that the illusions are real. Here, it is urged that one should know the *dharmadhātu* and the *dharma-nairātmya* aspect of each phenomena so that he can be freed from the dichotomous influence of the illusions created by perceptions.

Modern physics like the Buddhist philosophy agree on this aspect that the material world is ultimately essenceless and uncertain, but, at the same time, it is relatively real and true like the rope in the rope-snake example. The systematic analytical methodology, the method used by modern analytical sciences, is in agreement with the position of Mādhyamika that the objective world of things is dependent and essenceless ultimately.

2.6 "Uncertainty Principle" of Werner Heisenberg—Proof of *Dharma-nairātmya*

The empirically perceived rope (object), when analysed systematically reveals sub-atomic particles that never have the property of rope. The characteristics of the sub-atomic particles are beyond the comprehension of the normal human mind, for these unique particles do not give any sort of identity with regard to the objective phenomena originally perceived. The snake, rope, fibre, and particularly the incognisable particle that may be existing in the object, lead us to believe that there is a substratum from which the object is formulated. The conception of atomism originated from this view. But we have seen in this discussion that the existence of a substratum as the source of phenomenal realities is not the philosophical position of Mādhyamikas. There are many schools of philosophies, alluding that there is an inconceivable substratum that comprises the objects of the world; similarly, modern science too postulates an inconceivable substratum as the foundation of the phenomenal world.

The analytical methodology of modern science is based on the systematic analysis of the empirically perceived objects to find the truth about the phenomenal world. For many centuries, it has been believed that scientific methodology is the only way to find the truth that is manifested in the universe, and this method is capable of revealing that truth. But the uncertainty principle of Werner Heisenberg thwarted the notion that modern analytical science, as a system, is able to explain the world of things with absolute certainty. There are two important stages in the history of science, the first is the period when it has been assumed that science could explain the apparent world of realities with absolute certainty; and the second is the period that starts with the introduction of uncertainty principle, which has frustrated scientific determinism.[74]

The introduction of Newton's theories of gravity paved the way for scientific determinism, in order that a few sets of scientific laws can explain everything that would happen in the universe. French scientist, Marquis de Laplace argued that scientific determinism based on scientific laws not only would predict everything that would happen in the universe, but also predict with the support of similar set of laws everything else including human behaviour.[75] These findings have revolutionised the human thinking that there are no implied mysteries beyond the comprehension of the human mind. In addition, if the phenomena are analysed properly, it is possible to reveal all the mysteries in the world that appear before us. Specifically, the certainty that Newtonian laws would offer are based on the complete state of universe at one time; for instance, if we knew the position and speed of the Sun and the planets at one time, then we could calculate the state of solar system at any other time.[76] This scientific finding has enlarged the realm of human knowledge that if we could determine the position and velocity of the sub-atomic particles, we would precisely be able to determine the nature of the matter made out of them. In other words, we would be able to predict the nature and behaviour of the universe with the help of a comprehensive theory that is always true. But the introduction of uncertainty principle by Werner Heisenberg has unseated all such dreams.[77] According to Stephen Hawking,

> The more accurately you try to measure the position of the particle, the less accurately you can measure its speed and vice versa. Heisenberg showed that the uncertainty in the position of the particle times, the uncertainty in its velocity times the mass of the particle can never be smaller than certain quantity, which is known as Plank's constant. Moreover, this limit does not depend on the way in which one tries to measure the position or velocity of the particle, or the type of the particle. Heisenberg's uncertainty principle is a fundamental, inseparable property of the world.[78]

The uncertainty principle has really impeded the dream of having a theory that could determine the nature of future events with utmost certainty. Again, conforming this view of Heisenberg, Stephen Hawking opined in this regard:

> The uncertainty principle had profound implications for the way in which we view the world. Even after more than fifty years they have not been fully appreciated by many philosophers and are still the subject of much controversy.[79]

Here, the reason for bringing out this aspect from the findings of modern science is to show how difficult it is to find any theory that is valid, predictable, and true eternally.

The confusion created in the minds of thinkers about the uncertainty principle is tremendous and that contains in the famous statement of Einstein: "God is not playing dice with the world." Einstein thought that the uncertainty principle is a passing phase in the history of science and predicted that another theory, which is more deterministic, is going to replace it in due course of time. Even after seventy years of its discovery, the uncertainty principle still holds good. In a paper presented at the Department of Applied Mathematics and Theoretical Physics, University of Cambridge, Stephen Hawking elaborated this problem:

> The classical view, put forward by Laplace, was that the future motion of particles was completely determined, if one knew their positions and speeds at one time. This view had to be modified, when Heisenberg put forward his Uncertainty Principle, which said that one could not know both the position, and the speed, accurately. However, it was still possible to predict

> one combination of position and speed. However, even this limited predictability disappeared when the effects of black holes were taken into account. The loss of particles and information down black holes meant that the particles that came out were at random. One could calculate probabilities, but one could not make any definite predictions. Thus, the future of the universe is not completely determined by the laws of science, and its present state, as Laplace thought.[80]

We can find from our discussions that the uncertainty principle is completely in agreement with the views of the early Mādhyamikas, who argued that there could not be any theory or position that is ultimately valid in determining the true nature of world with the analysis of the objective phenomena appearing before us.

The wave-particle dichotomy and the fundamental character of uncertainty principle can be explained as the limitations of human faculties for discerning such a phenomenon; its realm may be beyond the instruments of true cognition or *pramāṇas*. Since human life is short and the knowledge that one can acquire through the true means of knowledge is limited, any conclusion and conceptual formulation, made out of them, has only limited purpose to serve. Thus, theories prove only conventional truth-value of the things of the world. In other words, what appears in the world of experience can be explained as a dependent entity, relatively true, but ultimately these phenomena are essenceless and insubstantial to formulate a theory that explains the universe in its totality and magnanimity. In the case of rope-snake example in the previous pages (62–66), this is clearly stated by Āryadeva that the rope perceived is relatively true to certain conditions but on careful examination the existent rope and the illusory snake ceases to exist, like the rope-snake particles too follow the rules of uncertainty principle. Nobel laureate and eminent nuclear scientist, Steven Weinberg views this problem in these words:

> For some who felt wounded by the reductionism and determinism of Newtonian physics, two aspects of quantum mechanics seemed to offer a welcome balm. Where human beings had no special status in Newtonian physics in the quantum mechanics humans play an essential role in giving meaning to the wave function by the act of measurement. And where the Newtonian physicist spoke of precise predictions the quantum mechanics now offers only calculations of probabilities, thus seeming to make room again for human free will or divine intervention.[81]

Mādhyamika is the first philosophical system, which introduced the concept of *śūnyatā* as the analytical essence of the world of things;

śūnyatā like the uncertainty principle is implicit in each phenomenon in the existent world, revealing its existence on close examination. The inefficiency of traditional epistemology to reveal the ultimate truth about the Universe is elaborately discussed in the literature of the Mādhyamikas; this has been proven by modern physics with its elaborate analytical systems, which too arrived at the limitations of our philosophical systems to reveal the truth.[82] This problem has put contemporary philosophers in a very difficult position. There are two ways they could solve this problem: either they must evolve new philosophical systems which must introduce new methodologies to understand the realities of the universe; or adopt a fresh and impartial look at the principle of philosophical systems like the Mādhyamika, who identified such problems well in advance and accepted scientific reasoning as one of the methods of understanding the phenomenal world. Specifically, it is admitted by modern scientists that the system they followed is inefficient or insufficient to explain the finer details about the world of existence, because epistemology never agrees with the expected metaphysical results.

The questions raised by Nāgārjuna against epistemology are not meant to assail our ways of knowing but to remove the theoretical positions and arguments that are chronic in philosophy. Mostly theories are highly speculative, based on weak premises of epistemology and inconsistent logic that are vulnerable enough to be repudiated by another theory.[83] Unfortunately, modern philosophy does not help the theoretical scientists in their endeavour to find the truth or the real nature of the universe. Stephen Hawking has rightly put this problem of contemporary philosophers' indifference to the findings of science:

> In the nineteenth century, philosophers considered the whole of human knowledge, including science, as their field and discussed questions such as: 'Did the universe have a beginning?' However, in the nineteenth and twentieth century, science become too technical and mathematical for philosophers, or anyone else except specialists? Philosophers reduced the scope of their inquiries so much that Wittgenstein, the most famous philosopher of this century, said, 'The sole remaining task of philosophy is the analysis of language.'[84]

Stating the fundamental dichotomy of scientists of modern times in finding the real nature of truth about the universe, Hawking says:

> Many scientists are like Einstein, in that they have a deep emotional attachment to determinism. Unlike Einstein, they have accepted the reduction in our ability to predict, that quantum theory brought about. But that was far enough. They didn't like the further reduction, which black holes seemed to imply. They have, therefore, claimed that information is not really lost down black holes. But they have not managed to find any mechanism that would return the information. It is just a pious hope that the universe is deterministic, in the way that Laplace thought. I feel these scientists have not learnt the lesson of history. The universe does not behave according to our pre-conceived ideas. It continues to surprise us.[85]

In the contemporary world, analytical science has taken the position of a religion and its promoters too behave like the religionists, where they pretend or behave that certain truths are inexistent or the existence of which, it says, would be proved wrong in later time. It is a very pious hope. In this context, it is interesting to note that the views of Mādhyamikas that are formulated centuries ago are relevant even today in understanding the nature of universe, which had puzzled the intellectual community for many years. From the above discussions, we could find that there is a recognisable similarity between the concept of *śūnya* and the findings of the uncertainty principle. However, the main discussion of this thesis is not concerned about that.

2.7 Śūnyatā as a Tool to Restructure the Phenomena (*Dharma*)

On discussing the characteristic features of Mādhyamika dialectics, T.R.V. Murti says:

> Criticism of theories is no theory. Criticism is but the awareness of what a theory is, how it is made up. It is not the proposing of a new theory. Negation of positions is not one more position. Dialectic, as analysis, does not impose any new thing; it reveals rather than adds or distorts. Its function is like that of lights which merely show things in their true character.[86]

If a theory is substituted with another theory, then theories form *ad infinitum* or cyclic justifications; there may not be any end to theories and their criticisms. In other words, if a theory of the *svabhāva* of things is substituted by another theory of voidness of things, then that leads to an extreme position and infinite regress. This is not the purpose of philosophy for the Mādhyamikas. The purpose of philosophy for Mādhyamikas, as Murti contended, is for seeing things in a better light:

> As a last resort we have to accept pure analysis or mere awareness without any trace of distortion at some ultimate stage. The knowledge of what

> theories are, cannot itself be a theory; Knowledge of what a hypothesis is not hypothetical. Analysis or criticism does not add to the stock of our existing knowledge. We gain in depth and not in extension. As no new fact is added, there is no necessity for launching on a regressive series of *śūnyatā*.[87]

Here, one thing is explicit and clear that *śūnyatā* need not be explained in the same form as a theory, but it should be understood as a tool of analysis in deepening our knowledge, so that the awareness would be enhanced. Consequently, one could gain internal strength to liberate oneself from the regressive formulation of the extension of theories. The theories that are supposed to explain the world of existences are mere thought constructs with no real foundation. As we have seen in the *Vigrahavyāvartinī*, the *pramāṇas* are not independent or substantial by themselves in explaining the phenomenal world. The realm of *śūnyatā* is truly universal, the whole reality, if it were a theory however exalted it is, it is determined and conditioned, a construction of the real into this or that mould.[88] The dialectical conflict is applicable only to a stage of conceptual formulations.

Mādhyamikas successfully introduced the hollowness of all theoretical formulations and asserted that it is very necessary for one to attain liberation from the *saṁsāra* that is conditioned and bound. It is well-described in the *Kāśyapaparivarta*:

> Those, Kāśyapa, that misapprehended *śūnyatā* as a negative fact, I consider them the forlorn, the irrevocably lost [...]. Better it is to entertain the substance view (*pudgala dṛṣṭi*) of the magnitude of the Mount Sumeru than the *śūnyatā* view of the nihilist (*abhāvābhiniviśnaḥ*). Why it is so? Of all theories Kāśyapa, *śūnyatā* is the antidote. Him I call the incurable who mistakes *śūnyatā* itself as a theory (*dṛṣṭi*). It is as if a drug, administrated to cure a patient were to remove all his disorders, but were to foul the stomach when remaining therein. Would you, Kāśysapa, consider the patient cured? Likewise Kāśyapa, *śūnyatā* is the antidote for all the dogmatic view; but him I declare incurable who misapprehends *śūnyatā* itself as a theory.[89]

It has been clearly explained by Nāgārjuna that the wrongly perceived emptiness ruins a person of meagre intelligence. It is like a snake that is wrongly grasped in the case of rope-snake example or knowledge that is wrongly cultivated.[90] The concept of *śūnya* is wrongly interpreted by the critiques of Mādhyamika; this is due to the inadequate reading of Mādhyamika philosophy or their (the critics) failure to consider the arguments against the epistemological positions, held by other schools, especially about the *pramāṇas*. In another verse,

Nāgārjuna clarifies the need of having a proper conception about *śūnyatā*, as emptiness is something that haunts a person.

> We say that you do not comprehend the purpose of emptiness. As such emptiness and the meaning of emptiness torment you.[91]

The meaning of *śūnyatā* torments a person, if he is not able to identify the purpose of *śūnyatā;* it is evident that the concept of *śūnya* has only a functional meaning, not an absolutistic meaning. To clarify further, Nāgārjuna goes on to say that

> the teaching of the doctrine by the Buddhas is based upon two truths; truth relating to worldly conventions and truth in terms of the ultimate fruit.[92]

In the *Vigrahavyāvartinī*, Nāgārjuna clarifies this point clearly that the phenomenal world is before us for our experience and understanding. At the same time, it may not give any positive result when we try to construct a theory based on the premises formulated by the *pramāṇas*. The *pramāṇas* themselves are insubstantial, dependent, and the basis of which is *śūnya*. The authority of the *pramāṇas* is true, as far as, for the world present before us and available for our observation and understanding, the *samvṛti-satya*, but these *pramāṇas* are not able to prove anything that is beyond the realm of the phenomenal world. The rules governing, what can be put forward as *pāramārtha-satya* (ultimate truth), are not supported by the truth validation based on *pramāṇas*.

Since the worldly convictions are formulated through dependence on the arising and ceasing nature of phenomena, they are not ultimately true or real, because when the causes and conditions are removed, the phenomenon also ceases to exist. Nāgārjuna says:

> We state that whatever is dependent arising, that is emptiness. That is dependent upon conventions. That itself is the middle path.[93]

The basis of the middle path, proving the conventional truth-value of things with the support of *pramāṇas*, sustains only when the extreme views are avoided. As a clarification to the non-intrinsic nature of phenomenal world, Nāgārjuna says:

> A thing that is not dependently arisen is not evident. For that reason a thing that is not empty is not evident.[94]

When the things of the world are not revealing the intrinsic nature or the unique characteristics, supposedly implicit in them on analysis, the ascribed intrinsic nature turns into *śūnya* or empty.

The philosophy of Mādhyamika, the concept of *śūnya*, the middle path, and other such ideas, can be understood only if we compare the dialectics of Nāgārjuna with the dialectics of other schools of philosophy. As we have seen, for the early Mādhyamikas the dialectics itself is philosophy. T.R.V. Murti rightly interprets this aspect in his effort to interpret the philosophy of Mādhyamika:

> Not having a content itself, Mādhyamika dialectics receives its orientation from its criticism of human thought at every stage of its history. The dialectic performs the high office of philosophy in analysing the absolute presuppositions of thought. As analysis, the application will not add to the presuppositions, but only make us aware of them.[95]

This contention of T.R.V. Murti is very important in our study of Mādhyamika dialectics and its application in Buddhist Tantrism. Murti has emphasized that the philosophy of Mādhyamika finds its strength from the unique dialectics, so as to interpret the limitations of human thought to understand the world of phenomena, as the way it appears before us. There are many presuppositions together with the true cognition of the objective world that forms our understanding about the apparent world. Mādhyamika dialectics questions both the true cognition of the objective world and the presuppositions that formulate the theories, which explain the world of reality. The dialectics does not introduce *śūnya* as a premise that would add to the collection of presuppositions.

2.8 The Characteristic Features of Mādhyamika Dialectics

There is an opinion among scholars that the system of dialectics is introduced into philosophy from India. The action and reaction of the opposites is the main concern of the dialectics and that is considered as the basis of our understanding about the world of existence. This is one of the widely discussed subjects in Indian philosophy and literature. This knowledge of the action and reaction of the opposites is, according to Edgar W. Pritchard, originally introduced into philosophy by Indians:

> From India, the Idea (about Dialectics) has passed to Egypt. It is well known that among the Greeks, Egypt was considered a repository of philosophical wisdom. Plato, among others, visited it and is said to have been initiated into its religious mysteries. Thus, the idea of the flow of life between two extremes was introduced into Greece.[96]

Dialectics forms an important division of classical Indian philosophy, and is an integral part of the philosophical methodology of the Indians.

The play of opposites is one of the main concerns of philosophy. In common parlance, out of these opposites one is good and the other is bad, one desirable and the other undesirable, one beautiful and the other ugly. In dialectics, both the opposites are necessary and contribute to the existence when balanced properly. In the philosophy of Aristotle, the ethics divided the opposites, from the view of conduct; courage is considered as the medium course between the extremes of foolhardiness and cowardice. In the Aristotelian system, courage is static in between the two extremes of foolhardiness and cowardice.[97] Another method adopted by the Greeks in the arena of dialectics is the method of dialogue or debate to arrive at truth. The Greeks have developed the science and art of dialectics in this manner and it is considered as an important aspect of Greek civilization. The main principle is based on the fact that there are two sides to every question. The protagonist introduces one aspect of the question; consequently, another protagonist of the other side raises questions and takes part in the dialogue in order to arrive at a conclusion, which is nearing the truth. The conclusion arrived by the Greeks is mainly based on the good, the true and the beautiful.[98] The Hegelian dialectics is also trying to solve the problem of opposites in a characteristic manner. T.R.V. Murti opines:

> The Hegelian dialectics tries to remove the opposition between the thesis and the antithesis by intimately relating and unifying them under a third concept in which, Hegel claims, their discord is removed.... Hegel takes synthesis as a newer, richer, more comprehensive, and, therefore, higher idea, providing basis for difference.[99]

One of the serious problems in accepting Aristotelian theory is that the extreme of courage can turn to foolhardiness; and the extreme of caution can lead to cowardice. Or, for the dialogue, the one who knows the art of manipulating dialogue could influence the results of conclusion. So it must not be a static state, but as T.R.V. Murti writes on the unique way of the Mādhyamika dialectics:

> Dialectics is a self-conscious spiritual movement; it is necessarily a critique of reason. This is not possible without the consciousness of the opposition of the thesis and the antithesis. There must be two viewpoints or patterns of interpretations diametrically opposite to each other. The dilemma is not "dialectic," for that is a temporary predicament to a particular situation. The dialectic is a universal situation affecting every sphere of things.[100]

This explanation of dialectics is highly suitable to the context of Mādhyamika Buddhism. It is not just arriving at a dialogical conclusion about truth, or arriving at a synthesis of a thesis and its antithesis, but a self-conscious spiritual movement that leads to liberation through the play of the opposites.

The *Mādhyamikakārikā* gives many instances of this subtle movement. This problem of the opposites in reason is the main concern of philosophies of the world. In order to redress this problem normally, various theories and counter theories are advanced. But from the perspective of Mādhyamika, the dialectics is the only solution to this problem. It highlights the inconsistencies implicit in the theories due to which conflicts in reason arise. The solution lies in looking at the inconsistencies without resorting to any apprehensions, soothing beliefs, or dogmas. Mādhyamika may be the first philosophical system that is strongly founded on a dialectical system, which consciously investigates the premises from where theoretical positions are formulated. As we have seen in the *Vigrahavyāvartinī*, Mādhyamikas direct their arguments to the truth-value of the *pramāṇas* from where the theoretical positions have been formulated. The text of*Mādhyamika-kārikā* cites this problem in a different manner:

> How is it that a cause will produce an effect, which comes to be on its own nature? How is it that a cause will produce an effect, which does not come to be on its own nature?[101]

Here, the statement and its opposite argument are untenable and hence dismissed. If the cause and effect are independently not discernible, then the following verse says the alternative is also not possible, "The identity of cause and effect is indeed not appropriate. The difference between cause and effect is indeed not appropriate."[102] The Mādhyamika view can be interpreted as neither the cause nor the effect, nor the combination of cause and effect, nor the difference of cause and effect where they base their arguments. Mādhyamikas question the very existence of cause or effect as true entities. The concept of *śūnyatā* is an evolution of the Mādhyamika dialectics, not a theoretical formulation. Nāgārjuna clarifies this point when he says:

> Everything is pertinent for whom śūnyatā is proper. Everything is not pertinent for whom the śūnyatā is not proper.[103]

2.8.1 *The Relevance of Negative Argumentation*

The actual dialectical position of Mādhyamika and the ontology of *śūnyatā*, cannot be explained within the confines of any language and, thus, to release from the conceptual formulation of language, any interpretation should follow the procedure of negative argumentation. The power of negative statements is that it expands the expanse of our logical thinking. As T.R.V. Murti rightly puts it:

> If it were a theory or view, however exalted and useful it might be, it would still be a determination and limitation, a restriction of the real into this or that conceptual mould. To analyse a proposition is not to make another proposition. If that were the case we cannot make a universal statement. [...] Hence, the true universal cannot be a viewpoint; and, conversely, all points of view and positions are particular, not universal.[104]

Here, it is very clear that *śūnyatā* is not a theory and never has been a theory. A theory is confined within the limit of a particular thought construct and serves only a limited purpose. The all-pervasive universal application of theories is what Mādhyamikas vehemently object to and not to the utilitarian purposes of such evaluations. As discussed earlier, the realm of *śūnyatā*, is not a final metaphysical proposition that explains everything, but it is a tool using which one could understand the nature of phenomenon better and make him aware of the limitation of human thinking. To quote T.R.V. Murti again:

> The Mādhyamika is exorcising the devil of dogmatism from his own soul. He employs the outward form of refutation so that he can dissociate himself from the inherent dogmatic tendency of the human mind. The Mādhyamika dialectic is actuated by the spiritual motive of purifying the mind and freeing it of the cobwebs and clogs of dogmatism.[105]

In short, the Mādhyamika dialectics is an analytical tool and its purpose is to redeem human thinking from the shackles of dogmatism and theorization which limit the spectrum of human activity, especially the thought process. In this context, the nature of activity of *śūnyatā* is similar to the activity of a medicine in the human body; it works to cure the disease, the disease of conceptualisation. The Mādhyamika uses the negative mode of argumentation to reveal the implicit difficulties in conceptual formulations, but they never accepted it as a method or position; therefore, the problem of nihilism never troubles them.

2.9 Mādhyamika Dialectics—From Sañjaya to Nāgārjuna

Using dialectics as a method to solve problems involves many difficulties as it considers only two alternatives. The problems of reasoning can have more than two alternatives; it can be the assertion of a viewpoint, or the negation of a viewpoint, assertion as well as negation, or neither assertion nor negation. While the Mādhyamika rejects all the four alternatives that can be applied to a problem: such as P, ~P, both P and ~P, neither P nor ~P,[106] with a view that when two alternatives are identified, one makes a mistake of configuring the phenomena in a certain mental mould. By the negative method, Mādhyamika achieves the purpose of opening the vista of our view about the world of phenomena.

The logical sceptics lead by Sañjaya Ballaṭṭhiputta introduced this view much earlier to the Mādhyamikas.[107] Opposing the views of the Vedic schools of philosophy which promote eternalism of the self, the Sañjaya school, as a contra-position, to reject eternalism, have introduced negative arguments. The rivalry between these two streams is only a part of the long history of refuting the views of Vedic schools in Indian philosophy. The repudiation of the views of the eternalists with the help of traditional logic is a difficult task and, in most cases, the dialectician falls into the trap set by the opponent. To redress the problem, the Sañjaya School, which is known as Amaravikkhepas in the Pāli Nikāyas, or logical sceptics (by commentators of Indian philosophy), advanced the fourfold negation, which is deduced from the sixteen questions to the arguments of the eternalists. The answers to these questions, for inferring the truth-value, are ambiguous and unclear. Thus, Sañjaya concluded that all the views about the world of appearance are ultimately insubstantial on its own predicaments; hence, arguments on the subject of eternity of the existence would only lead to confusion and unnecessary philosophical wrangling, which also can cast a shadow over our natural understanding about the world of phenomena. Sañjaya rejects all the positions regarding, existence of reality, eternity of consciousness, finiteness of soul and body, and the relationship between them.[108] On the basis of the fourfold negation, it is possible to assail any absolutistic positions held by the Vedic schools. Sañjaya has advocated the philosophy of absolute indeterminism of all positions about the existent world. The ethical practices introduced by them are significant, which is based on avoiding questions that create confusion in the mind and suggests pursuing the path of quietude in meditation.

As discussed in the *Vigrahavyāvartinī*, Mādhyamika not only cites the inconsistency of the epistemology to formulate a theory and its relevance as a valid tool of analysis, but how it also upsets the parameters of traditional Indian logic,[109] by questioning the authority of cognition and the premises made from *pramāṇas*. Mādhyamikas method of analysis is well-defined by Āryadeva in *Catuḥśatakā*.[110] Mādhyamika calls the curious mind to discard both the dialectically opposing views and the four alternatives that can be configured from them.[111] Āryadeva in *Catuḥśataka* systematically enunciated this problem such as,

> Existence, non-existence, (both) existence and non-existence, and neither existence nor non-existence'—this is the progressive method that intelligent people should apply constantly in regard to entity, and so forth.[112]

The apparent world can be explained only within the limits of these alternatives, the possibility of another fifth alternative never arises. The fourfold negation is the only method that can be applied to transcend all possible theoretical constructs. Transcending the play of thought constructs does not mean to abandon all views and stop thinking, but to adopt thinking as a method to redeem oneself from the web of thought constructions.

Regarding the question of metaphysics, both Sañjaya's view and the Mādhyamika view are similar, but there is a marked difference in identifying the problem and suggesting a solution. Sañjaya's view envisages acquiring quietude of mind from confusing thoughts; Mādhyamika, on the other hand, identifies that the mind is of the habit of getting attached to the objective phenomena, identifying with them and creating confusion. The method of the logical sceptics or materialists is found to be impractical since the mind has the habit of constructing thought patterns, and theories construed out of thought constructions. The Mādhyamika method is to identify the nature of thought construction with the help of *prajñā* (wisdom) and *upāya* (right means), so that the objective phenomenon (*dharma*) can be understood as the way it really appears before us. Mādhyamika position is not just avoiding the effects of thought construction, but understanding the nature of thought construction to find the essence of such mental configuration, by identifying the *dharmadhātu* of the phenomena. The *Hastavālanāma-prakaraṇavṛtti* introduces a method to understand this problem. The problem of *dharma-nairātmya* is viewed not as a theoretical standpoint, but as something that is implicit in every objective phenomenon that is experienced in the world of existence. Unlike Sañjaya and the other materialist and logical sceptics, Mādhyamikas use the phenomena or thought construction to transcend the influence of the objective phenomena on the mind. When this influence ceases, the mind retains it original nature of quietude.

2.10 Conclusion

For the Mādhyamikas, dialectics is the system that reveals clearly the framework of their philosophy, especially the arguments that prove the essencelessness (*dharma-nairātmya*) of conceived and cognised objective phenomena. To highlight this aspect, the discussion introduced here is centred on two of the important works of early Mādhyamika, the *Vigrahavyāvartinī* of Nāgārjuna and the *Hastavālanāma-prakaraṇavṛtti* of Āryadeva. The introduction of the uncertainty principle of Werner Heisenberg clarifies the point that Mādhyamika view is not based on any substratum of atomism or any other humanly definable subatomic particle.

The method of analysis used in the *Vigrahavyāvartinī* is focused not mainly on the ontology of the objects conceived but on the premises of those conceptions, the instruments of true cognition or the *pramāṇas*. This methodology is called regressive method of analysis because the analysis is not just ending at the epistemic premises of *pramāṇas* but even discusses the logical inconsistency of the *pramāṇas* as the tool for true cognition. The discussion of the *Hastavālanāma-prakaraṇavṛtti* is based on the ontological analysis of the conceived object, the snake, the cognised object, the rope and the insubstantial object of neither snake nor rope (*dharma-nairātmya*). The ontological verifiability of the objects of snake or rope is not completely certain. Here, the analysis follows a progressive method from the most dichotomous objective perception, the snake; the dependently discernible object, the rope; and the indescribable and uncertain objective entity, which is neither snake nor rope. Thus, the *dharma-nairātmya* of the objects of experience is confirmed. The systematic analytical method of modern science also proves that on analysis the ultimate object shows unpredictable behaviour and the object of experience is insubstantial and dependent. All these methods prove one thing in common that the object of experience is essenceless, and the human cognitive faculties are not able to ascertain the true nature of the phenomenal world.

In the *Vigrahavyāvartinī*, Nāgārjuna highlights two points; in the first part, the focus is on the impossibility to negate the means of knowledge (*pramāṇas*) without accepting its existence, because *pramāṇas* form the way to understand the apparent world of experience. The first twenty verses focus on this aspect. In contrast, the second part of the text categorically refutes the authority of *pramāṇas* to formulate premises for the theoretical understandings about the world of phenomena. The regressive analysis employed by Nāgārjuna primarily attacks the substantiality of *pramāṇa* as a premise for true cognition of the objective world. It is not the objective world (*prameya*) but the *pramāṇa*, which is insubstantial. So, as far as the objects (*prameya*) is concerned, its existence is eluding the faculties of human mind. In other words, to avoid the confusion arisen from the deluded existence of the objective world, one has to accept its insubstantiality. The last verse of the *Vigrahavyāvartinī* explains this aspect further: "All things prevail for him for whom prevails this *śūnyatā*. Nothing prevails for him for whom *śūnyatā* does not prevail."[113] The concept of *śūnya* is actually misinterpreted as a metaphysical position by critics and interpreters of Mādhyamika. On the other hand, Mādhyamika says that the *śūnya* is implicit in each phenomenon to express its dependent and conceptual nature. *Śūnya* works as a tool of analysis to express the insubstantial nature of the phenomena; but at the same time, it never forms a theoretical position that exists beyond the realm of each phenomenon. It has been said that

> The victorious ones have proclaimed that emptiness consists of escaping from all view-points. Those who hold emptiness as view point, they declared them to be incurable.[114]

The function of *śūnya* can be summarised as that it is similar to an antidote, which cures the illusions that are attached with the phenomena that can create conceptual formulations in the mind. Against this regressive analysis about the non-substantiality, even, of the *pramāṇa,* Āryadeva introduces a progressive method from the level of empirical perception of the objects.

In order to assail any notion that the objective phenomenal world is substantial, this discussion introduces Ārydeva's *Hastavālanāma-*

prakaraṇavṛtti. Here, the analysis started with the conceived object of snake, which was actually a rope, but on veridical perception (the conception of the object with the help of six senses), the object is a rope. The ontology of the snake in the rope is dismissed as illusory or insubstantial; in other words, the snake is void (*śūnya*) on the rope. Similarly, on close examination, the rope as an object is not ascertainable, because the rope is dependent on the finer constituents of fibre; again, the fibre too is not substantial, since the matter constitutes of subatomic particles. Even analysis of the subatomic particle doesn't discern any ultimate identifiable entity.

It is Werner Heisenberg who identified the uncertain behaviour of the subatomic particle and introduced his theory, which remains unassailable even after seventy-four years of its introduction, that the velocity and position of a particle cannot be evaluated at the same time. It is called uncertainty principle, which states that when one measures the velocity, the position of the particle changes, and when the position is ascertained the velocity changes. Because the particle receives energy from the light particle and moves away from its position, it is difficult to measure it; similarly, when one succeeds in measuring the velocity of the particle, its position remains elusive. This aspect of the particle makes it a mathematical hard nut, that it is impossible to predict the matter's behaviour.

In the Buddhist perspective, the matter may have an existence of its own, but determining the behaviour of such matter is difficult with the help of human experience. As for the human experience of the matter is concerned, the true nature of the objective phenomena is insubstantial, unpredictable, dependent, or empty. In other words, the systematic scientific analysis of the matter proves the *śūnyatā* implicit in them.

References

1. The conceived object of the mind is called *dharma*, which is susceptible to variation and corruption. Ordinarily, the object of mind is referred as *dharma* meaning "idea" or "concept." David J. Kalupahana, *A History of Buddhist Philosophy*, p. 79.
2. *Cittaviśuddhi-prakaraṇa*, v. 8.
3. Quoted from *Saṁyukta Nikāya* by Peter Della Santina, *Mādhyamika Schools in India*, p. 13.

4. Ibid., p. 4, cites from the *Majjhima Nikāya*.
5. T.R.V. Murti, op. cit., p. 40.
6. David J. Kalupahana, *Mūlamādhyamikakārikā of Nāgārjuna*, XV.10.
7. T.R.V. Murti, op. cit., p. 128.
8. Peter Della Santina, *Mādhyamika Schools in India*, p. 103.
9. The ways to acquire knowledge are called *pramāṇas*; perception, inference, analogy, textual knowledge, etc., are examples of *pramāṇas*.
10. *Prasaṅga* is arguing out a theoretical position by pointing out the inconsistencies in the theory itself. "Reductio ad abstradum" is similar to *prasaṅga*.
11. T.R.V. Murti, op. cit., p. 50, quoted *Majjhima Nikāya*, III.
12. Peter Della Santina, op. cit., p. 104.
13. The epistemic regress argument used in Western philosophy and the regressive method of the early Mādhyamikas have some fundamental difference: the epistemic regress argument is coming to show that knowledge and epistemic justification a two-tier structure as described by *epistemic foundationalism*, which again forms evidential chains. Mādhyamika on the other hand accepts the foundationalism temporarily but assails the foundation on which evidential chains could form as insubstantial. Rejecting the foundationalism is the unique method of Mādhyamikas. See, *Cambridge Dictionary of Philosophy*, p. 233.
14. H.V. Guenther, *The Tāntric View of Life*, p. 53.
15. T.R.V. Murti, op. cit., p. 250.
16. Kamaleswar Bhattacharya, E.H. Johnston, and A. Kunst, *Vigrahavyāvartinī of Nāgārjuna*, p. 95.
17. The purpose here is not just resorting to the traditional philosophical methodology of dividing the subject into Pūrvapakṣa and Uttarapakṣa as described by Peter Della Santina, op. cit., p. 103.
18. Kamaleswar Bhattacharya, E.H. Johnson, and A. Kunst, op. cit., p. 97.
19. Ibid., p. 99.
20. The proper explanation to the inconsistency in accepting perception as a valid means of knowledge is successfully refuted in the later discussions. In the initial verses, Nāgārjuna put forward the objections that can be raised against his view on the epistemology. (Ibid., v. 19, p. 46, also vv. 5–6.)
21. Ibid., p. 101.
22. Ibid., p. 51, v. 12.
23. Ibid., p. 5, v. 13.
24. Ibid., p. 104, vv. 14–16.
25. Ibid., p. 105, vv. 17, 18.
26. Ibid., v. 19.
27. Ibid., p.106, v. 20.
28. Nāgārjuna's criticism is primarily against the Abhidharma schools of Buddhism. See David J. Kalupahana, *The Philosophy of the Middle Way*, p. 81.

29. Kamaleswar Bhattacharya, E.H. Johnston, and A.Kunst, op. cit., p. 107, v. 21.
30. Ibid., p. 108, v. 23.
31. Ibid., p. 109, v. 24.
32. Ibid., p. 111, v. 27.
33. Ibid., v. 29.
34. Ibid., p. 115, v. 31.
35. The self, according to Buddhism, is a combination of various identifiable functions. Among that dispositions will be acting with ignorance and the person generates cravings (*tanha*)—or the opposite—for the experienced. Cravings lead to grasping and it conditions becoming. David J. Kalupahana, *The Philosophy of the Middle Way*, p. 78.
36. Peter Della Santina, op. cit., p. 107.
37. Kamaleswar Bhattacharya, E.H. Johnston, and A.Kunst, op. cit., p. 115.
38. There are very clear and certain explanations about the erroneous perception.
39. Kamaleswar Bhattacharya, E.H. Johnston, and A. Kunst, op. cit., p. 115.
40. Ibid., p. 116, v. 33.
41. Ibid., p. 117, v. 34.
42. Ibid., p. 118, vv. 35, 36.
43. Ibid., v. 37.
44. Ibid., p. 119, v. 38.
45. Ibid., v. 39.
46. Ibid., p. 120, vv. 40, 41.
47. Ibid., p. 121, vv. 43, 44, 46.
48. Ibid., p. 123, v. 49.
49. Ibid., p. 124, v. 51.
50. Ibid., p. 125, vv. 52–53.
51. Ibid., p. 127, vv. 54–55.
52. Ibid., p. 128, v. 57.
53. Ibid., v. 58. The name suggests some characteristic feature of a thing, such as cold water or strong wind.
54. Ibid., p. 129, v. 58.
55. Ibid., v. 59.
56. Ibid., p. 127, v. 55.
57. Ibid., p. 130, v. 60.
58. Ibid., v. 61.
59. Ibid., p. 79, v. 62.
60. Ibid., v. 63.
61. Ibid., p. 153, vv. 64–65.
62. Ibid., p. 133, vv. 66–67.
63. Ibid., p. 137, v. 70.
64. The *Hastavālanāma-prakaraṇavṛtti* of Āryadeva, in F. Tola and C. Dragonetti, ed. and trans., *On Voidness*, p. 5.
65. Ibid., p. 4.
66. Ibid., p. 10.

67. Ibid.
68. Ibid., v. 2a-d.
69. Ibid., p. 11.
70. Ibid., v. 3c-d.
71. Ibid., p. 12.
72. Ibid.
73. Ibid., p. 13.
74. Steven Weinberg, *Dream of a Final Theory*, 1993, p. 28.
75. Stephen W. Hawking, *A Brief History of Time*, 1988, p. 57.
76. The idea that the state of the universe at one time determines the state at all other times has been a central tenet of science, ever since Laplace's time. It implies that we can predict the future, in principle at least (ibid.). See also the paper presented by Stephen W. Hawking at the University of Cambridge, copy published on the Web: www.damtp.cam.ac.uk/user/hawking.
77. In order to predict the future position and velocity of a particle, one has to be able to measure its present position and velocity accurately. The obvious way to do this is shine a light on the particle. Some of the waves of light will be scattered by the particle and this will indicate its position. One needs to use light of a short wavelength in order to measure the position of the particle precisely. The minimum one quantum of light used for this purpose would disturb the particle and change its velocity in a way that cannot be predicted. Ibid., p. 59. See also Steven Weinberg, op. cit., p. 57.
78. Stephen W. Hawking, *A Brief History of Time*, 1988, p. 59.
79. Ibid.
80. The lecture given at Department of Applied Mathematics and Theoretical Physics, University of Cambridge, available on the Web: www.damtp.cam.-ac.uk/user/hawking. April 1998.
81. Steven Weinberg, op. cit., p.61.
82. Einstein was very unhappy about this apparent randomness in nature. His views were summed up in his famous phrase, "God does not play Dice." He seemed to have felt that the uncertainty was only provisional: but that there was an underlying reality, in which particles would have well-defined positions, and speeds, and would evolve according to deterministic laws, in the spirit of Laplace. This reality might be known to God, but the quantum nature of light would prevent us seeing it, except through a glass darkly. Paper by Stephen W. Hawking, "Does God play Dice," Source: http://www.pbs.org.
83. See, Thomas S. Kuhn, *The Structure of Scientific Revolutions*, quoted from the synopsis of the original by Frank Pajares, "How are paradigms created, and how do scientific revolutions take place? Inquiry begins with a random collection of "mere facts" (although, often, a body of beliefs is already implicit in the collection). During these early stages of inquiry, different researchers confronting the same phenomena describe and interpret them in different ways. In time, these descriptions and interpretations entirely

disappear. A pre-paradigmatic school appears. Such a school often emphasises a special part of the collection of facts. Often, these schools vie for pre-eminence." The Philosopher's Magazine TPM Online is *The Philosophers' Magazine* on the net. It is edited by Dr Jeremy Stangroom. http://www.philosophers.co.uk/

84. Stephen W. Hawking, *A Brief History of Time*, p. 185.
85. Paper by Stephen W. Hawking, "Does God Play Dice?" Source, in the internet: http://www.pbs.org.
86. T.R.V. Murti, op. cit., p. 161.
87. Ibid., p. 162.
88. Ibid., p. 163.
89. Ibid. as quoted from the *Kāśyapaparivata*, 164.
90. David J. Kalupahana, ed. and trans., *Mūlamādhyamikakārikā of Nāgārjuna*, p. 335.
91. Ibid., p. 330.
92. Ibid., p. 331.
93. Ibid., p. 339.
94. Ibid., p. 341.
95. T.R.V. Murti, op. cit., p. 165.
96. Edgar W.Pritchard, *The New Dialectics in Theory and Practice*, 1952, p. 18.
97. Ibid.
98. Ibid., p. 19.
99. T.R.V. Murti, op. cit., p. 301.
100. Ibid., p. 124.
101. David J. Kalupahana, ed. and trans., *Mūlamādhyamikakārikā...*, p. 289.
102. Ibid., p. 288.
103. Ibid., p. 337.
104. T.R.V. Murti, op. cit., p. 163.
105. Ibid., p. 146.
106. Tom J.F. Tillemans, *Materials for the Study of Āryadeva, Dharmapāla and Candrakīrti*, p. 72.
107. See Fumimaro Watanabe, *Philosophy and its Development in Nikāyas and Abhidharma*, p. 88. There are four kinds of metaphysical standpoints dealing sixteen questions. This can be summarised in to four kinds of patterns that is, Exists; not Exists; Exists and not Exists; neither Exists nor not Exists. Actually these 16 questions about the soul, *tathāgata*, *karma*, and rebirth were asked to Buddha, but he refused to answer them categorically. Watanabe contents that may be the pattern of thinking of Buddha and Sañjaya were same. Buddha refused to answer these questions with an opinion that this would lead to nihilistic thinking. The same is the position of the Mādhyamikas. They also refuse to answer or take positions in this argument but posing these questions to make us understand the limitations of our thinking processes.
108. K.N. Jayathilake, *The Early Buddhist Theory of Knowledge*, 1963, p. 338. Here, the purport of finding a new logical system is to view the world in a

different way and express a desire to view nature in her actual stage "a logic in pursuit."

109. Nāgārjuna has written a text called *Vaidalyaprakaraṇa* which highlights the inconsistency of accepting traditional Nyāya positions as valid tool of logical analysis. See *Nāgārjuna's Rafutation to Logic (Nyāya), Vaidalya-prakaraṇa*, ed. and trans. F. Tola and C. Dragonetti, p. 3.
110. T.R.V. Murti, op. cit., p. 129. Here, it is contended that though Nāgārjuna cites this problem in *Mūlamādhyamikakārikā*, ch. XXVII. Āryadeva has given it in order of the alternatives. Mostly Āryadeva's verses are widely discussed.
111. Ibid. See also Tom J.F. Tillemans, op. cit., p. 72. Here, he discusses in detail about the nature of Mādhyamika position in the light of Western logic. However, one thing is sure that Mādhyamika never adduces himself to any of the position that can be possibly a part of the argument, but he rejects all the alternatives as inconsistent inherently. The association to any of the position is an inherent weakness of the human being and it never means that the position held has any amount of truth in it
112. Karen Lang, *Āryadeva's Catuḥśataka*, XIV. 21, p. 133.
113. Kamaleswar Bhattacharya, E.H. Johnston, and A. Kunst, op. cit., p. 137.
114. *Mādhyamikakārikā*, 13.8, quoted from Guy Bugault, "On Śūnyata," *Journal of Indian Philosophy*, p. 67.

Chapter Three

Dharmadhātu—A Rational Reconstruction of "Phenomenon"

3.1 The Rational Structuring of *Dharma-nairātmya* and *Dharmadhātu*

The dialectical analysis of the apparent phenomenal world of appearance, as we have seen in the previous discussion, in the Mādhyamika way, could reveal the insubstantial nature of the world of things. This apparent world for many schools of philosophy is a reliable source to discern the fundamental truth about the world, existence, life, etc. The Mādhyamikas, on the other hand, desist from making any clear and certain opinion on this aspect, they just pinpoint the difficulties involved in formulating any position, because such positions based on partial views about the world would only lead to confusion and worry for the human mind. When we look at this problem in a broader sense, we can see that most of the conflicts in the world are a result of these articulated partial views about the world. Mādhyamikas' message should be seen as one which would not substantiate a single view but ready to look at all views. This is not a state of mind easily achievable without adequate training especially with regard to the dispositionally conditioned aspects of the human mind who like to cling on to something substantial. For the normal human mind, the insubstantial nature of the phenomenal world may be intellectually acceptable, but not emotionally. Hereafter, we follow the discussion of the text *Cittaviśuddhi-prakaraṇa*, where this discussion takes a new turn about the same problem of understanding the insubstantial nature of the phenomenal world. The text begins with an explanation to the unconditioned nature of the mind and its inherent purity; the purity through which one could view the phenomenal world without the problem of dichotomous conceptualisation (*vikalpas*). In other words, the discussion in the text leads us to achieve the original state of mind, the inherently pure mind. This is a common method in the philosophical tradition that certain ethical practices are inculcated with each tradition to prepare one to follow the doctrinal position of that tradition. Here, Mādhyamika method is different from other views since it does not accept any theoretical position, so the training is also meant to rationally restructure the mental faculties without damaging its stability.

In the last chapter, the nature of the voidness (*śūnya* or *dharma-nairātmya*) of the phenomenal world has been ascertained from three methodological tools. So long as the human personality functions as the knowing self, and under the control of various adjuncts, it is naturally, difficult to remove the negative effect of the phenomena on the mind, even though it accepts the essencelessness (*dharma-nairātmya*) of phenomena as a reality. This again leads to the formation of an eternally existing self. The notion of an eternally existing self would gestalt the phenomena (*dharma*) and that would lead to the formation of tentative theories with regard to the objects of the world. In this regard, it is essential to analyse whether knowledge of *dharma-nairātmya* alone leads to the realisation of *pudgala-nairātmya* or the insubstantial and non-eternal nature of the self. In the following pages, we would analyse three important trends in Indian philosophy which deal with this problem, the Materialist school led by logical sceptics, the Brāhmanical schools led by Sāṅkhya-Yoga, and the Mādhyamika school. These three strands of Indian philosophy follow certain subtle similarities.

A deeper dialectical analysis of the experienced objects reveals that theories are mere constructions on weak epistemological foundations, and that the objects of the world perceived are insubstantial and dependent. This truth is clearly explained in the *Vigrahavyāvartinī*, through the methodology of regressive analysis.

From another perspective, if the occurrence of erroneous perception is the proof of the existence of a (non-erroneous) true entity, then based on the arguments of the *Hastavālanāma-prakaraṇavṛtti*, it can be proved that both the erroneous perception (the snake) and the substratum (the rope) are insubstantial on closer analysis. We can examine the dichotomous nature of the object and later its insubstantial nature. The progressive method of analysis used here involves directing the conscious mind to the insubstantial nature of the phenomenal world. The systematic analysis, which is the method of the modern science, has also proved that the objects analysed are insubstantial; in other words, the closer we move towards the understanding of the real truth about the things of the world, the further that truth moves away from our understanding. They are not adequate to formulate a theory that truly explains the nature of the objective world. The finer entities after the analysis of a material objects do not hold any of the properties of the object which is originally analysed.

The parallels between modern science and the Mādhyamika view are, in fact, coincidental. Even though the methods of analysis adopted by them are dissimilar, both the systems were analysing the same phenomenal world. The similarity may be attributable to the fact that the purpose of these analysis was not to substantiate a metaphysical doctrine but to observe the world as the way it appears before us. For the Mādhyamikas, the existence of rope depends on the finer particles like fibre, etc.; the fibre depends on finer particles not having the nature of fibre or rope. Thus, the fibre, the rope, and the snake have only dependent existence. Modern science, with its most efficient and accurate method of analysis and calculation, is agreeing with the observations of the early Mādhyamikas: The objective analysis leads to finer atomic particles; the atomic particles on further analysis reveal subatomic particles of uncertain behaviour and nature, which are ultimately unpredictable. In other words, the seemingly real and predictable entities of the objective world are dependent on entities of unpredictable and uncertain behaviour; the apparent phenomenal world is discernible only relatively.

In the *Catuḥśataka*, Āryadeva expresses his views on the question of validity of the theoretical positions, which are formulated based on the perception of the apparent world of phenomena. If there is an inconsistency in concluding the authenticity of an argument, then it does not mean that the contraposition is valid. On the other hand, if there are conflicts in reasoning in any one of the positions that leads to a definite conclusion, then the same conflict prevails in all the four possible positions of existence: the affirmative (*sat*), the negative (*asat*), the conjunctive assertion (*ubhāya*) of the both, and the disjunctive denial (*anupāya*).[1] This is based on the fact that no theory or view is perfect in explaining the true nature of the universe. So, if there is an entity that is based on perfect premises of true cognition or on perfect unchangeable substratum or on mathematically perfect foundations, then the explanation to that entity's existence will be consistent in all the four positions of existence. However, such an entity is not discernible for human cognition. The only way to understand the actual way of the functioning of the phenomenal realities without interfering with the natural tendencies of the mind to cling and crave, is to have those faculties functioning in a very active manner. There, the rational structuring of the phenomena needs an enhancement in the analytical faculties of the human personality, which is possible with *Cittaviśuddhi* or cleansing of the mind.

3.2 *Cittaviśuddhi* for Realisation of *Pudgala-nairātmya* and the Experience of *Dharma-nairātmya*

The discourses of the Buddha are explicit in explaining the nature of the human personality and the objective phenomenal world and the experience of it; it never attributes any sort of substantiality for both objective phenomenal experience and the subjective human personality.[2] It is the five attributes of the mind (*pañcaskandhas*) that is alluded as the eternally existing self, where the wrongly alluded self configure the objective experience as real and certain. The method to free oneself from the excessive influence of the phenomenal experience and the naive practice of configuring the unreal as real, one should achieve purification of mind, *Cittaviśuddhi*. The procedure of purification (*Cittaviśuddhi*) is a method of active interaction with the five attributes of the mind (*pañcaskandhas*). The *Cittaviśuddhi-prakaraṇa* deals exclusively with the problem of *Cittaviśuddhi*. Elaborating this aspect, the text discusses the aspects of *Cittaviśuddhi*, *Bodhicitta*, *Vajrajñāna* in the first part; the *dharma* (phenomena), *dharmadhātu* (essence of phenomena), and *dharma-nairātmya* (essencelessness of phenomena) in the second part of the discussion. The text explains the value of Tāntric meditative practices in achieving spiritual virtues, especially the importance of *mantra-sādhanā*. It also argues that other spiritual practices are not efficacious to achieve any spiritual merit. Some of such practices, according to Āryadeva, bring only demerit and more bondage.

The Mādhyamika philosophy and the Tāntric method of spiritual developments are comparable because both avoid the extreme positions. Mādhyamikas introduce a unique philosophical system which apparently equips one to view the world as the way it appears, by declining to be specific on the question of the eternity of the human self and the existent objective world, and the contraposition of declamation of both the existent realities by projecting the conception of Nihilism. Tantra, too supports the middle position between the absolute ritualistic practices of the eternalists and the absolute withdrawal from all spiritual practices as advanced by some of the Nihilists. The Mādhyamika position and its relevance to the actual world of appearance can be better understood only by analysing the positions held by the rival schools of eternalists and nihilists.

3.3 The Materialists' View on *Pudgala-nairātmya*

The phenomenal world as an appearance of an eternally existing reality is the contention and position of most of the Brāhmanical schools of philosophy. The Materialist schools of Indian philosophy always held a contraposition, which assailed the views of the Brāhmanical schools, using fourteen *avyakṛtas* (inexplicable).[3] With the help of this method, the Ucchedavādins[4] belonging to Sañjaya Belaṭṭhiputta repudiate the existence of the world as real and the eternal existence of the self. He questions the very necessity of ritualistic spiritual practices as a method towards redemption and the efficacy of ritualistic practices to eradicate sufferings from the world of existence. Sañjaya's questions dialectically oppose the views of Brāhmanical schools, because of the lack of evidence to prove beyond doubt the eternally existing entities. The fourteen questions vehemently query the theorists' positions in the logical format of: P, not P, both P and not P, neither P nor not P. Each of these questions is asked against the realities of the self, the rebirth, the world, and the finiteness of existence.[5]

Two arguments and two solutions can be thought of in this regard. Firstly, if one realises that the eternalists' theories on realities are not substantial and which crumble on questioning, then there is no point in following the spiritual practices suggested by them. The alternative solution is based on the argument that the normal life is full of miseries and sufferings due to confusing thoughts, and the thought on contentious metaphysical questions might only be furthering the process of confusion. Sañjaya, thus, contends that anything that could retard the smooth conduct of life should be avoided. Differing from the traditional two-pronged logical approach (the truth-value assessed on acceptance and denial of a proposition), the fourfold system assesses the truth-value with respect to the possibility of assertions, the possibility of denials, the possibility of both assertions and denials, and the possibility of neither assertions nor denials.[6] A.B. Keith, the famous Buddhologist, gives credit to Sañjaya for initiating such a thought process. He describes that, "as Sañjaya agnostic to have been the first to formulate the possibilities of existence, non-existence, both, and neither."[7]

3.3.1 *Silencing of Mind-Spiritual Practices of the Ucchedavādins*

According to Sañjaya, a thorough analysis of the phenomenal world of things would rather confuse the mind than redeem it from the dichotomous nature of the world of existence. Thus, it is advised to keep the mind off from any contentious thoughts regarding existence etc. As K.N. Jayathilake explains:

> Sceptics merely considered it undesirable to be involved in belief based on one's likes or dislikes. They held this view not because such beliefs would be a source of worry and mental disquietude. In any case, this school of thinkers adopt scepticism primarily out of moral considerations rather than for intellectual reasons.[8]

The eternalists' view is in corroboration with different aspects that confronts human life in the world: it gives support to the mind's internal nature to acquire support from various aspects of the phenomenal world; it also gives meaning to life in the world where he is encouraged to do good so that his life in the next birth would be assured. This view never creates any problem if the follower believes in the teachings of the doctrinal position without questioning, but the problem originates when one begins to question the authenticity of the doctrinal position and the views of these schools of thought. This is the main worry of the people who oppose these views, the moral danger happens because following such confirmed views might be confusing the mind of a follower. It is evident from the Buddhist Nikāyas that the method of Sañjaya school tries to avoid to answer any question asked to them, in such a way that the questions themselves can create severe ethical problems for one who try to answer them. The dialogue between Ajātasatru and Sañjaya is a good example highlighting this aspect.[9]

However, Āryadeva finds a different reason for using the analytical technique of the Ucchedavādins like Sañjaya, because they use them to highlight the untenablility of extreme views of the realists. In the

Catuḥśataka, Āryadeva says: "just as one might say that a permanent thing exists if the continuum (*saṁtāna*) is perceived wrongly; similarly, one might say that a thing exists if the combination of causes and conditions is perceived wrongly."[10] The causes for articulating permanent things are many and complicated. Āryadeva uses views of the Sañjaya school of thought to verify the idea of the permanence of things philosophically.

3.4 Āryadeva's Refutation—the *Catuṣkoṭi* to solve *Avyakṛta* Problems

Introducing a view of insubstantiality with the help of fourteen *avyakṛtas*,[11] the Sañjaya school of logical scepticism highlighted the insubstantiality of the eternalists' adherence to metaphysics, and with an equal zeal they dismissed their ethical practices. Notwithstanding this position, the Mādhyamikas' question both eternalism and the contraposition of nihilism using the technique of *catuṣkoṭi*, which is derived from the fourteen *avyakṛtas*. They assert that both the positions are based on insubstantial foundations. In this chapter, the discussion is primarily based on the thesis that things we perceive exist only relatively, and that relatively existing things are not permanent. Since there is nothing which is independent, permanent, and eternal with our experience of the empirical world, the contra-position of nihilism is also not true, because the dependence of things does not substantiate its absence. As Āryadeva rightly says in the text, "Where a thing is in no way dependent upon another, its existence certainly would be established, but such a thing does not exist anywhere."[12] Here, the stated objective world of things exists in dependence of other things; nothing is independent in its existence. The stated *svabhāva* of things is apparent only because of our association with them. The nihilists' view on the voidness of things is also untenable and contradictory. The context in which Āryadeva uses the technique of *catuṣkoṭi* relates to show that both the eternalists' view of permanence of things and the nihilists view on voidness of things, are untenable. He says:

> Existence, non-existence, (both) existence and non-existence, and neither existence nor non-existence this is the progressive method that intelligent people would apply constantly in regard to unity and so forth.[13]

Mādhyamikas not only say that no theory in the world is able to explain the true nature of the world of phenomena, but also say that it is not proper to judge anything, with the available knowledge and information, which is insufficient for definite conclusions. Commenting on the real position of Mādhyamika, T.R.V. Murti says:

> The Mādhyamika is convinced that the conjunctive or disjunctive synthesis is but another view; it labours under the same difficulties. Rejection of all views is the rejection of competence of reason to comprehend reality. The real is transcending to thought. Rejection of views is not based on any positive grounds or acceptance of another view; it is the inner contradictions implicit in each view.[14]

It is not just the conflict in reason alone that is worrisome to Mādhyamika in accepting the theoretical stands of realists and the nihilists. He also is aware of inability of the theorists to comprehend the real nature of the human mind.

3.4.1 *Controlling the Thought Process—Not Absolute Silencing of the Mind*

One may be able to avoid conflicting arguments regarding metaphysical questions and attain quietude by abstaining from mental and verbal conflicts. But in real experience it is clear that the realities of life never allow him to stop thinking completely due to the incessant thinking process of mind. This is exactly the philosophical problem dealt with by the early Mādhyamikas. The ethical problems that can arise from accepting either the eternity of the world of existence or the opposite view of the voidness of existent things, are equally damaging. Accepting either of the views is like jumping to conclusions based on unconfirmed and insufficient information. The sceptics promoted stringent asceticism to stop the mind from falling into unnecessary wrangling on contentious issues, but they are not completely successful in controlling the incessant thought process of the mind. However, they could succeeded only partially, as complete cessation of thought process is almost impossible. The mind, by its very nature, according to Mādhymikas, is like a gem, devoid of conceptualisations (*vikalpas*); it is pure, beginningless, without any taint or *svabhāva*.[15] Here, the Mādhyamika method of spiritual training is important as it uses the technique of transcending the influence of thought by means of thought itself.

The spiritual disciplines and practices are beyond doctrinal difference. Different schools of Indian philosophy adopt the same practical methods, such that only the philosophical perspective differs from system to system. Thus, it is important for our discussion to understand the positions of the Brāhmanical systems, which all the heterodox schools of Indian philosophy categorically oppose.

3.5 Realisation of the Eternal Self—the Brāhmanical View

The Brāhmanical schools, in general, profess three types of spiritual practices which are basically in conformity with their philosophical positions with a primary view that the life in the world is a temporary phase one has to pass through and the ultimate aim of all spiritual practices is to find liberation for the indestructible soul which is manifested with life in this world. The spiritual practices are a part of continuum in corroboration with the teachings of the Vedas which are considered eternal like the soul. The primary aim of this school is to find adequate spiritual practice for finding liberation (*mukti*) of the soul. The prominent spiritual practices accepted by the Brāhmanical school for attaining *mukti* (liberation), are the *Jñāna-mārga*, the *Karma-mārga*, and the *Bhakti-mārga*. *Jñāna-mārga* has the capacity to reveal the nature of phenomenon and loosen the human soul's attachment towards them; *Karma-mārga* helps one to repudiate the ills of bad *karma* (dispositions) that are accumulated; and *Bhakti-mārga* is the total surrender of the individual soul to the creator of the universe. More specifically, the *Karma-mārga* and the *Jñāna-mārga*, indicate direct allegiance to the *Karma-kāṇḍa* and the *Jñāna-kāṇḍa* of the Vedas respectively. The *Bhakti-mārga*, on the other hand, is a later development.

The Brāhmanical philosophical systems follow certain fundamental convictions regarding the origin of the world. As noted by Indologist McDonnell, "The one regards the universe as the result of mechanical production, the world of carpenter's and jointer's skill: the other represents it as the result of natural generation."[16] The creator of the universe is an intelligent agent and the universe is being created with a definite purpose and an aim that the creator sets. At the same time, there is a phase in the evolution of the world that is natural and the progression of which one could observe in the apparent world. But the purpose set by the creator is not certainly clear and according to the Brāhmanical schools, this is beyond the comprehension of normal human understanding. Accordingly, the phenomenon that appears before us is nothing but a mere unformed and imperfect representation of the total reality, and also it is indicative of the nature of the ultimate reality. The passage from *Taittirīya Brāhmaṇa* says all about the nature of the Brahman and the architectural creativity of the Brahman, "Brahman the wood and Brahman the tree from which the heaven and earth were made."[17] The notion of Brahman is not explained completely in clear logical terms, yet the Brahman is understood as something that is, the agent of the action as well as the one on which the action is performed; or the subjective and objective aspect of the "only" reality that exists forever. The *Ātman* according to the earlier Vedic thought would be considered as the subjective faculty that is reflecting the phenomenal world. As Surendranath Dasgupta put it, "The Ātman is generally used to mean vital birth (*prāṇa*), *manas* (mind) which is the seat of thought and emotion and it is to be regarded as a dwelling in the heart."[18] Again he says: "The Veda teaches that the Ātman can be separated from the physical body and has the capacity to exist after death."[19] The pre-Upaniṣadic concept of *Ātman* is not philosophically clear, yet it has started the rational explication of the nature of life and the stages of consciousness. On this foundation, later philosophical theories have been formulated.

Philosophically valid and clear views have been shaped in the Upaniṣads that the idea of self and the supremacy of self are the only reality, and that everything else remains far below this reality. To illustrate further, "There is no relation here of the worshipper and the worshipped and no prayers are offered to it, but the whole quest is of the highest truth, and the true self of man is discovered as the greatest reality."[20] The teachings of the early Vedas and the Upaniṣads are very clear that an underlying reality is existing permanently, and the nature of the permanent reality transcends the strict realm of duality; the duality of subject and object, the worshipped and the worshipper; the true and false; and the right and the wrong, etc. It says that

> the fundamental idea which runs through the early Upaniṣads is that underlying the exterior world of change there is an unchangeable reality which is identical with that which underlies the essence in man.[21]

However, to give a verbal explication and narration on the nature of this reality is very difficult and the Brāhmans adopt various methods to verbalise the nature of Brahman. One such method is the negative method introduced by Yājñavalkya. He says:

> He (the Ātman or Brahman) is not this, nor this (*neti neti*). He is inconceivable for he cannot be conceived, unchangeable, for he is not changed, untouched, for nothing can touch him; he cannot suffer by a stroke of the sword, he cannot suffer any injury.[22]

This method of explanation transcends the normal logical method and analysis, and it leads to the inexplicable nature of the reality as we conceive it. The reality according to this view is beyond the comprehension of normal human understanding. It is explained as:

> That which is inaudible, intangible, invisible, indestructible, which cannot be tasted, nor smelt, eternal, without beginning or end, greater than the greatest, the fixed; he who knows it is released, from the jaws of death.[23]

The inexplicable nature of the only reality that underlies the apparent changing phenomena is otherwise described as of the nature of silence, and it is explained as, "I teach you indeed but you do not understand; the Ātman is silence."[24]

3.5.1 *Sāṅkhya School—Philosophisation inspired by the Vedas*

One of the important contributions of Sāṅkhya school is that it introduced a philosophical system based on the essential teachings of the Vedas and it successfully defended the positions of Vedas against the critiques that was chronic in classical Indian philosophy. The tenets of this system are revered by various schools of philosophy around the world because of its strong basis and referential importance.

From the Upaniṣads to the philosophical schools, the discussion in the Brāhmanical tradition has become more critical and analytical. This is due to the critiques by the Materialists and logical sceptics who vehemently opposed the extreme theoretical standing of the Brāhmanical thought that owes absolute allegiance to the teachings of the Vedas. According to Jayathilake:

> We find that metaphysics first develops out of mythology and it is when the metaphysical speculation attains a certain maturity and results in the formulation of a variety of theories that an interest is shown in the problem of knowledge and epistemological questions are first mooted.[25]

The origin of philosophical schools in the Vedic tradition of the Brāhmans first started as a counter critique to the critics. The schools like Sāṅkhya and Yoga had found a suitable space for its origin and development where it formed a suitable platform to counter the extreme critical position of the detractors and critics.

The Sāṅkhyan view is the direct answer to the epistemological questions advanced by the Materialists and logical sceptics: "Philosophical enquiries were, however, continuing in circles other than those of the Upaniṣads. Thus, the Buddha who closely followed the early Upaniṣad period spoke of and enumerated sixty-two kinds of heresies."[26] It is clear that although Vedas and Upaniṣads formed an important philosophical tradition, the opposing Materialists and logical sceptics too formed an important tradition, where critical analysis was the main method of philosophising, a refutation or clarification of their positions against the detractors' arguments and criticisms.

Sceptics argue that how an entity that is beyond the world of existence determines the conditioned existents. When we look into the nature of phenomena, we are not able to discern anything that shows any certainty about the world or universe.[27] Sañjaya's questions are considered as the biggest heresy in the history of Indian religio-philosophical traditions. Even the Buddhists, who refute the authority of the Vedas, opposed the views of Sañjaya fervently saying that it is untenable to refuse the existence of the phenomenal world completely. This is obvious from the answers given to the Sage Vacchagotra on the question of the existence of soul.[28] The Buddhists never agreed to the extreme views expressed by these rival schools, for the two views showing rival arguments are not agreeing to the real nature of life, its different effects and its manifestations. Therefore, it is concluded that all these philosophical wrangling causes more confusion to already confused mind and the best way for understanding the nature of the world is only through understanding of the nature of the world of phenomena. According to the philosophy of Yoga, an offshoot of Sāṅkhya, the *citta* (mind) is a collection of instincts and tendencies collected from various lives: "Apart from the perception and the life function, *buddhi*, or *citta* as Yoga describes it contains within it the root impressions and the tastes or tendencies of all past lives as man and as some animal."[29]

3.5.2 *Sāṅkhya and Yoga—Understanding of Cittaviśuddhi*

Citta[30] is a storehouse of previous birth's *vāsanās* (impressions) and tendencies that are carried forward into this life too. In order to understand the true nature of the world, according to fundamental convictions and beliefs, one needs to cleanse the *citta*. The philosophical system of Sāṅkhya-Yoga also addresses the problem of the mind and its importance in spiritual development. Surendranath Dasgupta is of the opinion that: "Sāṅkhya and the Yoga, like the Buddhists, hold that all experience is sorrowful," and he says that the purpose of philosophy is to show a way to eradicate the suffering that is imminent in human life.

> It is when a man ceases from seeking pleasure that he thinks how best he can eradicate the roots of sorrow. Philosophy shows how extensive is

> sorrow, why sorrow comes what is the way to uproot it, and what is the state when it is uprooted. The man who has resolved to uproot sorrow turns to philosophy to find out the means of doing it.[31]

There are some subtle differences in the analytical systems of the classical Sāṅkhya and the Yoga system of Pātañjali. The method adopted in Sāṅkhya system, is to dissociate the *citta* from the principal concept of reality, the *Puruṣa*. As for the Sāṅkhyans, because of the association of *citta* (mind, intelligence, etc.) with the eternal conscious principle *Puruṣa*, the process of conceptualisation begins to develop, leading to confusion and suffering. Using the technique of active analysis of the phenomena, one acquires the power to dissociate the *citta* and *Puruṣa*; this discrimination roots out the ignorance that causes suffering. One is able to experience life without suffering.

On the other hand, Yoga, one of the enduring systems of Indian philosophy, follows another method of analysis; it categorically rejects the notion that philosophy alone can root out suffering and help one attain liberation from the confusions of the life in the world. Some scholars are of the opinion that Pātañjali's version of Sāṅkhya is the Yoga system of philosophy.[32] In his version of Saṅkhya, Pātañjali addresses those contentious questions. The main question of Yoga system posed before the Kapila's Sāṅkhya school, is that if the process of philosophising can help one to liberate from the world and attain *mokṣa*, then *saṁskāras*, which one acquires from the series of births, would be neutral or active. Or in other words, Yoga would like to question the position of the Sāṅkhyans, that if the association of *citta* and *Puruṣa* are differentiated with the help of knowledge, what will happen to the *saṁskāras* of the *citta*, the habits acquired (*saṁskāras*) over a period of time. We can easily understand that if the *citta* is dissociated from the *Puruṣa*, it may fall itself into the grab of ignorance. The practical life addresses this problem almost regularly that even though intellectual discussion solves many human problems at the discussion level, in the actual situation of solving these problems, the intellectual solutions turns insufficient or impractical. Dasgupta explains this problem:

> To destroy the old *saṁskāras*, knowledge alone is not sufficient, a graduated course of practice is also necessary. This graduated practice should be disciplined in such a way that by such practices, one should be living a higher and better mode of life, and by steadying the mind on its subtler states, the habits of ordinary life might be removed. As the Yogin advances,

> he has to give up what he had adopted as good and try for that which is still better. Continuing thus he reaches the state when the *buddhi* is in its ultimate perfection and purity. At this stage, the *buddhi* assumes the form of the *Puruṣa* and final liberation takes place.[33]

This view of the Yoga school of Pātañjali is a major deviation from the stated stand taken by the Vedic systems, that if the *citta* (or *buddhi*) is important in discerning Brahman or *Puruṣa*, then the human intelligence is also enduring and important, and not rejected as a part of *Prakṛti*. The Yoga envisages equipping the body and preparing the mind to enjoy or suffer the fruits of *karma* in this very life itself.

In Buddhist literature, there is the mention of a wise man, having a high level of intelligence and practising spiritual practices, by critically analysing the pros and cons. Such a man is suited to attain the desired spiritual merits, he is called the Bodhisattva. To the Buddhists and the Pātañjali Yogis, the use of intelligence is absolutely necessary for the purification of *citta* (mind), as it eradicates the sufferings from the world. The definition given by Pātañjali for Yoga, "steadying the states of *citta*,"[34] as well as Āryadeva's Yogic methods for *Cittaviśuddhi*,[35] are practically the same. In the Pātañjali system of Yoga, a Yogi through disciplined practice attains the stage of *saṁyama*. Then, *citta* realises the conscious principle, the *Puruṣa*. Pātañjali says, "One doesn't have the differentiation of the word and its meaning and he understands the meaning of everything without being inferred into."[36] At this stage of perfection, one loses affliction to past *karmas* and to the play of the *Prakṛti*. This miraculous power of a Yogi, according to Yoga, elevates the practitioner to a unique stage of existence, where he is no longer confused by the play of *vikalpas*. The control of the mind and steadiness the mental functions, are possible only when *citta* realises the true nature of *Puruṣa*, because the *Puruṣa* alone knows the changing nature of the mind.[37] Pātañjali, on enumerating the final liberation, agrees with the Sāṅkhyan way and says that the *Puruṣa* need not be associated with the distortion caused by the *guṇas* (the expression of the *Prakṛti*), because the *Puruṣa* remains pure and pristine, as the *citta* does the job of discrimination.[38] There is an intrinsic similarity between the Pātañjali system of Yoga and the Āryadeva's *Citta-viśuddhi-prakaraṇa*, especially in describing the nature of *citta* and the necessity of purification of *citta*, for liberating the *citta* from *vikalpas*, either by purification or by steadying it through accepted

Yogic practices. Even though the philosophical system differs very much with regard to views about life, there is a similarity in the ethical practices of the logical scepticism of Sañjaya, the *Yogasūtra* of Pātañ jali, and the *Cittaviśuddi-prakaraṇa* of Āryadeva. All these systems are concerned with the human mind's attachment to the world of things and the problem of misconceptions (*vikalpas*) that can cause confusion and suffering.

3.6 The Importance of Middle Way in Spiritual Practice

Logical sceptics' attitude towards spiritual maturity by stopping thought can be explained as,

> If I were to join issue, argue and debate with them, I would not be able to explain to them. If I were unable to explain to them, that would cause me worry and be moral danger. Thus, because the fears and detests interrogation he doesn't pronounce this to be good nor that to be evil.[39]

It is very clear that the sceptics' attitude towards attaining mental stability by avoiding thought is that of escapism. It can be compared to a chase holding on to the tail of a tiger, in which a moment of failing concentration would cost him his life. And in fact this is the reality of spiritual life where falling concentration can be fatal. The sceptics call the Brāhmanical view as illusory and inconsistent, creating more confusion. K.N. Jayathilake explains:

> Some recluses and Brahmins wrangle like eels. For when a question is put to them on this or that matter, they resort to verbal jugglery and eel wriggling[40] on four grounds. The first of these schools is described as follows: Herein a certain recluse or Brahmin doesn't understand, as is really is, that is good or that is evil. And it occurs to him: I do not understand what is good or evil as it really is, if I were to assert that this is good and this is evil, which will be due to my likes, desires, aversions, or resentments. If it were due to my likes, desires, aversions, or resentments, it would be wrong, it would cause me worry, and worry would be moral danger to me.[41]

No one can disregard the contribution of Materialists and logical sceptics to Indian philosophy, as they shed light on the limitations of our ways of thinking and our adherence to certain set thoughts.

The Brāhmanical thinkers avoided questions from rival schools of thought, especially the Materialists. It is certain that their arguments are coloured by certain set theories and convictions, because for them, any thought system beyond the boundaries of these metaphysical positions is unacceptable. The structure of these metaphysical doctrines is marked by partial views configured from the phenomenal world; on the other hand, the Materialists and logical sceptics highlighted this aspect by questioning the consistency of these theories. They, therefore, conclude that most of the arguments advanced by the Brāhmanical schools, are based on the likes and dislikes; aversions and attachments; resentments and associations, leading to more confusion and suffering. Nevertheless, Buddhists and sceptics have similar views as far as the equanimity of the mind is concerned. It has been said that

> for the different schools of sceptics there seems to be some conception of good life, whether they believed in salvation or not, and the sceptical attitude seems at least to have been regarded as psychologically desirable in promoting one's peace of mind. [...] The sceptics believed in spite of their theoretical scepticism had the good sense to cultivate the tranquillity of mind, which was highly valued in Buddhism as well.[42]

It is very clear that the heterodox schools share a common ground at times in refuting the extreme theoretical views of the Brāhmanical schools.

Both the extreme views: the view of sceptics rejecting the influence of Vedic thought and the view of Brāhmans rejecting the expanse of human thought, agree on one point that their views are limited to conditions. But in the case of Mādhyamikas, they try to understand the nature of human thinking and suggest suitable methods to control them. The middle way adopted by the Buddhists enables them to understand that the mind is of the habit of thinking and formulating thought constructs, which hardly have any real rational foundation. The bubbling thoughts that form in the mind is the problem that is to be tackled, not by abstaining from the flurry of thoughts or forcing them to stop, but by handling them with proper spiritual disciplines and accurate graduated practices.

3.7 Phenomenal World and Means of Liberation

Unlike the Sāṅkhya-Yoga, which proposes the realisation of an eternally existing entity as the aim of the spiritual practices, the Mādhyamikas introduce a new spiritual tradition, based on their philosophical position and dialectics. The logic of that practice can be interpreted as: "All the evil actions by which the beings are bound, through those means they can be released from the shackles of Saṁsāra."[43] As explained earlier, the troubles due to the world of phenomenon are because of the mind's association and identification with them; the normal human mind doesn't recognise these aspects properly, causing suffering and confusion. As we have referred to earlier, the Sāṅkhya-Yoga accepts an eternally existing *Puruṣa*, which is reflected on the *citta*, an evolution of *Prakṛti*. The realization of *Puruṣa* is possible by discriminating *Puruṣa* and *Prakṛti*, such that the *vikalpas* would vanish. On the other hand, the Buddhists have elucidated in the canonical texts that the phenomenon (*dharma*) and mind that is devoid of *ātma* (*pudgala-nairātmya*)[44] constitute the *citta*.[45] If the elements that appear before us through our perception are the reason for bondage, then they can open a way for attaining liberation from that bondage. For the Vedic schools like Sāṅkhya and Yoga, certain things assist liberation; at the same time, certain others hinder liberation. The Mādhyamikas never make such distinctions, yet they identify that the problem of suffering is the main cause for bondage. According to the *Cittaviśuddhi-prakaraṇa*, false ascriptions or *vikalpas* are the real reason for bondage and suffering. The verses in the beginning of the text show a clear elaboration of this aspect; the path to cease the process of suffering is possible through the Mantra, the patent deity (the God), and the *guru*.

3.7.1 *The Arising of Suffering (Duḥkha-samudaya)*

Āryadeva proposes a new view that the very elements or things that are supposed to bind the mind (*citta*), have the ability to redeem the mind (*citta*) from bondage as well. The life that we experience is not just to be explained in terms of positive and negative aspects, but life itself is considered like a house infested by crocodiles; it has the capacity to push anything that comes in its way into its fold.[46] It is dangerous and unsafe. With this existence, there is nothing that is positive and good enough to depend upon; it is like a house, where one has to live with a beast that one should be very vigilant at all the time. Though the normal mind's attachment to the apparent phenomenal world is very dangerous, one can depend on the purified *citta*. The importance of *citta* is that it comes in direct contact with the phenomenon appearing before us. And, thus, *citta* has the power to understand and assimilate the nature of phenomena, for the problem arising due to the *vikalpas* or misconceptions can be eradicated. At the functional level, the phenomena are superior to mind, so the mind acquires a condition that makes it to act quickly and decisively.[47]

The mind overacts, remains quiet or might stay in a state of constant confusion, when it is influenced by the phenomena. The incessant thoughts come and go in the mind as they may not help one to deal with the world of phenomenon;[48] but, when the mind acquires purity in thoughts, this distortion vanishes, so one could see things in proper perspective and one's actions would be clear and certain. After all, most of human actions are contaminated by impure thoughts that are the product of a confused mind, leading to mental pain and suffering. Such actions are considered as sin, and the actions of a pure mind are sinless.[49] The quantum of sin and sinlessness is understood based on the state of mind of the beholder. The mind that is free from *duḥkha* has the power to understand the nature of all phenomena that appears before it. The idea of *duḥkha* has a deep philosophical ramification that it contains the basis of Buddhist philosophy. Here, the discussion can follow the path of the Āryasatyas.

3.7.2 *Cessation of Suffering (Duḥkha-nirodha)*

Duḥkha arises from the association of the mind with the phenomena or *dharma*, that are unreal and relative and not that are real and permanent. If those phenomena are real then the association of the mind never would create any confusion and suffering. Removal of *duḥkha* is possible only by destroying the conception that those phenomena are enduring and essentially independent; the true nature of phenomena, though it is not desired by the mind, has the ability to remove uncertainty and confusion leading to suffering. The situations leading to suffering are not just symptoms, not the real reasons, while most of the other schools elaborate on the symptoms of suffering and suggest methods to avoid such symptoms. The segregation of the world as good and bad implies that: goodness is sacrosanct, the one that should be followed; badness is sacrilege, the one that should be avoided, for creating desecration of one's faith in life. Buddhist schools of philosophy never support such partial views; on the other hand, it professes the view that everything in the world has the inherent power of infusing *duḥkha* into the mind, whether they are good or bad. The seemingly joyful horse ride, if continued for very long time can turn into a cause for severe suffering; similarly, an apparently difficult situation of living in a slum, wouldn't be so difficult when one decides to live there.

The inherent property of mind to align with the three aspects, generally, creates suffering that is the notion of permanence and the adherence to substance view. Removal of the notion of substance and permanence is very much necessary for the cessation of suffering, yet the individual minds that are the beholders of *duḥkha* tend to suffer irrespective of the situation they are in. There may be some situation in which one experiences less suffering, yet the suffering never leaves one permanently until one realises the true nature of the phenomena.

Nature of *pāpa* (sin) or *puṇya* (merit) is determined by the state of mind of the individual, not by any other factors; all other explanations leading to the determination of *pāpa-puṇya* will only lead to misconception and confusion.[50] Many schools of philosophy, in their ethical pronouncements, attribute too much importance to the question of *pāpa* and *puṇya*; they say that various human activities like bad *karma* (action), even unintentional, could bring downfall to the soul or accidental good *karma* could bring redemption to the soul. This view is severely criticised by Āryadeva. According to him, for a person with a pure mind which is freed from sorrow, even the gravest act committed by him does not accrue him any sin.

The relationship between mind and objects of the world is like a crocodile that has entered a house such that it would grab anything that comes in its way; one needs to be aware of this aspect for surviving in such a house. A moment of failing concentration would push a thing into the grab of the crocodile; there is nothing in that in this world where one could find a safe refuge, as everything is in a state of flux. When the mind is aware of its inherent nature to get attached to objects of the world, then the objects of the world themselves can be used to redeem the mind from its crocodile grab. A Yogi, like an alchemist who knows about poison, understands the working of the poison in the human system, is able to cure the disease of poisoning by administering poison in the right quantity.[51] In other words, it is possible to reconstruct the phenomena that create attachment and suffering, so that a Yogi would be able use the same phenomena to transcend the influence of those phenomena on his mind. The process of reconstruction should be based on the notion that: "The whole universe is illusory like a mirage, like a city in the dreams (*gandharvanagara*), or like a dream; by perceiving such a world, 'who' enjoys 'what' by 'whom'."[52] For the ordinary people, such things are real that they identify with them, but for the Yogi who understands the real nature of the objective world, they are like a dream, eternally unreal. Human beings suffer immensely from this false identification. This is a recurring phenomenon in human life, so the main endeavour of human life is to eradicate the suffering arising out of false identification with the phenomenal world. Āryadeva says that those who are enlightened with the knowledge of the real nature of the phenomenon, of its formation and of the law of dependent origination, are liberated from the *saṁsāra*.[53]

3.7.3 *The Means of Cessation of Suffering (Duḥkha-nirodhagāmini-paṭipada)*

The concept of God here is what supports the individual soul to redeem from the world of things (*saṁsāra*); God is in the nature of natural forces that are believed to support the existence. To put it differently, God is the perfected stage that an individual soul could identify with his notion of perfection. Thus, God is a supporter of a person's spiritual journey bringing him to the abode of perfection, and not an absolute reality controlling the world of things (*saṁsāra*) in an authoritarian way. At the empirical level, this journey is always supported and guided by a *guru* who suggests to the aspirant the nature of rituals and the patent God. At each level of his practice, the student seeks guidance from the *guru* on matters relating to the ritual and the patent God. Since the *guru* claims certain perfection with regard to the goal of the spiritual practice, he is considered as equal to God or another form of God. Moreover, such a spiritual practice would inevitably lead the aspirant to a stage, where he could liberate himself from the existence (*saṁsāra*) and the *vikalpas* that come out of them.[54]

According to the Buddhistic tradition, the term *mantra*[55] is described as the technique by which one could control the activities of mind. The etymological meaning of this word is "protect the mind."[56] As described earlier, Vasubandhu says in the *Bodhisattvabhūmi* that absolute meaninglessness is the real significance of the *mantras*. A *sādhaka* is to meditate on the objects of the world using these *mantras* as something absolutely meaningless and this constant meditation on the meaninglessness of the objects will gradually lead to a state of mind where he will be able to discern the ultimate nature of the phenomena (*dharmas*) as *śūnya*. This meaninglessness is the essenceless (*nairātmya*) nature of the phenomena (*dharmas*).[57] The use of *mantra* otherwise would help the aspirant to reconstruct the whimsical nature of phenomena into deconstructable deities so that he could liberate himself from its influence. Āryadeva instructs the aspirant for Bodhisattvahood:

> One has to ponder over all the schools and all the methods of worshipping the deities, and one should eat without any confusion after conforming that it is pure and in accordance with the prescribed Mantras.[58]

Based on the direction from the *dhāraṇīs*,[59] one needs to consume his food S.B. Dasgupta explains this aspect further making it clearer:

> *Dhāraṇīs* are not the textual directions to the dos and don'ts for the yogis, their mantras and *dhāraṇīs* are the prescribed method of practising spiritual disciplines accepted by the philosophical tradition they belong to.[60]

One should practise the spiritual disciplines according to the directions given by the *guru*, the custodian of the spiritual practices; the aspirant has to take directions from the *guru* in his eating of food, his practising of discipline, and his using of the *mantra*.

The process of constructing and deconstructing the deities is a method of spiritual training where one employs a deity to restructure his mental defilements and violations and it would be replaced by another deity of higher spiritual dimensions so as to retain the spiritual virtues of each deity in a very subtle manner. This activity of identifying the deity and relating it with a person's dispositions is the duty of a *guru*.

3.8 Cessation of Suffering and Freedom through *Bodhicitta*

The aspirant who attempts to be a Bodhisattva, the one liberated from the *saṁsāra* yet refused the *nirvāṇa*, should practice spiritual disciplines in the prescribed manner. However, Āryadeva clarifies further that for a liberated one, there is no distinction between *saṁsāra* and *nirvāṇa*; it is only for the average sentient beings there are such distinctions. For them, the *saṁsāra* and its illusory manifestations are real and certain.[61] What appears as real and certain for an average person is to an enlightened Yogi certainly unreal, illusory, and momentary. Accordingly, the Yogi, by transcending the uncertain and unsteady mind, understands the form and the nature of phenomena, so that he is neither bond nor released. The notion of *saṁsāra* or *nirvāṇa* is redundant for him.[62]

The *saṁsāra* is where we see the distinctions of duality that of the subject and the object, the good and the bad, and all such distinctions. However, for an enlightened person, such distinctions are redundant as they cease to manifest. The mind of the enlightened person is purified from all false ascriptions or *vikalpas*,[63] produced from the constant association with the phenomena and manifested from delusion. As it says that, "The original nature of mind is like a gem, devoid of any impurity in the form of thought chains. It is begginingless without any impurity and has no *svabhāva*."[64] The nature of the phenomena being superior to mind, the mind confuses in the presence of such phenomena, and, thus, *vikalpa* or false ascription arises. The nature of such ascription and identification is almost like a crocodile, which pulls one into the ocean of *saṁsāra*; when one understands this activity of the mind, one is able to redeem from such identification, and could be saved from the existence of *saṁsāra*, in the form of crocodile grab.[65]

The innate nature of *citta* is that it is like a pure and internally clear crystal, which shines forth, but another inherent nature of it is that it imbibes the colour of the object placed near it. So, the unblemished and pure nature of crystal when viewed from outside, would have the colour of the object placed before it. Like the crystal that seems to be tarnished, the *citta* also imbibes the objects of the phenomenal world of existence that has the superior power to influence the inherently pure *citta*.[66] Āryadeva is of the opinion that *citta* should be cleansed of the objects that tarnish it. It is the doubt generated out of misconception and false ascription that would create serious problems for the mind. Āryadeva categorically says, "Poison in the form of doubt affects people. By digging it out the compassionate one move forward without being affected by such *vikalpas*."[67]

A *sādhaka* (Yogic aspirant) after receiving his initiations from a competent *guru*, is allowed to practise spiritual disciplines that are normally censured for ordinary people. Such spiritual disciplines have definite purpose and systematic stages of development, which are known only to a *guru*. The *guru*, who has practised such disciplines and attained the desired results, is able to determine most of the spiritual practices. On describing the role of *guru*, John Woodroff, a great scholar on *Śāktatantras*, explains in the following manner: "Just as the wick of one lamp is ignited at the flame of another, so the divine

Śakti which is the Mantra is communicated to the disciple's body from that of the *guru*."[68] Āryadeva says that the method to purify the mind is possible only when a Yogi practises his spiritual disciplines with dedication to one's personal god.[69] As described by John Woodroff, the *guru* imparts the nature of God by the way of the *mantra* and the disciple internalises the *mantra* and *dhāraṇīs* that act as a vehicle for his spiritual journey.

It is common for Tāntric Yogis to practise human sexuality as a spiritual discipline where the woman who participates is considered as an embodiment of the Goddess supreme, the patent deity of the Yogi. He views the woman who participates in the sexual *sādhana* with high esteem and respect, normally given to the Goddess herself. As Herbert V. Guenther writes about the accomplishments of a Yogi:

> Just as Bodhisattvas embodying the magnificent vision of the Mahāyāna are good citizens, Tāntric Yogis are also extremely good citizens. Tāntric practitioners are the good mechanics in garages, who know the infinite details of the functioning of machines with clean and precise mind. Tāntric practitioners are good artists, who paint good pictures that do not try to con one. Tāntric practitioners are good lovers, who do not take advantage of their partners energy and emotion, but make love precisely.[...][70]

Āryadeva clarifies the virtues of the Yogi, in a different way: "The damsels, who have the poison in the form of the fire of desire, fill up the pure mind of Yogis with desires; they indeed bear the fruits of both desire and liberation."[71] The Yogi being a superior personality in all aspect of life is using the desire of his partner in the sexual practice, carefully, to remove that bondage from him, and he also helps his partner to redeem the bondage of desire without emotionally disturbing her. The fruit of desire is liberation, at least liberation at that moment of fulfilling the desire; normally a Tāntric Yogi works on that moment and controls the incessant occurrence of desire in him, which a normal human being finds difficult to practice. The *guru*, not allowing the disciple to practise this *sādhana* without his guidance, determines the nature of practise, the personality of the partner, the *mantras* of importance, and the nature of deity, etc. Such practices may increase the desire and bondage thereof, if performed without proper initiation and guidance; the Yogi may also become slave to sexual desires. A detailed description on "sexo-yogic *sādhana*" is given *infra*, chapter Six.

So, these practices should be very carefully performed; şimilar to a therapist curing poisoning (*viṣa-vaidya*) who uses the technique of sucking out the poison from the affected (poisoned) person, without himself being affected by the effect of poison. The therapist removes the poison from blood after completing his meditation on the deity Garuḍa.[72] The Garuḍa is the patent deity for a *Viṣa-vaidya* as far as the removal of the poison is concerned. Like the *Viṣa-vaidya,* the Tāntric Yogis too, should have right visualisation. Herbert V. Guenther details this process in this way:

> The right understanding of Tantra is crucial for visualisation. One *Nyigama* teacher said that understanding the practice of visualisation is like going to bed with a pregnant tigress. She might get hungry in the middle of the night and decide to eat you. On the other hand, she might begin to nurse you, creating the furry warmth and texture of basic space. Certainly, practising visualisation without the proper understanding is extremely destructive.[73]

The practise of visualisation in the Tantras is important that in the absence of right visualisation and understanding the *Viṣa-vaidya* himself may get poisoned; similarly, the Yogi who practise sexual *sādhana*, to liberate himself from the bondage of excessive passion that hampers his spiritual progress, may himself become a slave of the excessive passion and desire.

Right visualisation is the main methodology for the Tāntric Yogi who practises difficult *sādhanas*. The Yogi, for realising the *Bodhicitta* that is dormant in him and seeking manifestation, practises these spiritual disciplines; it is said to be of the nature of a wheel of twelve *yojanas* diameter which moves in the head, and which produces the *Bodhicitta* and then recedes by itself.[74] This is the experience of the practitioner at his meditative level, which is hard to explain; the language used here does not have any direct meaning; but at the same time, one could presume that the mind goes to a special phase and settles into its original state. This may be similar to the instance of deconstructing the mind from all its conceptualisation activity and restructuring it into its original form, which is pure inherently. The *Bodhicitta*, according to Āryadeva is of the nature of: "Pure from the beginning, non-originated, not having a nature of its own, no stains whatsoever. By perceiving such an entity as the world, one is neither bound nor liberated."[75] The mind, according to the Buddhist thinkers, is an entity that is pure in its original stage; its activity is such that it has the tendency to fall into the *vikalpas* or false ascriptions. It also agrees to the fact that only through constant and steady practice, one could redeem it and retain its original pristine nature. According to Herbert V. Guenther,

> These impulses (the impulses created due to false ascription) will only die out when the individual develops spirituality, and the spiritual development is essentially a restoration of the psychic equilibrium that has been disturbed by the emotional outbursts and that remains disturbed due to possible emotional outbreaks.[76]

3.8.1 *Bodhicitta through Sexuality and Martial Arts*

In the early Buddhist tradition, *vipāśana*, a meditation based on introspection, was employed in order to remove all impediments that restrict the mind in its progress for the realization of *dharma-nairātmya*.[77] In the later phase of development of this meditative practice, it has become evident that the basic human instincts are interfering with the active practice of meditation, so it has become inevitable to try out new methods for getting freed from those basic instincts. The introduction of sexo-yogic practices should be seen from this perspective. The use of sex as a spiritual practice and discipline is criticised by the critics of the Tāntric tradition as a system engages in inordinate methods. But, on the other hand, Tāntrism should be understood as a spiritual discipline that accepts all human activities and life in totality and states that there is equanimity in the virtues and vices; and that both virtue and vices are sacred and spiritually rewarding. In the case of meditation based introspection, such as *vipāśana,* there is good chances that the practitioner may fall back to the original dispositional tendencies of mind which actually very dangerous for spiritual wellbeing.

Since the purport of spiritual development is the destruction of all distinctions and barriers, the Tāntric traditions never reject or relegate any aspect of human life as untouchable. The fundamental view of this system is such that a phenomenal objective reality, which has the inherent tendency to bind the human mind to the existent world with a grip as strong as that of a crocodile, if used intelligently, has the power to liberate one from the bondage created out of that association. The Mādhyamika philosophy also envisages delineating all aspects of life to understand the true nature of life and phenomenal world; this is the meaning of the rejection of extreme positions that is introduced by the Mādhyamika. Herbert V. Guenther explains this crucial aspect:

> The most powerful emotions are linked up with the sex drive which, according to the Buddhists, sets in not at puberty but is in operation already prenatally, determining the selection of the future parents and of the actual sex in embryonic development. This acknowledgement of sex as a most powerful motive as well as the unmistakably sexual language of the Tāntrics might easily mislead a casual reader into a one-sided interpretation. That it is not merely a question of sexuality that is borne out by the many other injunctions given in the Tantras. Ever and again, we are warned against the irresolute yielding to biological temptation. Therefore, a correct understanding can only be achieved if, on the one hand we take the "sexual" language as a well meaning guide for a mind, optimistically setting out on high philosophical flight, but coming to a tragic and untimely end as soon as an attractive female crosses its path; and, on the other, as a symbol for human relationship in the most liberal sense. Thus, the Tantrics are not at all speculative but pre-eminently practical and up to the actual problems of life.[78]

The most powerful emotion that drives human mind is the sexual urge, but lack of understanding of this aspect creates a lot of misconceptions and anathema; however, the Tāntric systems understand this aspect perfectly and envisaged it as an accepted spiritual technique. The Tāntric view on this aspect can be explained as: both the excessive indulgence with the matters regarding sex and the total abstinence from this aspect, are irrational and retard spiritual growth. Thus, instead of abstinence or excessive indulgence, using the urge with a meditative mind is the most recommended way for releasing from the strong grip of that basic and most important human instinct. Normally, the philosophical teachings recommend abstinence because of foreseeing the dangers involved in excessive indulgence, but such practices always lead one to the difficult situation of inner conflicts and of sufferings.

This problem is well-discussed by Āryadeva in such a manner that a careful and resolute use of such negative urges could bring extraordinarily positive results. The practice of martial art as a technique of meditation also brings the same results, since the tendency to fight is inherent in every living being. Such instincts are manifested in every being as it gives a way to survive in the world. It helps a being, directly or indirectly, to assert its position in this world as a being. This unique blessing given by nature, in order to support a living being, may be anathema to the normal conduct of life, because it works often together with ignorance and strong feeling. Therefore, one must review the following aspects carefully: is it possible for any being to abstain completely from the influence of these basic instincts; nor is it advisable to follow them bluntly; nor is it good to develop positive virtues countering these instincts? According to the tenet of Tantra and the philosophy of Mādhyamika, the advisable attitude towards these aspects for a spiritual aspirant is to develop proper meditative methods to transcend from the whimsical influence of such instincts.

In many Buddhist monasteries, practice of martial art as a meditation technique continues even today. One of the grand masters of Zen and Japanese martial arts, Taisen Deshimaru clarifies this point further:

> The *dojo* (the martial art training centre) becomes now a meditation hall steeped in the quiet and tranquillity that emanate from the posture of *zazen*,[79] now a field of combat. But the great lesson of this session lay beyond any notion of winning or losing: it was that Zen and the martial arts alike are ways of learning life, learning death.[80]

3.8.2 *Other Important Spiritual Practices*

In the tradition of Buddhist Tantras, various special meditative techniques are employed to attain spiritual perfection. One such practice is called *śava-sādhanā*, where the practitioner meditates on a dead body, the body that just lost its life. It is believed that such a body produces sounds, which are fearsome and unusual. Meditating on the dead body, the Yogi attains powers that help him to quarantine first, and then protects himself, from any fear that can act on him in this life.[81] The practitioner should be under the protection of the *guru*; he should master *mantra-siddhi* to practise this special *sādhanā*. The purpose of this practice is to ward off the fear that is inherent in the mind. The most important thing is to use the knowledge and intelligence uninhibitedly, to perfect the mind from all *vikalpas*, or attain perfection in *Bodhicitta*. Āryadeva calls such an aspirant a wise man or a Yogi.

3.9 *Bodhicitta*—the Middle of Adherence and Aversion

The "wise man" or Yogi is one who has reached certain stage of wisdom (*Bodhicitta*), his mind not deluded, his actions not monitored by the basic instincts, and his knowledge uninhibited. On the contrary, an average human being gets attached to things, and wishes them to be eternal. To explain the mind of an average individual, Buddhaghoṣa writes in *Viśuddhi-mārga*:

> The thirst for the objects is called thirst for pleasure, when an object comes into the range of visual consciousness and when this thirst continues to absorb the object because of its pleasurable stimulus attachment. But when this thirst is continued with the idea of permanence, that is, when the subject desires that the object should be lasting and eternal then it is called "thirst for continued existence" for a desire accompanied by the idea of permanence is called "thirst for continued existence."[82]

Here, it is clear that the mind, with its innate nature of permanence and pleasurable stimulus attachment, desires to have continued existence of what has been apprehended which means the mind has a tendency to forego the nature of the actuality of things. This is one aspect. Another aspect of mind is that of "avoidance." On the conception of "avoidance," Buddhaghoṣa says in an almost similar manner:

> When (this thirst) is accomplished by the idea of annihilation that is, (when the subject desires that) the object should break up and perish, then it is called "the thirst for discontinued existence;" for the desire accompanied by the idea of annihilation is called "thirst for discontinued existence."[83]

The human mind falls into these traps of attachment and avoidance or attachment and rejection, where the reality of existence is overlooked. Such a mind is not an intelligent or wise mind. It is incapable of taking decisions that are extremely necessary for finding successful ways that lead to liberation. The mind is driven from one position to another that the true knowledge about the world eludes him. Habits and beliefs, having the innate nature of retarding spiritual growth, are formed due to the attachment and avoidance of mind. The Buddhaghoṣa says again,

> The core of every belief is prejudice; swayed by the emotions we make an unjusted generalisation. Habits which prevent us from applying our knowledge, and beliefs which prevent us from acquiring new knowledge, impair our spiritual growth considerably.[84]

Detaching oneself from the habits and beliefs and attachment and avoidance, is the way for acquiring enlightenment; the Yogi has to wake up from his inertia and transcend all the contraries that pull back him from true knowledge, by understanding the actual nature of the phenomena and the world of things.

When the Yogi attains the *Bodhicitta*, his misconceptions (*vikalpas*) are removed, he will be able to see the world in a better perspective, and his mind or *citta* no longer is impeded by the inhibiting thoughts, habits, and beliefs. He is free from the hard, bewildering, baffling, and teasing influence of the phenomenal world; so also, the suffering that comes up together with it will not affect him. He attains a stage where he can understand the nature of desire and would be able to control it with the help of the patent gods.[85] Then, he would be able to enjoy the object of desire, at the same time eliminating the negative influences that can be a part of the objects of desire. The greatest aspect of Āryadeva's thinking, taken up by the Tāntric Buddhist community in a big way, is the idea of rooting out the desire by practically using the "desired objects" and things. Here, the main difference is that the grappling power of the desired objects no longer affects the person, since he has completely removed its influence by purifying the *citta* through spiritual practices. After cleansing the *citta*, the Yogi reaches a position of perfection, where he has perfected his *citta* with adamantine knowledge or *vajrajñāna*, resulting in the complete annihilation of *vikalpas*.

3.10 *Bodhicitta*—Removal of *Vikalpas* and Realization of *Dharmadhātu*

Āryadeva clarifies his adoption of the Tāntric system saying:

> The power of existence is indeed confusing, especially with regard to what to do and where to obtain (liberation), yet somebody who is affected by poison can be de-poisoned by poison alone.[86]

The attachment to objects of desire is an inherent fundamental aspect of human life or the life in the world in general; abstinence or disregard to this fundamental instinct might retard not only spiritual growth, but also inculcate suffering and greater identification with the world of objects. As described earlier, the normal human mind's relation to the world of objects is not just attachment alone, but avoidance as well. Therefore, when a Yogi uses these techniques in his meditations, he would be able to understand the progressive movement of consciousness that leads to deep attachments and consequent avoidance. As Buddhaghoṣa opined, the cyclic aspect of attachment and consequent aversion may be the cause of perpetual suffering. Thus, abstinence from the world of things may not be an answer to this problem of suffering that generated out of clinging to them. The world itself offers solutions like using water to remove the water that got clogged inside the ear; or using a thorn to remove another thorn that has pierced the feet.[87] When we understand the functioning of *citta* and the thoughts that lead to the attachment of the objective world, then it is easy to unwind the thought chain that causes the attachment. Āryadeva says that, in practical (*saṁvṛti*) experience, one would be able to see that a washerman uses dirt[88] to remove dirt from the cloth that he washes,[89] or a mirror, which gathered dust for over a period of time, could be cleared with the dust alone, as dust is the best substance to clean a soiled mirror.[90] The dust that gathers on the mirror out of exposure to the dust, is removed effectively by dust alone, in order that the dust particles go effectively into the gathered dust particles and remove them, when one removes them with apt attention and proper concentration.[91]

Identifying with the objects of world, both adherence and avoidance can be compared to the metallic ball that always sinks deep inside the water, the water of existence; when that metallic ball is made into a vessel, it floats over the water, like the *citta* transforming into *Bodhicitta*. Like the metallic ball transformed into a vessel that can traverse people across the river, the *Bodhicitta* of a Bodhisattva also can help people who live in the world of ignorance, to liberation.[92] The performance of the spiritual disciplines acts like an external force that transforms the mind, which is like a metallic ball that is heavy and always shows the tendency to sink, when made into a vessel that never sinks into the water, for it shows a new character of floating over the water.[93] The mind thus transformed never drowns into the depth of existence in the world (*saṁsāra*) and suffers, but it helps the suffering minds with suitable means to redeem from the *saṁsāra*. When a blacksmith makes a vessel from the metallic ball, he takes care that the vessel floats always, yet it never flies away due to lack of weight, or partially sinks into the water due to excessive weight. Similarly, spiritual practices should be done under the directions of the *guru* (blacksmith), so that the mind will not get into *vikalpas* again or addicted to spiritual practices. The practices are meant only for purifying the mind and it has no intrinsic value that one should follow always. Once a vessel is made from a metallic ball, it, never, naturally, remade into a metallic ball again. The vessel is made with the fire of *vajrajñāna* (*prajñā*) and the most suitable means (*upāya*), the Tāntric spiritual techniques.

A Yogi (Bodhisattva), after attaining spiritual perfection, should help ordinary human beings, living under the influence of dichotomous existence, as he knows the secret to turning the mind from its most basic tendency of drowning into existence and suffering from that: it is a unique knowledge unachievable for others. He alone is able to help others who are in the whimsical effect of existence. Āryadeva explains the qualities of a Yogi more clearly:

> The objects of desire and its enjoyment, for an unwise person, could become a source of bondage (*bandhanam*); the same object of desire and their enjoyment, for a wise person, becomes a source of liberation.[94]

It is similar to the case of the milk consumed by a snake: it is well known that the milk has the power to cure poisoning, but at the same time the milk consumed by a snake, only increases its poison.[95] The spiritual practices are like the milk. If practised by a person who is not properly initiated or lacking innate interest then the whole practice would end up in the destruction of his personality; nevertheless, its proper application would help a good aspirant immensely. It is well known that a wicked Yogi is an embodiment of negative notions.

In this regard, H.V. Guenther aptly explains that

> the sacrifice of our petty and much cherished ego is not very difficult for us when we burn with passion for a great adventure. Moreover, there is more sublime and dangerous adventure than the renovation and remaking of man. It is correct to speak of a dangerous adventure, because no one knows what lies behind the walls of ego. The hidden potentialities may destroy the individual. In the case of the relationship of masculinity and femininity, they may lead to a hopeless disturbance of life by unnatural sexualization. On the other hand, they may open up new possibilities for life and lead to the realization of the highest aim.[96]

The spiritual discipline is meant to harness the aspirant to formulate correct attitude and guidance to make the practices in a proper manner so that the Yogi won't become a slave of practices but attain the highest realization through them. These spiritual practices may look very ordinary or naïve but in essence they are the most difficult and risky activities a man can encounter. It is very clear that improper practice of such activities would destroy a person beyond redemption. The reason for an adventure is to obtain pleasure from excelling the impossible; in that perspective, the spiritual disciplines would help one to transcend the nearly impossible task of purifying the *citta* from all its egoistic and instinctive tendencies.

The supreme attainment of a Yogi is the discriminating power attained through various spiritual practices, so that the world of phenomena will not confuse him, and he can be free from the world of multiple realities. The Yogi, according to Āryadeva is: "Like a swan, drinking the milk alone from a mixture of milk and water, a wise person enjoys the world of objects and he becomes liberated."[97] The celestial bird swan is blessed with the power of drinking milk alone from a mixture of milk and water; similarly, a Yogi who lives in the world of phenomena attains the spiritual merit of understanding the essence of each phenomenon the *dharmadhātu*, discarding the illusory aspect of phenomenon. Resembling the swan, segregating the milk from the mixture of water and milk, the Yogi will be able to segregate the essence of the phenomena, the *dharmadhātu* (cognised object) from the phenomena—conceived object (*dharma*). In the rope-snake example, the snake perceived in the place of rope is the most dangerous perception. The perceiver of that object may generate unnecessary fear and act accordingly; on the other hand, the perception of rope that can be verified with the support of the six senses is not dangerous as the illusory perception of snake. The veridical perception of rope in a way helps a person to take correct decisions, if he is afraid of rope; illusory perception, on the contrary, generates damaging fear and decisions thereof. As for the worldly convictions, the rope forms the *dharmadhātu.* If a person develops spiritual merit then he is in a position to see the *dharmadhātu*, he will not be deluded by the illusory manifestations of the phenomenal world.

Since a liberated man can see the *dharmadhātu* of each phenomenon, he is neither bound nor liberated; he is unaffected by the notion of *saṁsāra* or *nirvāṇa*, so life in the world is a pleasant experience for him, of being freed from all confusions. It has been proven that,

> Even the poison can turn into nectar (*amṛta*), if consumed according to the injunctions associated with it; whereas, the sweet made out of ghee can turn into a poison, if consumed improperly.[98]

This is possible, only if the poison is used expeditiously, according to the injunctions from the texts or the directions of the masters. The working of a vaccine too follows the same principle: small quantities of disease causing germs are administered into the body, so that the body attains the power to defend itself from the same disease. Similarly, arsenic, which is poisonous, is used for curing snake poisoning. Any human activity improperly done can create many problems: over-eating of sweets can be the cause for diabetes; carbohydrates and starch, which are essential for a healthy body, can turn out to be the causes of diseases that can kill the body; likewise, a prolonged ride on the horseback can turn out to be a miserable experience. When one realises the *dharmadhātu* of the *dharma* (phenomena), he understands that there is nothing arouses permanent happiness and nothing destroys harmony permanently. It can be interpreted as: "The mind, purified by auspicious means (*upāyas*) become independent, *nirvikalpa* (from the influence of the world of objects) and manifests in a naturally pure form,*prkṛtinirmalam*."[99] The purified mind after proper spiritual practices, will become independent, freed from false ascriptions (*vikalpas*) and other manifestations due to association with phenomena; the mind retains its pristine nature, in order that it never falls into the trap of false ascriptions. Validating the importance of spiritual practices, various views are available for active consideration, some questioning the merit of such practices and others differing on the acceptability of those practices.

The Brāhmanical schools of Indian philosophy, in general, are of the view that the apparent world is a reflection of the eternally existing reality, and when one understands the true nature of reality, the influence of the apparent world becomes redundant. Instead of reaching out to the reality through strenuous spiritual practices, one could realize the reality through various ritualistic practices. On the other hand, the Materialist schools of thought is of the view that the world is not worth to be known in its entirety, because it is full of dichotomies and unresolved questions. Attempting to solve these questions might end up as a futile exercise. Hence, live a life which is trouble-free and smooth.

Āryadeva differs from both these views; like the other Buddhist thinkers, he is of the opinion that life is full of suffering and one needs to find suitable spiritual practices to eradicate the notion of suffering from the world. The Yogi, aspiring to find the real nature of the phenomenal world, should take the initiative in order to solve the troublesome problems of life and he, in turn, should help them who are less meritorious to cross the *sāṁsārika* life. The one who realises that the phenomena that appear in the apparent world of existence are insubstantial and dependent, will be endowed with the power of deep compassion (*mahākaruṇā*). He is like: "As the fire though having a thin flame when manifested by oil, wick and the like becomes bright and still and thus destroys the pervasive darkness."[100] Since the knowledge of the Bodhisattva is like tiny lamp in a huge room, it spreads far and wide destroying the pervading darkness. He then attracts the ones who are looking for help and compassion. He is a banyan tree, taken birth from a tiny seed, grows far and wide with branches, roots, and fruits; gives stability to the ground; shelters those who need a bit of shade; and gives birth to small seeds that can produce mighty trees.[101]

3.11 The *Dharmadhātu*

The dialectical systems introduced by the early Mādhyamikas effectively question the validity of the authority of sense perception and the instruments of true cognition to formulate theories that could explain everything. They are of the opinion that any theory that can be formulated possesses an element of speculation that is considered an internal weakness of man.[102] So the aim of spiritual practices should be to transcend this internal weakness of human beings; consequently, one is able to see the world of appearance in its true nature and in its entirety, which is called the discernment of *dharmadhātu* of the apparent existent world. Āryadeva says when a Yogi attains the spiritual merit to see the true nature of things, he can be compared to the following:

> Mixed with turmeric powder, any substance changes its colour; similarly with the association of *prajñā* and *upāya*, a Yogi could discern the source of all phenomena, the *dharmadhātu*.[103]

Unlike many philosophical systems in the world, Mādhyamika, following critical analysis as the foremost methodology to discern truth, introduced an analytical system to reveal the truth of the world of phenomena. This system is based on two aspects: one, on the methodology of critical and intellectual understanding, known as *prajñā*; and the other, on a clear understanding about the functioning of the world of phenomena, called *upāya*. Commingling of the both through suitable spiritual practices could reveal the real nature of phenomena, the *dharmadhātu*. T.R.V. Murti opines that, "Spiritual discipline is of the nature of purification or removal of the hindrance and defilement that cover up the real. Beings are found in various stages and degrees of purification, though they are essentially one as Buddha."[104]

It is interesting to note whether *prajñā* (wisdom) alone could remove the causes of suffering and leads to *mokṣa*, or it is required to be augmented by the *prajñā* with *upāya*. This is a big discussion that was taken up by Āryadeva and other Mādhyamika thinkers, which forms the philosophical basis of Tāntric Buddhism. Murti says:

> Considering that opportunities for the cultivation of the spiritual life are rare and the obstacles many, the votary must make up his mind to cultivate the Bodhicitta at the earliest. He should direct all, the contention of the Mādhyamika that freedom cannot be attained without the realization of the unreality (*śūnyatā*) of things.[105]

This is possible through critical analysis on the basis of perfection of knowledge. This also was the argument between Sāṅkhya and Yoga, but the Buddhist way is different. It is not the same as in the case of Yoga, the integration of *buddhi* with *Puruṣa*, but it is possible with the integration of *śūnyatā* and *karuṇā* or *prajñā* and *upāya*, resulting in the arising of *Bodhicitta*. Thus, one could redeem his mind that is in the captivity of the world of existence.

References

1. Karen Lang, Āryadeva's *Catuḥśataka*, XIV.21.
2. *Cittaviśuddhi-prakaraṇa*, v. 8.
3. Watanabe Fumimaro, *Philosophy and its Development in the Nikāyas and Abhidharma*, p. 89.
4. *Ucchedavāda*: Nihilism, Materialism; the theory that denies freedom (freewill and its responsibilities), *karma* and *karma-phala*. T.R.V Murti, *The Central Philosophy of Buddhism*, p. 350.
5. T.R.V. Murti, op. cit., p. 38. See the introduction for more clarifications.
6. Ibid., p. 134.
7. A.B. Keith, *Buddhist Philosophy in India and Ceylon*, 1964, p. 303.
8. K.N. Jayathilake, *Early Buddhist Theory of Knowledge*, p. 127.
9. Sāmaññaphalasutta of *Dīghanikāya*. v. 33.
10. Āryadeva'*s Catuḥśataka*, XIV.22.
11. Fourteen *avyakṛtas* means fourteen in explicable questions asked by the logical sceptics and materialists to the Vedic position of eternity of self and other entities.
12. Āryadeva's *Catuḥśataka*, XIV.22.
13. Karen Lang, op. cit., p. 133.
14. T.R.V. Murti, op. cit., p. 128.
15. *Cittaviśuddhi-prakaraṇa*, v. 27. It might be a common view shared by almost all schools of thought in India that time. On this point, K.N. Jayathilake also gives a similar opinion of the use of *catuṣkoṭi*, on this he says that all schools share the idea of *catuṣkoṭi*. See K.N. Jayathilake, op. cit., p. 135.

16. Surendranatha Dasgupta, *A History of Indian Philosophy*, p. 23.
17. Ibid.
18. Ibid., p. 26.
19. Ibid., p. 25.
20. Ibid., p. 33.
21. Ibid., p. 42.
22. Ibid., p. 44.
23. Ibid.
24. Ibid., p. 156.
25. K.N. Jayathilake, *Early Buddhist Theory of Knowledge*, p. 23. This has been quoted from Burnet, *Greek Philosophy-Thales to Plato*, 1943, pp. 3ff.
26. Surendranath Dasgupta, *A History of Indian Philosophy,* p. 65.
27. Sañjaya Belaṭṭhiputta and other logical sceptics advanced their arguments based on the certainty that Vedas offered in the case of the world. The fourteen questions advanced by Sañjaya are meant to repudiate the very arguments of the Vedas that offer certainty and eternity of the principle that exists both in the human mind and the principle force that is controlling everything possible to understand. The sixteenth questions can be put into four categories, they are: (1) Does the other world exist? (2) Does it not exist? (3) Does it both exist and not exist? (4) Does it neither exist and not exist? (5) Do beings reborn exist? (6) Do they not exist? (7) Do they both exist and not exist? (8) Do they neither exist nor not exist? (9) Does the result of good and bad *karma* exist? (10) Does it not exist? (11) Does it both exist and not exist? (12) Does it neither exist nor not exist? (13) Does he thus gone exist after death? (14) Does he not exist after death? (15) Does he exist and not exist after death? (16) Does he neither exist nor not exist after death? See Fumimaro Watanabe, *Philosophy and its Development in the Nikāyas and Abhidhamma*, p. 88.
28. David J. Kalupahana, *Mūlamādhyamakakārikā of Nāgārjuna*, p. 1.
29. Ibid., p. 263.
30. *Buddhi* (intelligence), *ahaṁkāra* (ego), and the senses are called *citta* in Yoga. (Ibid.)
31. Ibid., p. 262.
32. Ibid., p. 221.
33. Ibid., p. 267.
34. *Yoga cittavṛtti nirodhaḥ, Yogasūtra of Patañjali*, trans. Swami Prabhavananda, 1953, I.2.
35. *Cittaviśuddhi-prakaraṇa*, v. 127.
36. Pātañjali, *Yogasūtra*, III.17.
37. Ibid., IV.17.
38. Ibid., IV.33.
39. K.N. Jayathilake, op. cit., p.127.
40. Vācavikkhepa is given for verbal jugglery and Amaravikkhepa for eel wriggling in the Nikāyas. Brahamajālasutta of *Dīghanikāya*.
41. Ibid., p. 122.

42. Ibid., p. 133.
43. *Cittaviśuddhi-prakaraṇa*, v. 6.
44. As the *Buddhist Hybrid Sanskrit Grammar and Dictionary* says the *pudgala* refers to as a locality or the locus centre, p. 347. According to T.R.V. Murti, *pudgala-nairātmya* means non-substance view and *dharma-nairātmya* means the denial of elements or phenomenon. Op. cit., p. 26.
45. *Cittavśuddhi-prakaraṇa*, v. 8; see the concept of *dvādaśāṅga* where the five aggregates, six elements, and twelve factors are considered as the part of the human personality. Realizing the *dharma-nairātmya* and *pudgala-nairātmya* are the internal activity of the mind, and the real person is not beyond description.
46. *Cittaviśuddhi-prakaraṇa*, v. 9.
47. Ibid., v. 10.
48. The Buddhist texts divide the objective world as the—(1) objects seen, (2) objects heard, (3) objects conceived, and (4) the objects cognized; in this group the objects conceived creates confusion in the mind. David J. Kalupahana, *A History of Buddhist Philosophy*, p. 79.
49. *Cittaviśuddhi-prakaraṇa*, vv. 13–14.
50. Ibid., v. 15.
51. For the cure of poisoning, poison alone was used in ancient Indian medicine. The traditional doctor used poison for this purpose. The alchemist should have had good knowledge of the working of poison; otherwise, he could risked the life of the patient.
52. *Cittaviśuddhi-prakaraṇa*, v. 18.
53. Ibid., v. 19.
54. Ibid., v. 16.
55. According to *Buddhist Hybrid Sanskrit Grammar and Dictionary*, the term *mantra* means "formula."
56. *Manastraṇābhūtatvād mantram ity ucyate*? Herbert V. Guenther, *The Dawn of Tantra*, p. 63.
57. S.B. Dasgupta, *An Introduction to Tāntric Buddhism*, p. 50.
58. *Cittaviśuddhi-prakaraṇa*, v. 20.
59. *Dhāraṇīs* are the practical disciplines an aspirant has to follow, and it is an unwritten law, normally prescribed by the *guru* together with the *mantras*.
60. The innumerable *dhāraṇīs* seem to be an early form in which the Mantra elements begin to be used extensively in Mahāyāna. The word *dhāranī* literally means that "by which something is sustained or kept up," i.e., the mystic syllables that have the capacity of keeping up the religious life of a man. S.B. Dasgupta, *An Introduction to Tāntric Buddhism*, p. 56.
61. *Cittaviśuddhi-prakaraṇa*, v. 22.
62. Ibid., v. 23.
63. The term *vikalpa* according to *Buddhist Hybrid Sanskrit Grammar and Dictionary* is a false discrimination between true and false, real and unreal, T.R.V. Murti says the *vikalpas* are *a priori* forms, which the uncritical mind superimposes on what really are momentary particular elements of existence. Op. cit., p. 57.

64. *Cittaviśuddhi-prakaraṇa*, v. 27.
65. Ibid., v. 24.
66. Ibid., v. 26.
67. Ibid., v. 25.
68. Sir John Woodroff, *The Principles of Tantra*, pt. 2, p. 206. Most of the Tāntric systems have the same method of practice the difference is only at the level of philosophy.
69. *Cittaviśuddhi-prakaraṇa*, v. 28.
70. Herbert V. Guenther, *The Tāntric View of Life*, p. 49.
71. *Cittaviśuddhi-prakaraṇa*, v. 29.
72. Ibid., v. 30.
73. Herbert V. Guenther, *The Tāntric View of Life*, p. 49.
74. *Cittaviśuddhi-prakaraṇa*, v. 32.
75. Ibid., v. 34.
76. Herbert V. Guenther, *Philosophy and Psychology of Abhidharma*, p. 11. The text *Aṭṭhasālinī* is philosophically interpreted in this work.
77. David J. Kalupahana, *A History of Buddhist Philosophy*, p. 219.
78. Herbert. V. Guenther, *The Tāntric View of Life*, p. iii.
79. A Japanese way of sitting in meditation. See, Taisen Deshimaru, *The Zen Way to the Martial Arts*, 1982, p. 120
80. Ibid., p. viii.
81. N.N. Bhattacharya, *The History of Tāntric Religion*, 1982, p.137. The *śavasādhana* is performed on a new moon night, the aspirant has to secure the dead body of a robust person belonging to a lower caste preferably a Caṇḍāla. The corpse should be un-diseased, of the one who has died of an accident.... The aspirant then goes to a burial ground. He washes the corpse, offers worship and utters the *mantra*, which invokes a patent deity, he sits on it close all doors of his sensory organs and contemplates the figure of the great Goddess. The inner perception will then begin to function. At the first state of his meditation, he will have the vision of temptation in the form of wealth, beautiful damsels, etc., and if he is moved by all these, his efforts will be lost and he may become insane. At the second stage, he will have fearful experiences, too terrible to bear. If he is successful in enduring these the Goddess will come to him generally in the form of a little girl, and reward him for his efforts.
82. H.V. Guenther, *The Tāntric View of Life*, p. 21.
83. Ibid., p. 22.
84. Ibid., p. 23.
85. *Cittaviśudhi-prakaraṇa*, v. 35.
86. Ibid., v. 36.
87. Ibid., v. 37.
88. A kind of mud is used in ancient times to wash cloths and it is said that, thus, washed cloth would be shining with brightness.
89. *Cittaviśuddhi-prakaraṇa*, v. 38.

90. Ibid., v. 39.
91. This had been done at a time when there were no chemical substances that could act internally and disintegrate the gathered particles.
92. *Cittaviśuddhi-prakaraṇa*, v. 40.
93. Ibid. v. 41.
94. Ibid., v. 42.
95. Ibid., v. 43. Milk was used as an antidote to poison in ancient times. Even today, the practice of Siddha and Ayurvedic medicines the use of milk as a purifying agent is well-known.
96. Herbert V. Guenther, *The Tāntric View of Life*, p. 41.
97. *Cittaviśuddhi-prakaraṇa*, v. 44. *Haṁsa* is a celestial bird, which is endowed with a perfect nature as far as the world of existence is concerned, it is as perfect as God is.
98. Ibid., v. 45.
99. Ibid., v. 46.
100. Ibid., v. 47.
101. Ibid., v. 48.
102. T.R.V. Murti, op. cit., p. 256.
103. *Cittaviśuddhi-prakaraṇa*, v. 49.
104. T.R.V. Murti, op. cit., p. 257.
105. Ibid., p. 262.

Chapter Four

The Intersection of Tantra and Mādhyamika Philosophy

4.1 The Philosophical Significance of *Prajñā*

The earlier part of our discussion has indicated that introduction of Tantrism into Mādhyamika Buddhism is a natural development, where a natural space has been created in the socio-religious praxis of this tradition. The two extremes Mādhyamika tries to avoid: the transcendental reality which is eternally existing or the perfect emptiness that is inexplicable as the basis of philosophical arguments. In such a situation, it is difficult to introduce a suitable ethical system with a strong metaphysical foundation; it found a suitable space for Tāntric systems supplementing that requirement. Accordingly, the Mādhyamika ethics have evolved as a way of life, rooted in the actual experiences drawn from the life in the world, cultivated using the system of Tāntric spiritual practices which have its own time tested praxis. This synergy of two enduring systems has benefited both the systems in such a way that the Mādhyamika could bring out an ethical system which is not a set of coded moral principles but a set of practices through which a person can realise the teachings set out by the Mādhyamika philosophy. Likewise, the Mādhyamika philosophy contributed to the Tāntric practices a philosophical system which justifies the relevance of their spiritual practices. The dual principles of Tantra, as per Mādhyamika tradition, are represented by *śūnyatā* and *karuṇā*. Commingling these entities would reveal the *dharmadhātu* of the *dharma*, or the phenomena without illusions. In this context, S.B. Dasgupta explains the nature of that relationship:

> *Śūnyatā* and *karuṇā* are widely termed *prajñā* and *upāya* respectively in Tāntric Buddhism. *Śūnyatā* is called *prajñā* simply because it represents perfect knowledge. So far as the individual *sādhaka* is concerned, this perfect knowledge is rather a state of negative state of mind which separates the individual from the world of suffering beings; *karuṇā*, on the other

> hand, acts in his mind like a dynamic force—the moral inspiration that prompts one to find oneself universalised in an emotion of deep compassion.[1]

Prajñā or wisdom is considered as the most important spiritual attainment for a Buddhist. Only through the perfection of knowledge and wisdom (*prajñā*), a Yogi is able to realise the *Bodhicitta* concealed in him, which remains unmanifested because of the illusion of the world of phenomena; thereby he transcends the notion of bondage and liberation. Spiritual disciplines remove the *vikalpa* or false ascription in the minds occurring due to poor understanding of the nature of phenomenon. Discerning the nature of phenomena independently without any misconception is the basis of any spiritual practice that leads to the *Bodhicitta*. *Prajñā* opens up a way to reach that level of understanding.

The philosophical systems at the time of the early Mādhyamikas either propounded an eternally existing reality as the basis of the *saṁsāra*, or rejected the authenticity of such an entity. Mādhyamika, on the other hand, envisaged a system for analysing the nature of phenomena independently to arrive at the truth about *saṁsāra*. Both the Sāṅkhyan view of the eternity of *Puruṣa* and *Prakṛti* and the logical sceptics' view of voidness of all entities were considered to be partial views formulated without proper understanding about the world of conceived objects (phenomena).[2] The Mādhyamika view is based more on clear understanding of the phenomenon and of the mind that conceives it. As K.V. Ramanan explains this point clearly:

> To be aware of the possibility of different formulations of one and the same truth from different standpoints is to rise above the exclusive clinging to any one of these formulations as absolutely true. This is the non-exclusive understanding that lies at the root of the Buddha's skilfulness.[3]

Having expressed the skilfulness in repudiating an argument by citing its internal inconsistencies to explain anything conclusively, Nāgārjuna introduced his dialectical system in the *Vigrahavyāvartinī* and stated that no theory is consistent in explaining the world of things:

> This situation seems to have provided for Nāgārjuna but one instance of the inveterate tendency of the Human mind, the tendency to cling, to seize. This tendency, which functions with a false imagination and not on right understanding, is the root of suffering in life and dead ends and conflicts in understanding.[4]

The dialectical system that was introduced by the Mādhyamikas not only repudiated the authenticity of any theory to explain the world of phenomena, but also pinpointed the mind's inveterate nature of identifying with the objects of the world and to gestalt them as real. Thus, it has become essential to have perfect knowledge about the world of phenomena (*prajñā*), and perfected techniques devised from a proper understanding about the nature of the phenomenal world (*upāya*).

4.1.1 *Theravāda and Mahāyāna Views on Prajñā*

The Theravāda tradition of spiritual practices involves three important aspects, namely, *śīla, samādhi*, and *prajñā*. *Śīla* means the disciplining of the senses, body, and mind; *samādhi* is the concentration inculcated in the mind after disciplining of the senses, body, and mind; and *prajñā* is a stage of perfect knowledge of mind about the nature of things in the world of phenomena. In contrast, the Mahāyāna tradition of spiritual practices follows a system called *ṣaṭpāramitā-naya*, a sixfold path of spiritual discipline. The six *pāramitās* are *dāna, śīla, kṣānti, vīrya, dhyāna*, and *prajñā*. It also provides a minute analysis of the highest stages of spiritual life into *bhūmis* or planes of Yoga culminating in complete realization of Buddhahood.[5] The interpretation of these six *pāramitās* in terms of Buddhist Tantrism is quite different and it forms a part of the practitioners' meditation scheme.[6] Through the meditation of the *pāramitā* scheme, one is able to realize the *prajñā* perfectly.

In the Mahāyāna schema of the *pāramitā*, there is no deviation from the traditional Theravādin concepts of *śīlā, samādhi*, and *prajñā*, but two more important aspects are included as *dāna* (charity) and *kṣānti* (forbearance). T.R.V. Murti opines that

> the place of *prajñā* as the guiding and controlling factor to which all other *pāramitās* tend is made abundantly clear. Though in the earlier system too, *prajñā* was taken as the culmination of the discipline, there was a tendency to regard the spiritual path as the almost mechanical performance of virtues and practice of concentration. Here, *prajñā* informs and inspires the entire spiritual discipline; every virtue and each act of concentration is dedicated to the gaining of insight into the real.[7]

Attached with no obscurity, requiring no doctrinal postulations or metaphysical delineation, the Mādhyamikas' views on spiritual development are completely based on analysis of the apparent world, where *prajñā* plays an important role. It makes the Yogi's mind fit for viewing the world as it appears, for all the *pāramitās* play an important role in achieving *Bodhicitta*.

The meaning of the word *prajñā* really goes beyond mere wisdom; it signifies the intellectual process through which we understand the nature of phenomena and beyond. The all-penetrating aspect of *prajñā,* going to the root of each phenomenon, is what a Yogi achieves through his spiritual practices.

The *prajñā* or the intellectual enterprise, and its magical power to solve human problems are accepted by most of the philosophical systems in the world. Whether it is the realisation of an eternal entity that transcends the normal sense faculties, or the critical understanding that there is no eternal entity beyond the explanations of the apparent phenomenal world, it is *prajñā* that helps one to formulate or dispute views about the world of things.

4.1.2 *Buddhi and Prajñā to Understand the Nature of Phenomena*

For the Sāṅkhya system, the realization of the conscious principle *Puruṣa*, is the purpose of philosophical and spiritual endeavours. The Yoga system, on the other hand, envisages perfection of *buddhi*, a facet of *Prakṛti*, as the medium through which one could reach *Puruṣa*. The Sāṅkhya system denigrates the importance of *buddhi*, because it envisages that the realization of *Puruṣa* is directly possible and that is the right method.[8] This doesn't mean that the Sāṅkhyans do not use *buddhi* in their spiritual practices, but they refuse to accept its importance in graduated practices for realizing the *Puruṣa*. On the contrary, the Yoga system accepts the authority and importance of *Prakṛti* (*buddhi*) and acknowledges that it is through the material world, the way to redemption is possible. Like the *buddhi* for Yoga system, knowledge about the *śūnyatā* of things is important for the Mādhyamikas in their endeavour to discern the world of things and *Bodhicitta*. H.V. Guenther explains:

> It is true, *śūnyatā* appears to the superficial mind as nothingness, because it is nothing to which we could apply the rigid laws of our reason, the systematic ideologies which often come perilously close to those that flourish among the paranoid cases in our insane asylums. *Śūnyatā* is not nothingness, not emptiness. It is not negation and withdrawal from reality. It is emptiness of illusion. Moreover, illusion does not mean the illusion of perception but the false conclusions we base upon perception. It is the superstition of permanency, which we develop about in permanent things, the illusion of possession we create about things that are only given to us for use. It is the illusion of life and immortality, which makes it so difficult for us to accept the reality of death and it is the illusion of death, which makes us wear guns

> with which we shoot our neighbour or kill whole nations, because we think that they are death in disguise. It is the illusion of ego, which makes us believe to be more important than another.[9]

The *śūnyatā* of things can be understood only through the perfected intelligence or *prajñā*. Aśvaghoṣa is the first Buddhist thinker who explained the nature of configuring the conceived or cognized phenomena in the mind, that there is an element of *karuṇā* existing in each phenomenon, and that can be understood only through *prajñā* or wisdom.[10] The mind with its inherent nature to depend on something as an escape route to annul its confusion is naturally forming thought chains that configure the phenomenon as something close to his mind but the conceptualization by those phenomenon creates confusion in the mind again. Understanding that all the conceptualized phenomena are essenceless or *śūnya* would be something very favourable to human mind; thus, each phenomenon has an element of compassion (*karuṇā*) associated with it. This can be understood only through active *prajñā*; it is not to dismiss the idea of the *śūnyatā* as voidness, but to understand the phenomenal world as devoid of *vikalpas*, since *vikalpas* are the real reason for suffering.

4.2 Conception of Duality as *Karuṇā* and *Śūnyatā*

It is not very clear whether Mādhyamikas accept the notion of *mahākaruṇā* as the substratum of the phenomenal world, but they implicitly agree with this concept as the basis of each phenomenon that appears in the existent world. The existence of *karuṇā* and *mahākaruṇā* is understandable only to a *vajrasattva*, a Yogi who perfected the spiritual practices, by combining *śūnya* and *karuṇā*. The Mādhyamika accepts *karuṇā* as the basis of the phenomenal world, as it is through *karuṇā* one can see the illusory nature of things (*śūnyatā*); bringing them together in each perception is the greatest achievement of a Yogi. *Śūnyatā* without *karuṇā*, or *karuṇā* without *śūnyatā* do not exist in pragmatic sense.[11] Professing doom and fear of the unknown is not the philosophizing methodology of the Mādhyamikas; for them *śūnyatā* is not something which is profane, but favourable as it removes sufferings. Contextually, T.R.V. Murti says:

> *Śūnyatā* and *karuṇā* are two principle features of Bodhicitta. *Śūnyatā* is *prajñā*, intellectual intuition, and is identical with the absolute. *Karuṇā* is the active principle of compassion with the absolute. *Karuṇā* is the active

> principle of compassion that gives concrete expression of *śūnyatā* in phenomena. If the first is the transcendent and looks to the absolute, the second is immanent and looks down towards phenomena.[12]

It can be interpreted that *śūnyatā* with the association of *karuṇā*, is actualized as the phenomenon devoid of illusions, the *dharmadhātu*; and a Yogi who is endowed with deep compassion can interpret the true nature of *śūnyatā*. Neither through intellectual predicaments, nor through interpretations about the nature and meanings of *śūnyatā*, but only through the Yogic spiritual practices, the true meaning of *śūnyatā* can be understood. A Yogi who has gone through such practices spreads the light of compassion and love.

4.2.1 *Spiritual Dimension of Dharmadhātu*

In the Buddhist philosophical traditions, the word *dharma* has many meanings. The etymological meaning is from the root verb *dhṛ* which means "to hold," "to bear," "to wear," "to have," "to support," etc.[13] The meaning of the word *dhātu* is "element." Therefore, the meaning of this *dharmadhātu* word can be construed as the "element" that holds or supports. Another meaning for *dharmadhātu* is the "space," the "expanse," the "sphere," etc. and also that in which massed in compass.[14] Surendranath Dasgupta describes it as "the totality of things:"[15]

> The performing of the pure *dharma* (*tathatā*), however, works on to eternity without any interruption. For this, thatness is the effulgence of great wisdom, the universal illumination of the *dharmadhātu*, the true and adequate knowledge, the mind pure, and clean in its own nature, the eternal, the blessed, the self-regulating and the pure, the tranquil, the inimitable and the free, and this is called the *Tathāgatagarbha*.[16]

The phenomena exist on a foundațion on which life can survive and progress; a small change in this foundation can lead to severe complications, which can lead to even complete annihilation of life itself. A deep compassion supports the universe to survive as far as human life and life in the world in general are concerned. Understanding the world of things without illusion is the essence of the internal urge that exists in the human mind, for that is revealed through the *mahākaruṇā* in its totality. In its manifestations, *mahākaruṇā* is very similar to the Brahman of the Brāhmanical schools; however, *mahākaruṇā* is not the controller of the universe.

Though there are many explanations that can be given to *dharmadhātu*, here it is used as it is suitable for the discussion and appropriate for the philosophical position of the Mādhyamikas. The nature of *dharmadhātu* can be understood only after one attains perfection in *Bodhicitta*, by commingling *prajñā* and *upāya*. Mind in its original state is pure; it is beyond *vikalpa* and in unity with the *dharmadhātu*.

The analytical knowledge has it own premises and constants, but in practical life this analytical knowledge is of little or no use. These constants or premises could explain only partial views of things, but in the case of Mādhyamika view the *śūnyatā* and *karuṇā* work together to redeem the mind (*citta*) from the conceptualizations (*vikalpas*). The duality as *prajñā* and *upāya* could bring the same results and it is absolutely efficient knowledge which is not just conceptual knowledge alone.

Prajñā replaces *śūnya* at the meditative level; similarly, the *upāya* replaces *karuṇā*, such that it explains the actual nature of the working of the phenomenal world. The functioning of the phenomenal world is based on certain rules that are discernible to human mind, as it manifested as *karuṇā*.

4.2.2 *Optimum Intermingling of Prajñā and Upāya*

Commingling of *prajñā* and *upāya* should not be an aberration such that it leads to yet another set of theoretical positions, as in the case of later Mādhyamikas, who accepted the theoretical position of the critics, especially the school of Svatantra Mādhyamikas.[17] The union of these two entities should be like:

> When mixed with honey, *ghee* and meat become poison, but the same 'meat' when taken in accordance with proper prescribed rules (*vidhi*) becomes a good rejuvenating tonic.[18]

It must be understood that improper use of any of the duo (*prajñā* and *upāya*) would lead to negative results. The problem with *prajñā* (intellectual understanding) is that it has its own way of analyzing the world of phenomena, which may not be in agreement with the functioning of the world of phenomena; *upāya* also has similar problems, as it forms only the means to reach the *Bodhicitta*. Using *upāya* improperly leads to confusion; *prajñā* too can lead to confusion generating out of the interaction between dispositions and feelings, manifesting the egocentric personality. These things can be observed in actual life, at times, as educated and knowledgeable people behave egocentrically. Such inconsistencies in the working of *prajñā* and *upāya* can be solved only through correct bringing together of these two aspects that lead to *Bodhicitta.*

It is only knowledge that can reveal the illusory manifestations associated with a phenomenon. When knowledge and suitable means are synergistic to each other, another stage of knowledge, *Bodhicitta*, is attained. It is similar to the instance of unalloyed and pure copper, when rubbed with mercury, turns to gold, if rubbed according to the injunctions.[19] Purifying the mind from the afflictions such as ignorance, illusory manifestations, gestalt of unreal as real, and clinging to *vikalpas*, is possible with the invocation of *Bodhicitta*. Mercury is similar to *prajñā*—knowledge; the process of rubbing is the *upāya*; and the gold is the *Bodhicitta*.

Āryadeva is always critical of the view that *nirvāṇa* is a transcended stage of *saṁsāra*, and like other Mahāyānists, he too rebukes the views of Hīnayānists in this regard. Hīnayāna practitioners are obsessed with the notion of attaining *nirvāṇa*, as it is the transcendence of *saṁsāra*; while the Mahāyānists do not consider *nirvāṇa* as the transcendence of *saṁsāra*. To one who is in the grab of *saṁsāra*, which forms due to the interaction of dispositions, feelings and ignorance, *nirvāṇa* appears as real, but to a Bodhisattva, who has realized *Bodhicitta*, the *saṁsāra* and *nirvāṇa* are redundant. According to T.R.V. Murti.

> The Arhat rests satisfied with achieving his own private salvation; he is not necessarily and actively interested in the welfare of others. The ideal of Arhat is smacks of selfishness; and there is even a lurking fear that the world would take hold of him if he tried here too long. The Bodhisattva makes the salvation of all his goodness. He shuns retiring into the final state of Nirvāṇa, though fully entitled to it, preferring by his own free choice, to toil for even the lowest of beings for ages.[20]

In the words of Āryadeva:

> Concerned by the fear of the death that would impede his chances to attain Nirvāṇa, a Hīnayānist practitioner suffers in each moment of his life; instead of freedom, he is living and attaining more bondage. In fact, after winning a war, a warrior should stay away from fighting, as for him winning and losing are inessential.[21]

Āryadeva has no apprehension in saying that those who follow the path of Mahāyāna are protected by *karuṇā*, the supreme internal power of an individual that drives him to the sufferingless stage of mind; the Buddhist *dharma* that stays with him as a protector; and the wisdom (*prajñā*) in the form of a bow, from which an arrow can be shot which could liberate the world from the suffering.[22] The Buddhist *dharma* (teachings) would act like a shield, protecting one from the problem of misconceptions (*vikalpas*); *prajñā* acts like a tight bow-string from which an arrow can be shot that has the power to remove misconceptions from the mind, revealing the essence of phenomena (*dharmadhātu*). Though the string has tremendous power, it stays in its place quietly; similarly, the mind of a Bodhisattva remains calm, not engaging in any form of speculative thinking. Remaining quiet, desisting from speculative thinking, and not showing the intellectual vigour, the Bodhisattva is always vigilant against the mind falling into the web of conceptualizations and confusions.

4.2.3 *The Bodhisattva's Mind*

The Bodhisattva is a courageous man with firm convictions and mental resolves; he not only keeps a steady mind, but also keeps his intellect sharp like a dialectician. Again, because he is never interested in speculative philosophizing, his observations are based on his experiences deduced from the facts of the world of phenomena, his intellectual faculties and his intuitions. Knowing the fact that *mahākaruṇā* supports the world of existence, he is never deluded by the dichotomies of the existent world. His convictions based on firm resolutions, his personality transcending the realm of existence and non-existence, the attitude of the Bodhisattva is developed after a prolonged and dedicated spiritual practice, which will not change according to situations.[23] Selfish attitude is a product of conceptualization (*vikalpas*), for it takes away the happiness from life. Āryadeva goes on to say that

> by taking care of one's own selfish ends, even the animals are affected. The blessed ones are scarce those who follow the welfare of the world.[24]

It is certain that animals and other lower level beings are free from the problem of conceptualization, and they have the inherent capacity to react directly to situations, satisfying all internal instincts. Even though they have such internal strengths, animals too are liable to suffer, if they are selfish. On the other hand, having been endowed with the power to think about the three stages of existence, the past, the present, and the future, human beings are bound to suffer the worst, if they are selfish. The human mind loses its power to react naturally like the animal, because of its innate nature to gestalt the apprehended phenomena in all the three stages, leaving it to suffer based on illusory manifestations. The perfected, cultivated, tamed, and unselfish articulation of the Bodhisattva's mind never falls into the grip of such illusions and it acts like an antidote to sufferings of the world.

Since most of the human activities are centred on personal choices and preferences, a normal person is not able to react naturally and, thus, not in a position to withstand the changes in nature like, heat, cold, winter, summer storm, cyclone, etc. Naturally, the mind over-estimates the effects of such natural forces and generates a fear psychosis about such happenings. A Bodhisattva, dedicating his whole life for the benefit of the world, is not affected by natural forces such as heat, cold, winter, summer, autumn, cyclone, etc., and is not bothered about the fear generated out of it.[25] His mind is free from fear created by illusions from the world of things. His concern goes to the suffering *per se* around him, not to the presumed suffering of nature and natural processes.[26] The Bodhisattva, endowed with the power of compassion, could accept the suffering even equal to that of a hell, without himself being affected by any fear.[27] The achieved *Bodhicitta*, after combining the *prajñā* and the *upāya* would insulate him from the illusions that cause suffering, because he could realize the *dharmadhātu*, the illusionless phenomena. A Bodhisattva enjoys a harmonious life in its fullest sense.

4.3 Importance of *Cittaviśuddhi*

In the realm of ethical praxis, majority schools of classical Indian philosophy promote external purification practices like bathing, refraining from eating certain food substances, rituals, penance, and the like; but the Mahāyānist's spiritual tradition introduces direct, objective, and rational practices which are result-oriented.[28] They reject the notion of acquired purity through *svadharma*, the spiritual practices of the Brāhmanical schools. Specifically, the Mādhyamikas bring to notice of the traditional Indian physiology that the human body is created from the semen of the father and the blood of the mother: the father's semen transforming into the nail, teeth, bones, and the marrow and the mother's blood transforming into flesh, blood, and the hair.[29] Here, they challenge the view of the Brāhmanical schools that the body can be purified by external purification methods. The validity of this argument, based on modern scientific paradigms, is not relevant here; in fact, it tries to explain only the nature of distribution of organs in the human body and its relation to the parents. Even the modern science with all its claim of being a systematic and advanced system, is able to explain only the development of life from the foetus, accepting the obscurity of the pre-foetus life, and failing to explain the actual process of creation. However, the attempt of Āryadeva is to show that the body is not pure in any sense, and it is not easy to purify it in any manner, and he categorically rejects all purifying spiritual practices as invalid.

4.3.1 *Pūrvamīmāṁsā View on Physical Purity*

The Brāhmanical systems of Indian philosophy, based on the injunctions of the Vedas, advocate strong adherence to the rituals prescribed in the Vedas. One of the prominent among the orthodox systems is the system of Pūrvamīmāṁsā, basing its philosophical inquiries on the *Karma-kāṇḍa* tradition of the Vedas. Since the Pūrva-mīmāṁsā is mainly concerned with spiritual practices that could help the practitioner to liberate from the world of existence, Āryadeva focuses his discussions on the advantages of his system of practices over the Pūrvamīmāṁsā system especially the latter's adherence to the *śabda-pramāṇa*, as the pre-eminent epistemological principle that reveals truth about the eternity of the soul. M. Hiriyanna explains their position as:

> The main object of the Mīmāṁsaka is to establish the authority of the Veda; but he does not like to do so solely on dogmatic consideration and, therefore, tries to seek rational ground for it. He contends that his system does not consist merely in delivering settled judgements, but is a reasoned inquiry.[30]

Proving the authority of the Vedas as the revealed truth, the Mīmāṁsaka seeks to establish this authority through rational means, not through dogmatism and superstitions. This special purpose has made them introduce many theories whose validity is not established properly.[31] This system has formulated many speculative assertions, which are not philoso-phically erudite. One good and famous example for this is that of Jyotiṣṭoma sacrifice, where heaven is held out as the end.[32]

The sacrifice assures the performer a place in heaven. The performer has to follow all the injunctions as given in the Vedas and perform the *karma* with utmost dedication and devotion. As a result of the intrinsic nature of such a holy action, the performer is assured the highest goal of life. Here, he is not allowed to think of anything else at the time of performing this sacred *karma*. Explaining this aspect further, S.N. Dasgupta says:

> When a sacrifice is performed according to the injunctions of the Vedas, a capacity which did not exist before and whose existence is proved by the authority of the scriptures is generated either in the action or in the agent. This capacity or positive force called *apūrva* produces in time the beneficent results of the sacrifice (leads the performer to heaven). The *apūrva* is like a potency or faculty in the agent which abides in him until the desired results follow.[33]

Though the rituals are performed according to perfect rational foundation, with regard to the results of these rituals, there are many obscurities; with regard to the expression of *apūrva*, it may be conceptually true but the realization of which is essentially irrational. Mādhyamikas refute these arguments of the Pūrvamīmāṁsā schools vehemently and confute them as mere superstitions. An important aspect of Mīmāṁsaka rituals focuses on cleansing of the body, as a spiritual discipline. The importance given to the removal of physical impurities is that the body is the dwelling place of the sacred and eternal soul, as though it could be tarnished by physical impurity. On the other hand, Mādhyamikas are of the view that since human body is created out of impure substances, such external purification practices would not yield any positive results, and, therefore, they attribute no importance to such purification practices.

4.3.2 *Dharma (Spiritual Virtue) through Rituals—the Difficulties*

As a clarification to his objections to the acceptance of accepting physical purification rituals as a method to achieve *dharma*, Āryadeva asks:

> Since the body is originated from impurities and contained full of impurities, how could it be purified by a bath in the Gaṅgā?[34]

The predicaments of the Brāhmnical School are certainly not intelligible to normal human rationale, as it heavily depends on its metaphysical assertions. According to S.N. Dasgupta,

> The importance of the Mīmāṁsā literature for a Hindu is indeed great. For not only are all Vedic duties to be performed according to its maxims, but

> even the Smṛti literature which regulate the daily duties, ceremonies, and rituals of Hindus even at the present day is all guided and explained by them.[35]

The social, cultural, and religious life of a community is strongly based on the maxims determined by this all-important philosophical system where the results depend on metaphysical assertions. The Mādhyamikas give less importance to such ritualistic practices, but the Mādhyamikas' rituals are meant to achieve the purity of *citta*, the *Cittaviśuddhi*, where unreasonable assertions on rituals are not considered. The rituals, practised as a part of cleansing the mind (*Cittaviśuddhi*), are formulated from the direct experiences of a *guru*, a Bodhisattva, or a very learned person who wishes to share his experience with a wider community. The extraneous dependence on Vedic rituals makes Mīmāṁsakas' view different from the Mādhyamikas. Āryadeva asks again that: "A pot that is impure inherently cannot be purified, even washed repeatedly by water. So also a body that is filled with impurities can never be purified by washing."[36]

The system of *puruṣārtha* is important as a division of the ethical doctrine of the Indian philosophical systems for determining the meaning of life; the *dharma* (righteousness), *artha* (wealth), *kāma* (desire), and *mokṣa* (liberation) interact with each other. Of these, *dharma* is the most important aspect as it leads the way to liberation. If one is certain about the nature of *dharma*, then he is naturally driven in the right path to *mokṣa*, because the other two aspects of *arta* and *kāma* are internal urges of a human being.[37] Spiritual practices aim towards the perfection of *dharma*, since achieving *dharma* is the most virtuous action of a human being. Āryadeva criticises the beliefs of the Brāhmanical schools, such as bathing in the Gaṅgā can accrue *dharma*; a dog may swim across the Gaṅgā, not receiving any merit; similarly, those who practise, bathing in Gaṅgā as a *dharma* also do not receive any virtue. Thus, it is futile to have bath in the holy places.[38] The water has no intrinsic power to purify the mind of an aspirant, and hence, taking bath is a futile exercise for acquiring spiritual merit. If the bath taken in Gaṅgā has spiritual merit, then the dog swimming across the Gaṅgā too should receive that.

In the philosophy of Mīmāṁsā, textual knowledge from the Vedas is given highest importance. Adherence to the textual injunctions of the Vedas is authoritative practice for the Brāhmanical systems like Mīmāṁsā, and they reject the rational analysis or criticism of the authority of the Vedas. Thus, they accept the validity of practice such as bath in the Gaṅga, without verifying the rationality. Āryadeva's criticism is not against the sincerity of the Yogis who practice "bath in Gaṅgā" as a spiritual practice, but against the validity of the bath in Gaṅgā as a method to achieve *dharma*. It is certain that any human activity if it is performed with dedication and complete submission could yield spiritual merit, but such practices also could corrupt the performer because he may believe such practices *per se* could bring *dharma*. This can lead to contempt and spiritual debasement. The extraneous dependence on rituals and on the belief of the eternity of the Vedas as a source to supplement directions to the spiritual practices is exactly what Mādhyamikas confute, and not the sincerity of the practitioner; sincerity of the mind of a practitioner would help him to achieve certain spiritual merit. Nonetheless, Mādhyamikas and the other Buddhist schools in general, give importance to introspection of all the *dharmas*.[39]

Āryadeva further comments:

> If one accrues *dharma* by taking a 'holy bath,' all the fisherfolk in the world be the gainers. What to talk of the fish, etc., who reside in the water day and night?[40]

In the perspective of critical analysis, this argument is correct, as it is not possible for all those who are in contact with the Gaṅgā water to attain liberation. There is a logical discordance in accepting bathing as a credible spiritual practice. On the other hand, in defence of the Brāhmanical school, one could argue that the holy bath is one of the *karma*, having intrinsic power leading one to *mokṣa*. The fisherfolk may be in constant contact with the "holy water," but they are not endowed with kārmic support, and also are not eligible for practising other rituals leading to liberation. Therefore, a bath in Gaṅgā is only one of the activities among many graduated practices. Āryadeva answers this observation in the next verse:

> It is certain that the removal of the sin is not possible by a 'holy bath.' The people, who have taken bath in the holy places, seem to have more attachment and the like.[41]

The knowledge from the holy texts deals with the revelations of the experiences of people who practised spiritual training. These are contextual, time-bound, and personalised individual experiences. Hence, it is absolutely necessary for an aspirant to look into the merit of such practices in a critical manner; if not, it could damage his personality with negative notions such as hatred, attachment, and the like.

What really impedes a practitioner from acquiring spiritual perfection? It is definitely not the lack of scriptural knowledge or the injunctions from Vedas, but the roots of all the sins are attachment, aversion, delusion, jealousy, and craving. It is said in the Abhidharma literature that the real reasons for suffering are these five negative notions of the mind, that can retard the spiritual harmony and create the suffering. So, a spiritual aspirant (*sādhaka*) should overcome these negative influences, rather than engaging in symbolic gestures like ablution in Gaṅgā water. It is rational and practical to inculcate spiritual practices that could remove those negative notions directly. Purification with water may be good for removing dirt from the body and for stabilizing the temperature of the body, but it may be of little use to cleanse the mind which is inherently attuned to the five negative notions that retard spiritual growth.[42]

4.3.3 *Cittaviśuddhi and Removal of the Notion of the Eternal Self*

Buddha's advice to the venerable Kātyāyana which we find in *Kātyāyanāvadānasūtra* goes thus:

> Without approaching either extreme, the Tathāgata teaches you a doctrine by the middle. Dependence upon the ignorance (*avidyā*) arises dispositions; dependence upon dispositions arises consciousness; dependence upon consciousness arises the psychophysical personality; dependence upon psychophysical personality arises the six senses; dependence upon the six senses arises contact; dependence upon contact arises feeling; dependence upon feeling arises craving; dependence upon craving arises grasping; dependence upon grasping arises becoming; dependence upon becoming arises birth; dependence upon birth arises old age and death, grief, lamentation, suffering, dejection and despair. Thus arises the entire mass of suffering.[43]

As stated above, mistaken identity of the non-self for the self is the real reason for rebirth, which is due to ignorance. As we have explained the intermingling of the dispositions with feelings which is deluded by ignorance is the real reason for the notion of an eternal self. When one ventures to remove ignorance, he can remove the notion of an eternal self. This mistaken identification of non-self for self imbues the being to take births and to find extinction in death, which is the reason for suffering.[44]

Liberation (*mokṣa*) for Brāhmanical schools, in general, is based on the redemption of the self from its karmic bonds; the self in association of the physical body (*prakṛti*) views the unreal as real and the real as unreal, causing suffering and rebirth. Quite the opposite, the notion of self, to the Buddhist schools is due to the ignorance, the ignorance of mind to identify with the psychophysical personality as an eternal self (*Ātman*), which otherwise is discernible only in association with the body. The independent existence of *Ātman* is not accepted. Liberation for the Buddhists is the removal of *avidyā* (ignorance) so that the notion of self ceases to exist.[45] Explaining the Buddhist view on this problem, Kalupahana writes:

> The principle of dependent arising is intended as an alternative to the Brāhmanical notion of an eternal self (Ātman) as well as to the conception of self nature (*svabhāva*) presented by some of the heterodox schools. As an alternative, it not only avoids mystery but also explains phenomena as being in a state of constant arising and ceasing. The Buddha realized that even though such a principle is verifiable, it is not easily perceived by ordinary human beings, who are engrossed and who delight in attachment to things as well as views.[46]

If the reality is beyond the human cognition and the flux of the things of appearance, then that entity is irrelevant for human existence, as it does not remove the sufferings of the world. The mind, because of its association to the things of the world, is always curious in searching for the "hidden something" that leads to the major cause of anxiety, frustration, and sufferings. Buddhists teach one to look at things as not "mystery of something," but perceive things as "what it comes to be."

The ontology of erroneous perception should be explained properly to explain the validity of the arguments of the realists' schools, who propound metaphysical doctrines to explain the phenomenal world, for these metaphysical doctrines are formulated out of non-erroneous perception. Advaita views the ontological status of the erroneous perception as well as apparent world, as neither real nor unreal, inexplicable (*anirvacaniya*) introducing the doctrine of illusion (*māyā*). The illusion is created out of misconception of the real; this means the ontology of erroneous perception and the ontology of the apparent world are inexplicable. Mādhyamikas, not upholding any metaphysical position with regard to the existence of universe, view this problem of erroneous perception as the establishment of the doctrine of *dharma-nairātmya*.

> As the erroneous perception of shell as silver gets removed after the realisation of the shell; similarly, the notion of the self gets removed by the realisation of the *nairātmya* (essencelessness of all the phenomena).[47]

The concept of *śūnya* or *nairātmya* is actually not the philosophy of emptiness, but it is the realization that the essence of all phenomena is not substantial for the formulation of any theory that is always true. The internal urge of the mind to view things as real, creates the notion of silver in the shell; when the mind is cleansed of the impediments, it would be able to perceive the essence of the conceived object, the shell (*dharmadhātu*) and the consequent essencelessness (*dharma-nairātmya*) of the shell. The next verse is a clarification to the problem that has not been explicated earlier:

> Just as with the perception of the rope, the notion of the snake in the rope is removed. As a result, the notion of snake instead of rope would not come back in this birth.[48]

When the mind is cleansed of the notions that create illusory perceptions through proper spiritual practices, then the notion of illusory perception never recovers in this birth.

4.4 The Vastness of Phenomenon and the Idea of *Śūnyatā*

The conceived phenomenon cannot be interpreted as void or *śūnyatā*, which is actually the position of the Nihilists. The perception of an individual object is confined to a limited space, and at the limited space we articulate an object, which again take a mental space. The object temporarily exists in the mind and excludes everything else. It is similar to the mind of a man in the desert, creating the illusion of water from mirage with the influence of his thirst, as he gestalts the idea of an oasis by looking at the vast horizon. When the attention is focussed on the particular object keenly to ascertain its ontological status, it turns into void, like in the case of analysis of the object to subatomic particles. The definition given by H.V. Guenther on the meaning of *śūnyatā* is very appropriate to note here:

> *Śūnyatā* can be explained in a very simple way. When we perceive, we usually attend to the delimited forms of objects.[49] However, these objects are perceived within a field. Attention can be directed either to the concrete, limited forms or to the field in which these forms are situated. In the *śūnyatā* experience the attention is on the field rather than on its contents. By "contents," we mean here these forms, which are the outstanding features of the field itself. We also might notice that when we have an idea before

> our mind, the territory, as it were, delimited by the idea is blurred; it fades into something, which is quite open. This open dimension is the basic meaning of *śūnyatā*.[50]

This openness can be seen in every determinate form, because every determinate form originates from something indeterminate, for this indeterminateness is inherent in all determinates. There is a subtle movement between the determinate and the indeterminate as the *śūnyatā* is implicit in every determinate form. On close observation, every phenomenon is not independently sustainable; it begins to vanish into something totally different, merging into openness. It is called *śūnyatā*. The openness of a phenomenon reduces its essence into essencelessness. It is called *dharma-nairātmya*.

4.4.1 *Knowing Śūnyatā through Perfected Knowledge*

In the meditative mind, the apparent phenomenon of the snake vanishes into rope, and on further observation, it opens into the vastness of *dharma-nairātmya*. There is a subtle difference between the understanding of an aspect and the knowledge about an aspect. Understanding serves only a temporary practical purpose, while knowledge serves an all-pervasive universal purpose. Āryadeva says:

> The dawn of *Vajrajñāna*, the adamantine knowledge achieved through constant meditation based on introspection of various phenomena, is liquidating the notion of permanence of entities as real, since no sprout germinates from fried seeds.[51]

Vajrajñāna is the culmination of the cumulative understandings of each phenomenon and its implicit nature as *śūnya*. It stops the mind from configuring further with illusions and forming thought constructs. On this, S.B. Dasgupta says:

> Āryadeva says that as the perception of silver in the shell is effected only when one perceives it to be nothing but the shell, so all our ignorance vanishes after the realisation of the void (*Nairātmya*); as the perception of the snake is contradicted by the perception of the rope as rope, so also all perception of phenomenalisation are contradicted by the *śūnyatā* or *vajra-jñāna*.[52]

We can look into the concept of *vajrajñāna* to know its usefulness. What is the real meaning of this *vajrajñāna*? Is it the knowledge of higher order; the knowledge that transcends all other knowledge; or the synthetic knowledge that removes misconceptions; or the simple, direct, and certain knowledge that arises from seeing the bracelet in hand? H.V. Guenther contends that

> Being related with these active characteristics, *śūnyatā* is clearly not a state of trance or absorption of some kind. It is a fearless state. Because of this fearlessness, one can afford to be generous. One can afford to acknowledge a space which does not contain any conflicts of that and this or how and why. No questions of any kind exist at this point. However, within this state there is a tremendous sense of freedom. It is an experience.[...] Therefore, a tremendous sense of conviction begins to develop with the *śūnyatā* experience. *Śūnyatā* provides the basic inspiration for developing the ideal, so to speak, of Bodhisattva like behaviour.[53]

The fear in an individual originates from his attachment to the world of things and the identification with it. The ego sense, a property of mind, pulls the mind towards fear in losing and over-joy in gaining of the things of the world. A Bodhisattva, who purified the mind of all impurities such as ego sense, on the other hand, gets rid of these fears or over-joy through the understanding of *śūnyatā*, because the knowledge (*vajrajñāna*) provides the power to see things as they are. The conceptual frame of mind that locates the things into a specified area and the thought on those things would be formulating a very limited perspective or creating a partial view of those things. Consequently, the mind moves together with these perspectives, and compels to view things at the limits set by these perspectives. In short, these perspectives are based on one's choices, such that the most favourable is the most intimate, and less favourable is less intimate and so on. Thus, we see different things in a categorized manner. However, the knowledge of *vajrajñāna* transcends these limits of choices and preferences and makes one to view not different things but things differently.

4.4.2 *Realizing Selflessness through Tāntric Practices*

The purport of spiritual practices to a Buddhist Tāntric Yogi is to realize the nature of *dharma-nairātmya* of the experienced objective world, and also to realize the *pudgala-nairātmya* of the individual self. It is only through the realization of *pudgala-nairātmya* that one could realize the *dharma-nairātmya*. The purpose of spiritual practices is meant to realize the *pudgala-nairātmya*, and the spiritual practices devised are simple and easily adaptable; however, some Yogis of average intelligence torment their body as a part of their training, which, according to Mādhyamikas, is not necessary. They are of the view that tormenting the body as a ritual would not bring any favourable result, unless he understands properly the meaning of *śūnyatā.*[54] The reason for bringing perfected knowledge (*prajñā*) and suitable spiritual practices (*upāya*) together is the real way of Mādhyamika spiritual tradition. It is not that the Mādhyamikas are against the spiritual tradition of enduring pain, using certain techniques, but they are certainly against the adaptation of such practices as a ritual. The underlying meaning of a practice is more important than the ritual. To substantiate this position, Āryadeva says:

> There is a meaning behind everything in the world. For example, the calendar is based on movement of moon; day and night are based on rising and setting of the sun; and so the things like *Graha*, the four directions, stars, and the *Rāśi*, are meant to explain the happenings in nature. Humanity has innovated these things to explain satisfactorily the world of appearance.[55]

The seasons like summer, winter, monsoon, etc. are also creative imaginations of a person, implying that, the enjoyments of the different seasons are due to the good and bad *karma* of the enjoyer.[56] On closer examination, one can see that there is nothing called season or seasonal changes, if the enjoyer (the one who experiences the season) does not acknowledge that. The meanings for such things are purely interpretative. Āryadeva's contention in this regard justifies the position of Mādhyamikas that their philosophy is not concerned with concepts and theories, but with the specifications such as the experience of the world of phenomena and a clear analysis of them. When the mind is deluded, the happenings in the apparent world would appear as real like in the case of seasons. Āryadeva again says:

> The mind (*Cittacintāmaṇi*) is like a gem, which has been soiled by the impurities in the form of '*Avidyā*'. If a wise man endeavours to cleanse it up, then it is impossible for somebody to make effort to increase the volume of*Avidyā*.[57]

The fundamental assumption of the Mādhyamika is that the mind in its essential nature resembles a gem,[58] which is pure, untarnished and steady; however, the incessant thought process, identified together with the world of things, tarnishes this purity of mind. At the same time, if man endeavours to cleanse the mind, then nothing can stop him from doing so, because he can ignore the presumed influences such as *graha*, *rāśi*, *karma*, etc., as something that is created for convenience.

The world of duality that makes a man afraid of his existence, and that he does not feel left out, for not achieved anything in this world.[59] Therefore, man who decides to pursue the path shown by the Buddha feels and acts according to His teachings. Besides, after having realized *Bodhicitta*, he understands the true nature of sense organs and he responds to them accordingly, with a sense of non-attachment. He frees himself from the influence of the sense organs, and inculcates the notion that everything is a manifestation of the Great Renunciate, the Buddha.[60] The *Vairocana* Buddha controls his eyes; the *Vajrasāya* Buddha controls the ears; the *Parameśvara* Buddha controls the nose; the *Padmanarteśvara* Buddha controls the mouth; the *Śrī Heruka* Buddha controls the body; and the *Vajrasattva* Buddha controls the mind. Thus, a Yogi is free from all afflictions and impediments that the sense organs, normally, can create on the mind.[61]

4.4.3 *The Personality of a Bodhisattva*

There are certain important questions asked about the conducts and activities allowed for a Yogi, such as, is he allowed to live a normal life like ordinary human beings; or should he live as a recluse until his death for the final redemption? Here, Āryadeva differs from many other thinkers. He says that a Yogi who understands the real nature of the world of phenomenon is allowed to conduct a normal life, since the influence of such things would never affect him in any manner. And the Buddhas protect him.[62] Since he receives protection from his own spiritual attainments, the Yogi is allowed to conduct his life in accordance with his wishes. He, however, is not compelled to live a life according to certain religious edicts.

Āryadeva clarifies the nature of Yogi:

> He has determined views (*Saiddhanthi*) about the world, he is free from all dichotomising conceptualisations (*Vikalpas*) and he is firmly established in his wealth, which is his intellect. His contemplation and activities are in accordance with his volition and hence he can enjoy everything and perform everything.[63]

This statement may be perceived as a major deviation from the common understanding of the basic teachings of Buddhism, which denounce desire. But, in fact, the desire one has to relinquish is the desire that is originated out of one's ignorance and passion. As the Yogi has destroyed the *avidyā*, the desire in him is not maligned by ignorance. In *Kātyāyanasūtra*, it was stated that desire originated from ignorance leads to suffering.[64]

> Even if he gets into a place which has no boundaries, or kept in a place where he is bound all the time (as captive), he enjoys his existence because of his association with his duties.[65]

The Yogi agrees with the life situation that he is destined to live, whether it is in the most adorable situation or whether it is treacherous like that of a hell. He is completely in agreement with his *karma*.

The contribution of the Mahāyāna system is the introduction of a new spiritual tradition and a new view of life by bringing in the idea that realization of *nirvāṇa* is possible in this life itself.[66] It is understandable, cognizable, and possible for anyone who aspires for redemption. At the same time, he need not be born in a particular caste or community for practising the spiritual disciplines[67] nor need he attain a certain age for practice. The spiritual practices are such that they can equip anyone to the path of spiritual maturity. Contrary to the views of the other orthodox and heterodox schools, the Mahāyāna system introduces the concept of spiritual merit accessible for aspirants. Āryadeva says:

> As ordinary world doesn't get sublated because of the world of Yogis; however it can be sublated by the special mind of the Yogi in due course of time.[68]

This verse argues against the presumption that there is a world of Yogis and another world of ordinary human beings, and the former is superior to the latter. However, the mind of a Yogi has the power to remove the afflictions such as ignorance, illusions, and misconceptions that are a part of the life in the ordinary world of experience. Here, Āryadeva criticises the views of Jainas, Ājīvikas, and Brāhmans.

The Yogi is not a human being different from the other human beings; nevertheless, his mind is superior to the minds of ordinary human beings as he is not affected by the dichotomous manifestations of the world of phenomena. The most important part of this argument is that the life of the Yogis in the phenomenal world is not tarnished by the desire coupled with ignorance, which makes the apparent existence of phenomena as real.[69] The Yogis never deny the ordinary world of phenomena, but at the same time, they are not influenced by the illusory manifestations of the ordinary world. Unaffected by such ill-effects, a Yogi enjoys normal life in the experiential world of existence.[70]

By introducing such a revolutionary view, the Mahāyāna School has achieved prominence over other schools of philosophy, because many of them teach that liberation is difficult to achieve and one has to live through innumerable births in its pursuit. Mahāyāna, on the other hand, teaches that one could realize *nirvāṇa* in this life itself, because the doctrine of *mahākaruṇā, mahāprajñā, mahopāya*, and *mahāsattva* are taught only in this school of philosophy.[71] This unique teaching of Mahāyāna transcends all those misconceptions about irrational theories and concepts about *nirvāṇa* or *mokṣa*.[72]

4.5 Referential Importance of Textual Injunctions

Contrary to the popular belief, the philosophy of Mādhyamika is not against the efficacy of texts as a documentary evidence of one's spiritual experiences, but it declines to accept texts as an unassailable authority to direct and decide one's spiritual practice. All the Brāhmanical schools accept the Vedas as an authority in one way or other, and in some cases, the only authority.[73] Adherence to the teachings of Vedas is absolutely necessary for a Yogi to attain *mokṣa* as per the Brāhmanical systems.[74] Āryadeva introduces the position of Mādhyamika:

> The Mahāyāna schools accept the authority of the *Bauddhāgamas*, which are authoritative texts for them. Because of the different dispositions of the mind to the attainment of the objects, there is a difference in the path leading to enlightenment.[75]

Bauddhāgamas are the texts giving experiences and opinion of the practitioners who followed the spiritual practices of the Mahāyāna system. They are sources of knowledge and inspiration to the new practitioners; but, at the same time, one must understand that these texts could provide only a general outline, not authoritative injunctions that are eternal. Declining the authority of textual injunctions, but at the same time accepting the reverential authority of the *Bauddhāgamas*, Āryadeva expresses the view that each human being is inherently different with his experienced world, his personalized viewpoints, and his generalizations about the manifested experiences. Thus, any generalisations into these aspects will lead to fallacies and difficulties. Āryadeva clarifies this view again:

> According to Mahāyāna schools, the theory relating to enlightenment is different; the practices for getting the enlightenment are different; the mental purification (*Cittaviśuddhi*) is different; the results spoken are also different.[76]

This may be the most rational explanation on "why" and "how" the textual injunctions are unsuitable for one to follow and formulate one's own spiritual practices. To summarise: the subtle natures of the humans are not amenable for any generalization or theoretical codification. In the opinion of Sañjaya, one has to withdraw into silence, leading the life of a recluse for finding harmony and happiness. Mahāyānists hold a different view that, even if one decides to withdraw from unnecessary discussions on trivial issues, his internal urges impel and drive him to think about such issues, as thinking unoriginated and uncaused.

The reflected image of a person is limpid if the mirror is clean and the eyesight of the onlooker is clear.[77] Similarly, the Yogi's mind also reflects the perceived objects like in a clean mirror, if he has cleansed his mind of distractions due to imaginations from the gamut of imagination through proper spiritual practices.[78] The results of all Mahāyānistic spiritual practices are directly discernible to a Yogi in this life itself. It does not elevate one to a higher level, but makes him realize something that is immediately available within him, which is natural and subtle. It rids his mind of the visualizations of multitudes, by providing clear and certain understanding about the nature of phenomena that the *śūnyatā* is implicit in every phenomenon.

4.6 The Vehemence of *Prajñā* to remove Misconceptions

Elaborating on the nature of a Yogi's attainment, Āryadeva introduces the example of Sūryakāntamaṇi,[79] a gem with unique properties:

> The gem called *Sūryakāntamaṇi*, when exposes to sunlight, produces fire, and the fire is capable of achieving its purpose of revealing itself and other objects. Similarly, when the mind is associated with *prajñā* burns away the totality of imaginations, liberating itself and helping others minds to be liberated.[80]

The substance in the gem Sūryakāntamaṇi is like the totality of imaginations (*vikalpas*) inherent in the mind. The nature of Sūryakāntamaṇi is identifiable with the matter content; likewise, the mind is normally understandable only with the totality of thoughts (*kalpanājālam*). The mass in the Sūryakāntamaṇi burns and shines as long as the sun shines; similarly, the mind also burns away the thought constructs (*vikalpas*) when the *prajñā* shines in the mind.[81] When thought constructs are burnt away, the *Bodhicitta* dawns in the mind, revealing the *dharmadhātu* of things.

A Yogi always should be vigilant against all types of afflictions, and he should constantly engage himself with reflections of all his activities. And he must inculcate right means (*upāyas*) that could help him in spiritual progress. The *upāyas* are understood from looking at the actual functioning of the phenomenal world which based on the concept of *mahākaruṇā*, configured as *karma*[82] and it rooted in *karuṇā*.[83] With the introduction of the concept of *mahākaruṇā*, Ārya Aśvaghoṣa started the fundamental philosophy of Mahāyāna. It can be construed that the action rooted in compassion should be the path of a Yogi. The *upāya* is a very important aspect of Buddhist Tantrism. Thus, Āryadeva rightly points out that

> when two pieces of wood are rubbed against each other the fire originates, and the fire is pure in the beginning, middle and end. It illuminates the objects of the world. Similarly it is known that *prajñā* and *upāya* together produce Yogic knowledge (or *Bodhicitta*).[84]

The knowledge of a Yogi is not just theoretical which is formulated from intellectual reckoning, but it is a perfect commingling of wisdom and action rooted in compassion. In the *Jñānasiddhi*, the difference between these two types of knowledge is explained:

> A distinction is drawn between ordinary knowledge (*jñāna*) and the knowledge of the highest truth (*tattva-jñāna*). Distinction is ultimately the same as that between *prajñā* and the combination of both *prajñā* and *upāya*. The former is *Nirvikalpa* i.e., free from all the false constructions; but the later *tattva-jñāna* should never be taken as the complete cessation of consciousness for in the *tattva-jñāna* there is the existence of universal compassion (*Karuṇā-bhāva*).[85]

The knowledge of a Yogi is capable of ceasing all mental modifications and doubts about the nature of phenomena. He can feel and enjoy the pure silence from all thought activities.

4.6.1 *Removal of Suffering with the Realization of Dharmadhātu*

Since a Bodhisattva refuses his personal *nirvāṇa*, the relevance of his strenuous Yogic practices can be questioned.[86] This is not irrelevant. As Āryadeva explains that the Bodhisattva is like a lamp which illuminates the objects around it in the place where it is situated.[87]

The presence of a Bodhisattva in a society is a blessing to that society as at least one person in the community could understand the real nature of suffering so that he can advise others about the path of peace, console the ignorant about the reasons and causes of suffering, or commiserate with one who requires spiritual help.

With the perfect commingling of *prajñā* and *upāya*, the Bodhisattva invokes the omniscience that is the manifestation of *Bodhicitta*, and then only he could destroy the multiplicity of things.[88] Earlier, we have seen that through *śūnyatā* one acquires the power to see things differently, not different things. The plurality of existent things would increase and multiply if the mind, with its inherent notion of attaching and identifying to different things, leads to confusion and suffering. The blossoming of *Bodhicitta* can be compared to a man who has the ability to know the way to extract nectar from the milk, which is non-defective and cool, soothing for the hearts, and panacea (*amṛta*) for all diseases.[89]

The Yogic knowledge is perfect, non-defective, non-confusing, and never lead to any form of conceptualizations (*vikalpas*). It helps all beings who suffer under the web of innumerable problems of existence as it is filled with compassion; it is rooted in compassion, and it cures like *amṛta. Prajñā* (wisdom) is like an ocean of milk, which is churned using *upāya* (means), and what comes out is called *dharmadhātu* (the *amṛta*); it is pure and destroys all distinctions and even transcends the differentiation between *sukha* (happiness) and *duḥkha* (suffering).[90]

The *dharmadhātu*, like a creeper moving on to a tree blossoming with flowers and fruits, dawns in the minds of the Yogis, since the enlightenment happens instantaneously when the *prajñā* and *upāya* interact perfectly through meditative practices.[91] The *Bodhicitta* dawns in the minds of the Bodhisattvas when the intermingling of the two aspects, namely, analytical knowledge and practical appreciative knowledge, take place as a result of the meditative process.

The Yogi, through his disciplined spiritual practice, acquires a certain level of insularity with regard to the world of things and normal human activities. However, the practice of Tantra as a spiritual discipline involves subtle spiritual practices that have special meanings of their own and could corrupt a person if wrongly practised. Āryadeva says:

> A Yogi can engage in activities like controlling (*vāsīkarānā*), creating jalousie (*dveṣa*), movement (*gati*), stoppage (*staṁbhana*), making contact for attracting things towards him, eating meat, drinking alcoholic drinks, and engaging in sexo-yogic practice (Despite practicing all these), he is not affected by bad effects of these objects and activities.[92]

When a Yogi acquires sufficient control on his mind, he would be able to do things which are not able for other people to do; like a magician's actions can be spellbinding and awe-inspiring. These are very difficult and strenuous practices and care should be taken, in consultation with a *guru*, to protect oneself from the ill-effects.

4.7 Significance of Mantras to Protect *Bodhicitta*

Indian philosophical systems can be broadly divided into two important sections. The first one is concerned with the intellectual understanding about the world of existence; the second one is concerned with the practical application of what is intellectually inferred. The first part comes under the section called Darśana, while the practical application of the *dārśanika* view is called Tantra. As we can see the Sāṅkhya philosophical system finds Śaiva-Tantra, and the Mahāyānistic systems are rooted in the philosophical tradition of Mādhyamika, which caused the origination of Buddhist Tantras.[93] The Tāntric system has independent spiritual practices irrespective of the philosophical school it belongs to. For example, the practice of Mantra is a very important aspect of the Tāntric systems. As H.V. Guenther opined on the meaning of Mantras.

> The word 'mantra' comes from the noun *manas* and the verbal root *tra* ('to protect') according to the Indian explanation. The full explanation runs as follows '*manastrāṇabhūtatvād mantram iti ucyate*' (meaning)—since it has become a protection of mind it is called mantra.[...][94]

Āryadeva says that the real teaching of Mahāyāna is to inculcate the nature of protection of mind through *mantra*, not the Yogi who acquires unusual powers by practising spiritual practices such as *vaśīkaraṇa, staṁbhanā*, etc.

> In order to see a bracelet in one's own hand one doesn't need a mirror. Similarly in Mahāyāna, one can have the enlightenment through the efficacy of Mantras. It is certain and clear.[95]

The philosophical message of Mādhyamika is to understand the world of appearance without illusions or *vikalpas*, the way it appears before us. Mantras help one to protect the mind from the incessant thought that forms in the mind, which may corrupt the mind. A man who understands the true nature and working of the existents, even relationships as intimate as that of mother or sister, will not influence.[96] A person's attachment towards his mother or other female members of the family is emotionally intense; even though a Yogi has perfected his mind through Mantras, he may also be influenced by such worldly attachments; but a Mahāyānist Yogi will have the mental tenacity to protect himself from any such influences. Also, he should protect himself against the notions of racial superiority or caste hegemony, because these afflictions are most damaging to human personality.[97]

Based on traditional Indian physiology, it is believed that a baby is born from the semen of the father and the blood of the mother.[98] Both the semen and the blood contain only forms of *pañcabhūtas*; even if it is the semen of a learned Brāhman[99] or the blood of a Caṇḍāla, it makes no difference, because it contains only same elements.[100] As we have understood, the knowledge of *dharmadhātu* removes the misconceptions from the mind of the Yogi about the conceived phenomena. Human personality is the aggregate of the five *skandhas*. They are: (1) *rūpa* (four elements of the body and senses), (2) *vedanā* (feelings—pleasurable, painful, (3) *sañña* (conceptual knowledge), (4) *saṅkhara* (synthetic functioning of compound feelings), and (5) *viññana* (consciousness).[101] The basic constitution of the body, which is made of the six elements[102] (the material aspect) and the *skandhas* (the personality aspect), does not bestow any speciality to an individual on his birth, or ascribe any superiority over other human being.[103] A Yogi who realizes this subtle nature of existence through his meditations, transcends the stage of *sukha* and *duḥkha*, his mind transcending suffering (*duḥkha-śūnya*), his consciousness cleared of all doubts. After introducing this argument, Āryadeva criticizes the superiority of Brāhmans as a superior caste as the only people allowed to perform any spiritual practice.

The Vedic schools consider the Brāhmans as "twice born" (*dvija*) human beings, having superiority as the chosen people, and also authorize them to perform sacrifices for the entire community that results in their personal redemption too. There is no difference in the constitution of the human personality of the practitioner. In fact it is the birthright and choice of a human being to practice any spiritual discipline and seek his personal emancipation and the societal redemption. There are instances in history that a man born to a fisherwoman or a Caṇḍāla, after performing penance, assumes the position of a Brāhman, is allowed to practise spiritual disciplines.[104] The distinctions such as caste, creed, etc. are man-made for enjoying certain conveniences and privileges; other than that such distinctions have no essential value.

4.7.1 *Sexo-yogic (Kriyātantra) Spiritual Practices and Transcendence of Dualism*

The introduction of Tantrism into Buddhism, made Buddhism to accept certain practices and beliefs that are part of Tāntric systems. In case of Tāntric spiritual practices, female deities are very important.

Moreover, the womenfolk in the society are considered as the human form of the Goddess. Tāntric spiritual practises, cutting across religio-philosophical lines, accept the worship of Goddess.

> Because of the knowledge and influence of '*Vajrasattva*'[105] a person (Yogi) would always worship the bodies like that of sister, mother, mother-in-law, daughter, neice, sister's daughter or a lady who belongs to Brāhmin, *kṣatriya*, *vaiśya* or *śudra*, or even somebody handicapped on her limbs, or one who is condemned by the society, or a lady from the lowest caste.[106]

The worship of woman and her use in the spiritual training has very deep spiritual meanings. The perceivable life in the world is sustained through the male and female principle, and this is more pronounced in the case of mammals,' etc., where each principle contributes actively to the procreation and substance of life in a very methodical way and the importance of the female principle is very decisive. It is her natural compassion and love, and dedication which is protecting life. Tāntrics use this aspect of femininity as their core of spiritual training. The active involvement of bisexual dual principle in procreation is pronounced only in higher species of plants and animals. Nevertheless, we can observe such activity in case of single-cellular organisms too. According to H.V. Guenther:

> Since the bisexual differentiation of an organism is already latent in a single cell's bio-dynamics, it is safe to assume that, in the same way as a living cell anabolically deficient in any way is chemically driven to work repetitiously to acquire and anabolise adequate and right qualities of nutritional substances, an individual which is either predominantly male or female is driven to seek the completely opposite type.[107]

Just as the single-cell organism seeks right quantities of nutritional substance to sustain and procreate, a developed organism seeks its female or male counterpart to sustain and procreate. To illustrate this aspect further, it is an internal urge of the being to seek its existence and sustenance.

> A man will seek the woman as well a woman the man. Such selective deficiencies or needs and cravings prove that every partial aspect is in want of its complement.[108]

In the *Kriyātantra* practice,[109] a Yogi uses this aspect for the spiritual development and the purpose of such training is that:

> The dualism is the cause of all the worries, all the miseries, all the conflicts that are going on in this world. Man must be remade. The remaking of man consists in regaining the integrity veiled only by the contraries.[110]

A Yogi who seeks to attain the spiritual perfection has to master the basic instincts of being a man. And once the remaking of man is done, he is in no way bound by the limitations that a normal human being has to go through. The remaking of man, in other words, is done by helping him to transcend the limits sets by nature to seek the female part for involving in the procreation process. The formulation of such practices are such that the Yogi would eventually transcend the basic instinct towards sex; however, it should not be doubted that he would destruct that instinct in him but he could control such instincts effectively. The remade man has attained the way to liberation. The systems of sexo-yogic practices are well-explained in this manner. A Yogi, as a practice and a way of life, should learn to respect the womenfolk as they give him a path to redemption.

4.8 Not Destruction of Desires but Appeasement of Desire

When the Yogi transcends the influence of dualism with the help of various spiritual practices, he is no longer bound by anything that binds a normal human being in this worldly existence.

> Always keeping a smiling face, bright eyes and broad vision, a Yogi moves towards perfection; by practicing of his Mantras, he is opening his mind into the '*Saṁbodhi*,' the perfected enlightenment. His perfected meditations towards the personal God, revealing what is to be perceived in the world of existence.[111] He listens to all that has to be listened; keeping himself quiet, he speaks a little that transcends the realm of true or false.[112]

Perfected enlightenment (*saṁbodhi*) for a Yogi is that his mind transcends the realm of good and bad; true or false; right and wrong; and all such dichotomies. He listens and responds only to things that are to be listened and to be responded, for he never falls into the trap of meaningless speech or actions.[113]

A Yogi (*sādhaka*) should perform all the rituals in a prescribed way, observe self-cleanliness, smearing of oil, wearing of clean cloth, and eating and drinking good food. These are done with a devotion to the personal God.[114] Āryadeva explains these aspects plainly.

> And a Yogi, after completing the spiritual training, needn't live like a recluse; he can live a normal life like any other human being, because the good effects of the spiritual achievement and the Mantras would be protecting him. A Yogi is even allowed to enjoy music (both vocal and instrumental), because he is observing the prescribed injunctions with a purity of mental purpose. Besides, he will not get attached to either to the enjoyment or to the objects of enjoyment.[115]

One of the reasons for such declaration that a Yogi should live a normal life, after realizing the *saṁbodhi*, is that he has to spend his time properly and effectively without considering himself as a special person. To illustrate further, though a Yogi destroyed the (*vikalpa*) power of desire in him that might have destroyed his spiritual life, however, he should find the positive effect of that desire which is offering a continuum to his life.[116] Activities like enjoying music and dance could contribute to the harmonious existence of spiritual achievements. He lives a normal life without being attached to the ill-effects of desires.

4.9 Realising *Pudgala-nairātmya* Through Tāntric Practices

Enlightenment does not mean abandonment of the normal life. It is not realized with the destruction of the physical body, but it is realized by augmenting the harmonious spiritual unity. However, the Yogi protects himself from being attached to relative and non-eternal nature of apparent phenomenal world; or he cogitates over the apparent phenomena as real and eternal. The Mādhyamika propounds neither self-mortification, nor advocates the doctrine of eternalism or nihilism; he puts forward the doctrine of the destruction of the notion of the self. For him, happiness comes from objects of happiness and enlightenment has no origin at all.[117] It is clear from this verse that the notion of enlightenment is not from systematic spiritual progression as many other schools are propagating.[118] Moreover, tormenting the body is considered as an act that could earn the practitioner the much-desired spiritual perfection and realization of the eternal self. Mādhyamikas reject torturing the body as a spiritual discipline. On the other hand, though Mādhyamika accepts spiritual realization through disciplined practices learnt from a *guru* and the texts *Bauddhāgamas* and others, it never envisages the notion of enlightenment as a systematic development. Since tormenting the body brings only pain and unhappiness, the expectation of a pure and omniscient self-originating from such practices is contradictory and improper to follow.

> Having successfully controlled the internal urges of desire, cravings, etc., as a normal human being, a Bodhisattva is allowed to enjoy the objects of world because he would not be attached to the confusing influence of such world of things.

With the enjoyment of all the objects of pleasures of the world, one can enjoy himself; there is nothing to be afraid of and no sin is attached to his activities. This is the way one has to pass on the time.[119]

The negative aspect of enjoyment of worldly pleasures is that one has a tendency to be attached to things he or she is associated with, which the Mādhyamikas remove from the mind using Tāntric spiritual practices. Āryadeva says in this regard that

> Even a piece of wood when consecrated with proper Mantras, can attain the state of Godly divine nature; therefore imagine, what Mantra can do to a man endowed with knowledge.[120]

The power of knowledge can help a human being remove the adjuncts that can create afflictions, which, in turn, generate illusions in the minds. The perfect knowledge, *vajrajñāna,* reveals the *dharmadhātu* of each apprehended *dharma.*

The most interesting aspect of this spiritual training is that one could destroy the notion of ego by commingling *prajñā* and *upāya.*[121] Ego is another form of matured ignorance,[122] as it propels the mind into heights by configuring unreal as real, the momentary as eternal, and temporary as permanent. The problem of ego is the theme of discussion of many philosophical systems. Some systems even recommend strict vigil and highly articulated spiritual practices to annihilate the notion of ego.[123] It says that

> the mind of a Māhāyānist Yogi is like a lotus, born in mud but never tainted by mud (impurity), because he has cultivated the *Bodhicitta* by commingling *prajñā* and *upāya* perfectly. The impurity of the worldly life such as the pluralities of impressions never taint the mind of a Yogi, and the mud in the form of beginningless *vāsanās* (impressions) also never corrupt his mind. The mind retains its pristine nature and illumines in its original nature.[124]

The nature of *Bodhicitta* is such that it helps one to retain the original nature of the mind, by removing the notion of a permanent self, establishing the conception of essencelessness of the soul or *pudgala-nairātmya.*

4.9.1 *The Removal of Ignorance clears the Notion of Permanent Self*

Like a gem fallen in the mud, the *Bodhicitta,*[125] remains unaffected even in the world of deceiving identities and the plurality of impressions, because the mud is too weak to tarnish the purity of a gem. The mind of a Bodhisattva apprehends only the essence of phenomena (*dharmadhātu*) on the conceived phenomena (*dharma*). Just as the moon reflected on water is unaffected by the defects of water, the essence of phenomena (*dharmadhātu*) reflects in the mind. In other words, the perception of the object is clear and the defects of eyesight never delude it.[126] The *Bodhicitta* is like the water, and the *dharmadhātu* is the moon; the reflection of *dharmadhātu* in *Bodhicitta* is perfect and clear. It is said that

> a wise person,[127] associated with own personal God, having a steady vision, is clearing of the clouds of ignorance (from his mind); in such a person the sun (in the form) of *Citta* (*Bodhicitta*) shines forth.[128]

When the clouds are removed, the sun shines perfectly; similarly, when the cloud of ignorance and misconceptions are removed, the *Bodhicitta* shines revealing the *dharmadhātu* of the objects conceived. The reason for the mind to identify objects as real is as follows:

> When the mind is delimited by assigned objects, there arises the certitude about an existing object. One has to accept *dharmadhātu* in order that the mass of *avidyā* is removed.[129]

If the perceived objects are confined because of the illusions attached to them, then the knowledge about those objects are limited; but when the mind realizes the *Bodhicitta*, then the limitations attached with the objects are removed and it could have the knowledge of *dharmadhātu* perfectly. It is not nihilism that Mādhyamikas try to profess, but the limited vision about the world of objects. As we have discussed earlier, the *dharmadhātu* is the subdivision of the *skandhas*.[130] The *prajñā* in the form of a hammer can break the pot created by the mud of illusions (*vikalpas*), for it can reveal the knowledge that is kept in the mud pot.[131] It is clear from the discussions that the influence of the world of objects on the human psyche can be removed with the help of proper spiritual practices. In other words, there is an end to the sufferings that are caused by the mental activity of conceptualization and false ascription.

4.9.2 *The Removal of Permanent Self with the Mastery of Mantras*

Mantras protect the mind from various aspects, especially from wondrous thought and the conceptual structures created by the phenomenalizational activities. Thus, it is able to find quietude and peace. However, at the same time, one should not forget the three *ratnas*,[132] normally the *guru*[133] who attained the *Bodhicitta*; non-injury, one should not kill or harm any living being; and adhere to the teachings of the masters.[134] Mādhyamikas are always explicit in their positions on the question of liberation and the duties of a Yogi. These duties are meant to keep the mind protected in the world of deceiving identities, but it does not mean that one needs to follow any strict regimen as a ritual, but accepts it as a practice.

It is now clear that the multiplicity of the objective world is not real. It is said:

> Everyone knows that the elements of the nature are earth, fire, water and air. The wise people because of their mastery over the Mantras transform by relinquishing all the conceptualizations. (Therefore) one should resort to Mantra-Vāda.[135]

The perfect stage of *saṁbodhi* is achievable only by perfecting the art of *mantra-vāda*, the technique of protecting the mind from conceptualisation; because one realises that the world of objects is nothing but the conglomeration of earth, fire, water, air, space, and consciousness, the six elements (*ṣaṭ-dhātu*).[136]

4.9.3 *The Yogic Practices that facilitate the Mastery of Mantras*

On the practical level, one has to show complete allegiance to what one has to do as practitioner of the Tāntric system of Yoga. "One has to take resort to *Madhu*, *Raktam*, Pure Camphor (*Karpūram*) added with red sandal, these five things are very important."[137] As we have discussed earlier, since the Mādhyamika philosophy was introduced into the Tāntric system, it was bound to accept the directions of Tāntric systems, where the practitioner should be showing complete allegiance and respect to this system. These practices are necessary for elevating the *citta*. One has to quieten the mind by controlling the airs in the body,[138] and eliminate the imbalance in the body."[139] With the help of *mantras* and *prāṇāyāma* (control of vital airs), one can keep a sound mind, because the distorted airs in the body would lead to mental complications. The Āyurvedic medicine accepts both control of vital airs and mental stability as important adjuncts for determining a treatment system. One should feel comfortable with his body.

> Because of the operation of the *Vikalpas* (alternatives), one should not think that he is impure. Having an equipoise mind, one who has mastered Mantra shall perform everything in the world.[140]

Because of the false ascriptions (*vikalpas*), one may feel that impurity exists in the mind and body, such that his body lacks cosmetic beauty and his mind has unsteady orientation. However, one who mastered the technique to control the mind and its activities is able to see the real nature of the things of the world with a harmonious mind. Such a physical and mental stability can be thwarted by inordinate mental activities. Just as a minute quantity of poison generated with the fall of a fly (on food or something), can create substantial problems for man; similarly, an iota of doubt in the form of fly-poison that generates in the mind of a man could cause fear of death and suffering.[141] Doubting will not always lead to clear thinking; actually, it could lead to situations that are more complicated. This is in contrast to the Descartes' submission to the understanding of doubt; he used doubt as a tool to analyze the belief systems existing at his time. The tenets of those belief systems are supposed to be unquestionable and one's duty is to follow such systems without any doubt or questions in this life.[142] In our discussion about the purified mind, which is clear of any misconceptions, if it begins to doubt further about the phenomenon, then the mind may fall into the process of conceptualization again.

For achieving perfection in spiritual training, development, and maturation, one needs to follow certain disciplines and self-control, which needs courage and strong conviction. "A wise man can either fight out a battle or make an honourable exit; the stage in between is bad as it leads one to fall."[143] It is not really required that one has to follow any spiritual discipline and live the life of a recluse; however, if one decides to conduct the life of a Yogi, he must succeed in his endeavours to find perfect *Bodhicitta*. As it has been said by the learned, a warrior should die fighting, or he should make an honourable exit, but the in-between stage is reprehensible.

The essential thing that leads to a successful completion of a spiritual training is the support of a competent *guru*.[144]

> One should not transgress the commands of one's preceptor, nor his mudras, nor even his shadow; his merits or good qualities are to be followed, not demerits or bad qualities; he is the supreme deity for an aspirant, and thus to be worshipped; he is none other than the king with the vajra in the hands and can be directly perceived (the *Vajradhara*).[145]

The supreme deity of Buddhist Tantrism is the Vajradhara Buddha. He can be compared to Śiva of the Śaiva Tantras. The *guru* is to be considered as the personalized form of the supreme deity that one can perceive directly, because his directions are absolutely necessary for one to follow a spiritual path. The Buddhist philosophy never accepts a Supreme God as the controller of the world of existence, but in Tāntric systems, the patent deities are important for the completion of a spiritual discipline, so the concept of Vajradhara Buddha as the supreme deity is accepted. The introduction of the deity is effective for the realization of *prajñā* at each stage of a practitioner's development. As suggested and recommended by the *guru*, the adept meditates on a particular deity in order to accomplish a certain spiritual maturity. In order to accomplish the set purpose the adept leaves the deity, after a certain level of perfection, and chooses another one that is more accomplished for higher spiritual perfection. Finally, he reaches the Vajradhara Buddha.

4.10 Right Concentration (*Śraddhā*) as the Supreme *Upāya*

The most important aspect in one's spiritual journey is the accomplishment of concentration (*śraddhā*), for it is acquired with the help of *prajñā* or wisdom. The purposes of spiritual practices become abortive with the lack of *prajñā*, so one should ponder it in the texts of Āgamas and Adhigamas to acquire more knowledge.[146] A person who attained active concentration, *śraddhā*, is like the gem called Udakamaṇi, which has the power to cleanse impure water; *śraddhā* (like the Udakamaṇi) acts on the deluded mind and cleans it, from all the *vikalpas*.[147] It is interesting to note that Āryadeva described the importance of *śraddhā* as the last phase of his discussions. Many such narrations normally highlight this aspect first before enumerating the system of practices.[148] Āryadeva considers concentration as the supreme *upāya* that can cleanse the mind, but to attain concentration one needs to have constant training and practice. One needs to go through many *upāyas* directed by the *guru*. Almost all systems agree that concentration is the key to one's spiritual attainments.

The one who is learned (*bahuśruta*), wise, and endowed with natural compassion by his very nature only finds good *upāyas* to destroy the suffering of mankind.[149] What a Bodhisattva, after his spiritual attainment, should do is to find suitable *upāyas* that could help the sentient beings to live a happy life in the world. This does not mean *sarvamukti* to all the people of the world. Here, Ārydeva introduces the doctrine of supporting and helping the less fortunate to pass though the *saṁsāra* successfully. After using various *upāyas* for redemption in his spiritual training, the Yogi identifies suitable *upāyas* that any sentient being can follow, his compassion to the world of existence being supreme. Āryadeva concludes his discussion on this subject by saluting the readers. He states that by attaining purification of the mind (*cittaviśuddhi*) he attained happiness and prays that such happiness be attained by everyone through *cittaviśuddhi*.[150]

References

1. Sasibhushan Dasgupta, *An Introduction to Tāntric Buddhism*, p. 90.
2. The conceived and cognized objects are susceptible to variation. The conceived object refer to the object cognized by the mind. The object of mind is referred to as *dharma* (phenomena). David J. Kalupahana, *A History of Buddhist Philosophy*, p. 79.
3. K. Venkata Ramanan, *Nāgārjuna's Philosophy*, p. 38.
4. Ibid.
5. T.R.V. Murti, op. cit., p. 263.
6. There are ten gods to represent the ten *pāramitās*. The *pāramitās* are *dāna*, *śīla*, *kṣānti*, *vīrya*, *dhyāna*, *prajñā*, *upāya*, *prañithi*, *bala*, and *jñāna*. The corresponding gods are: Pramuditā, Vimalā, Prabhākarī, Arciṣamatī, Abhimukhī, Duraṅgamā, Acalā, Sādhumatī, and Dharmamegha. S.B. Dasgupta, op. cit., p. 78.
7. T.R.V. Murti, op. cit., p. 267.
8. *dṛg-darśana-śaktyor ekātmatevāsmita*. *Yogasūtra* of Patañjali, Sādhana-pāda, v. 6.
9. H.V. Guenther, *The Tānric View of Life*, p. 53.
10. S.B. Dasgupta, op. cit., p. 90.
11. Ibid., p. 82.
12. T.R.V. Murti, op. cit., p. 264.
13. Fumimoro Watanebe, *Philosophy and its Development in the Nikāyas and Abhidhamma*, p. 11.
14. Ibid., p. 12.
15. This has been derived from the notion of *tathatā* (thatness) doctrine of Aśvaghoṣa, from whose initiation the Mahāyāna School of Buddhism started. The meaning of *tathatā* is described as the totality of things that cannot be thought of or spoken of. But that which appears as the existents before us a manifestation of that totality. The false ascriptions (*vikalpas*) are made on the *tathatā*. Surendranath Dasgupta, *History of Indian Philosophy*, p. 130.
16. Here, an implied existence of something exists beyond the realm of one's ways of understanding, which is very close to the views of Brāhmanical schools. Ibid., p. 137.
17. Peter Della Santina, *Mādhyamika Schools in India*, p. 156.
18. *Cittaviśuddhi-prakaraṇa*, v. 50.
19. Ibid., v. 51.
20. T.R.V. Murti, op. cit., p. 263.
21. *Cittaviśuddhi-prakaraṇa*, v. 52.

22. Ibid., v. 53.
23. Ibid., v. 54.
24. Ibid., v. 55.
25. Ibid., v. 56.
26. Rajesh Bedi shows the unusual spiritual practices of the *sādhus*, most of them are an expression of the endurance of the Yogi to withstand any adverse situation. For example, the practices like *Pañcāgni Tapasyā* is equipping the practitioner to withstand heat. *The Holy Men of India*, A Photo Illustration Book, 1957, pp. 57-70.
27. *Cittaviśuddhi-prakaraṇa*, v. 57.
28. The bathing done as part of the spiritual training is condemned here, not the bathing as a daily routine of cleaning the body. Many Brāhmanical schools especially the groups which give emphasis to *Karmakāṇḍa* part of the Vedas have various purification practices which are suppose to have subtle spiritual meanings. Abstaining from eating some food is very much in practice today. The meaning of avoiding certain foodstuffs also is not well explained by these schools. The foodstuff should be avoided if they cause diseases or not fit for a person to eat or drink if that is not fit for his body. But that is not the real issue here certain food stuff are considered as a taboo because of certain obscure reasons, that are not explained by the practitioners and the promoters of these schools satisfactorily. The Mīmāṁsā School of orthodox Indian philosophy has many rituals in practice, as a part of the spiritual training. Since their emphasis is on the aspect of *karma* as the way for redemption, it is believed that such practices have very obscure meanings. Penalizing the body by way of torture also accepted as a spiritual practice in the ancient times. Such penances that were performed by Sāṅkhyans and Ājīvikas were a subject of criticism. Ibid., v. 58.
29. Ibid., v. 59.
30. M. Hiriyanna, *Outlines of Indian Philosophy*, 1993, p. 307.
31. It asserts the self-validity of knowledge both in respect of its origin and ascertainment. If the knowledge originates from causes then the causes themselves explain the validity. The validity of knowledge is known when the knowledge itself is known; no additional means is required. (Ibid.) We must remember that in *Vigrahavyāvartinī* Nāgārjuna refuted this view categorically.
32. Ibid., p. 328.
33. Surendranatha Dasgupta, *History of Indian Philosophy*, p. 405.
34. A bath in the Gaṅgā is not just another bath in any normal river, it is considered as the most auspicious bath that has purification properties. This bath not only purifies the body but it could purify the soul too and eventually the soul acquires the power to attain liberation. The Brāhmanical systems and the Hindu community even today consider the bath in Gaṅgā is a step towards liberation. *Cittaviśuddhi-prakaraṇa*, v. 60.
35. Surendranath Dasgupta, *History of Indian Philosophy*, p. 371.
36. *Cittaviśuddhi-prakaraṇa*. v. 61.

37. The internal urge that directs man to acquire wealth is very natural since one is required to find food and living conditions for his survival; *kāma* (desire) is also internally driven notion, for procreation and satisfaction are drawn from the fulfilment of desire.
38. *Cittaviśuddhi-prakaraṇa*, v. 62.
39. The meaning of the word *dharma* here is "doctrine," "custom," and "justice." Fumimaro Watanabe, op. cit., p. 11.
40. *Cittaviśuddhi-prakaraṇa*, v. 63.
41. Ibid., v. 64.
42. Ibid., v. 65.
43. As quoted from *Kātyāyanāvadānasūtra*. David J. Kalupahana, *A History of Buddhist Philosophy*, p. 58.
44. *Cittaviśuddhi-prakaraṇa*. v. 66.
45. In the Yoga philosophy, this doubting of the psychophysical personality for self is considered *ahaṁkāra* or Ego. Here, the intelligence and mind (evolute of *prakṛti*) doubts the reflection of conciseness in mind as real, creating *ahaṁkāra*. However, by ceasing the existence of psychophysical personality opens the true nature of self (*Ātman*) with *buddhi* (intelligence one acquires the power to cease Ego and, thus, move to the liberation of self).
46. David J. Kalupahana, *A History of Buddhist Philosophy*, p. 59.
47. *Cittaviśuddhi-prakaraṇa*, v. 67.
48. Ibid., v. 68.
49. Delimited here means "assigned by boundaries."
50. H.V. Guenther, *The Dawn of Tantra*, p. 27.
51. *Cittaviśuddhi-prakaraṇa*, v. 69.
52. S.B. Dasgupta, op. cit., p. 40.
53. H.V. Guenther. *The Dawn of Tantra*, p. 55.
54. *Cittaviśudhi-prakaraṇa*, v. 70.
55. *Graha*, the planetary positions that decide human fate. *Rāśi* is considered in the traditional Indian astrology that a person's like is pre-decided and that can be discerned by investigating the planetary positions. This, according to Āryadeva, is a human innovation and does not hold any value. Ibid., vv. 71, 72.
56. Ibid., v. 73.
57. Ibid., v. 74.
58. Gem here means a pure and untarnished hard substance, or, in other words, something, which has unassailable purity and has the strength to remain so.
59. *Cittaviśuddhi-prakaraṇa*, v. 75.
60. Ibid., v. 76.
61. Ibid., vv. 77, 78.
62. Buddhist philosophy has a very definite view as far as the nature of gods is concerned. God for them is a friend and supporters in their spiritual journey are concerned. The God helps the aspirant to redeem himself from the web of *vikalpas* (alternatives).
63. *Cittaviśuddhi-prakaraṇa*, v. 79.

64. David J. Kalupahana, *A History of Buddhist Philosophy*, p. 58.
65. *Cittaviśuddhi-prakaraṇa*, v. 80.
66. Ibid., v. 81.
67. In the Vedic tradition, it is believed that only Brāhmans are allowed for spiritual practices, such that they are the only people who could perform *karma* according to the injunctions of the Vedas.
68. *Cittaviśuddhi-prakaraṇa*, v. 82.
69. David. J Kalupahana, *A History of Buddhist Philosophy*, p. 79.
70. This is a common question asked to the Advaita School of Indian Philosophy. What will happen to the world of *jīvanmukta* (one who realizes the Brahman in this life)? The answer is different here that the *jīvanmukta* remains as human being in the world of experience that the *prārabdha karma* remains with him. Though there are striking differences these two schools of Indian philosophy, yet holds many similarities.
71. *Cittaviśuddhi-prakaraṇa*, vv. 82-85.
72. Mostly some of the Brāhmanical schools promote restriction for the attainment of liberation. With the exception of the Advaita Vedānta most of the Vedānta schools do not accept *jīvanmukta*. Some Pūrvamīmāṁsaka schools even go on to say that liberation is attainable only for people who were born in certain creeds and that too only after death of the body. S. Radhakrishnan, *Hindu View of Life*, 1927, ch. 4.
73. M. Hiriyanna, op. cit., p. 299.
74. Ibid., p. 90.
75. *Cittaviśuddhi-prakaraṇa*, v. 86.
76. Ibid., v. 87.
77. The importance mental reflections of human activities are considered an important spiritual accomplishment for a Yogi. It would lead him to take right decision on right deeds. Buddha's discourses to Rāhula is clarifying this point. David J. Kalupahana, *A History of Buddhism*, p. 108.
78. *Cittaviśuddhi-prakaraṇa*, vv. 88-90.
79. Sūryakāntamaṇi is a precious gem, which can produce fire when it is associated with sunlight. The gem might be very important since fire-making was a daunting task in ancient world.
80. *Cittaviśuddhi-prakaraṇa*, vv. 91-92.
81. There can be questions on the propriety of this example, such as the *prajñā* is an outside entity or what shines in the mind is not *prajñā*, etc.? However, one must see this example stands out from the text; it works well with the logic of argumentation propounded by Āryadeva.
82. H.V. Guenther, *The Dawn of Tantra*, p. 68.
83. The word meaning of *karuṇā* is "compassion." But, for this context, we should understand *karuṇā* is not just compassion in the moral sense, it should have deeper philosophical meaning based on Buddhist philosophy.
84. *Cittaviśuddhi-prakaraṇa*, v. 93.
85. As has been directly quoted from *Jñānasiddhi*. The *Jñānasiddhi* is, in the opinion of Dasgupta supposes to give a very clear and rational explanation

to many of the practices of Buddhist Tāntrics. S.B. Dasgupta, op. cit., p. 39.

86. The Bodhisattva who do spiritual practices never aspires for self-liberation, but he strives for the liberation of the whole world. Doing service to the society may be a very common thing in the modern world, but such an activity even from a Yogi, in the ancient India would have been seen as an insane activity. A yogi normally strives for his own liberation. Charity of this kind may not have an accepted practice in the ancient world. Charity was considered as the duty of the rulers and kings.
87. *Cittaviśuddhi-prakaraṇa*, v. 94.
88. Ibid., v. 95.
89. Ibid., v. 96.
90. Ibid., v. 97.
91. Ibid., v. 98.
92. Ibid., v. 99.
93. S.B. Dasgupta, op. cit., p. 1.
94. H.V. Guenther, *The Dawn of Tantra*, p. 63.
95. *Cittaviśuddhi-prakaraṇa*, v. 100.
96. Ibid., v. 101.
97. See David J. Kalupahana, *A History of Buddhist Philosophy*, p. 79.
98. The knowledge of the actual process that of the intercourse of male sperm with female ovum may not have known at the time of Āryadeva, may be that is the reason why it has been said so here. But Āryadeva acquired this knowledge later. Even today there are many researchers working in this most important area of biological knowledge.
99. In the Pūrvamīmāṁsā tradition, it has been contented that only a Brahman is allowed to practice *saṁnyāsa* and not the other people e.g., *Caṇḍāla* (S. Radhakrishnan, *History of Indian Philosophy*, ch. 3).
100. *Cittaviśuddhi-prakaraṇa*, v. 102.
101. Surendranath Dasgupta, *History of Indian Philosophy*, p. 94.
102. In the perceivable universe, all things that appear before us could be explained on the basis of *pañcabhūtas*. The physical body is constituted of the five elements and the consciousness. David J. Kalupahana, *A History of Buddhist Philosophy*, p. 73.
103. *Cittaviśuddhi-prakaraṇa*, v. 103.
104. Ibid., v. 104.
105. *Vajrasattva* is the mental stage of a Yogi who acquired the knowledge of *dharmadhātu* and nature and play of *vikalpas*. It is the personality of a Bodhisattva.
106. *Cittaviśuddhi-prakaraṇa*, v. 105.
107. H.V. Guenther, *The Tāntric View of Life*, p. 30.
108. Ibid., p. 31.
109. S.B. Dasgupta, op. cit., p. 64.
110. H.V. Guenther, *TheTāntric View of Life*, p. 32.

111. The meaning of personal God here should be that the spiritual entity that helps one to realize a particular spiritual journey. It should not be seen as the supreme spiritual reality that controls the universe. Such a God is not relevant here.
112. *Citt..viśuddhi-prakaraṇa*, vv. 106-7.
113. Ibid., v. 108.
114. Ibid., v. 109.
115. Ibid., v. 110.
116. It is considered that desire forms after dispositions and feelings of the human personality (the *pañcaskandhas*) works together. The removal of disposition is, according to David J. Kalupahana (*History of the Buddhist Philosophy*, p. 73), an epistemological suicide, one needs to appease dispositions not complete destruction.
117. *Cittaviśuddhi-prakaraṇa*, v. 111.
118. In the perspective of Sāṅkhya, the liberation comes after a steady spiritual practice and only after the destruction of the notion of *Prakṛti* one could attain liberation. The realization of the *Puruṣa* is simultaneously removes the influence of *Prakṛti* on the self, and, thus, the self attains its pristine nature
119. *Cittaviśuddhi-prakaraṇa*, v. 112.
120. Ibid., v. 113.
121. Ibid., v. 114.
122. The dispositions can function in an extreme way and create an egoistic tendency when it works together with ignorance. The ignorance can determine the way of human disposition functions, either creating the belief in permanent existence or denying the value of the human personality altogether.
123. The Sāṅkhya-Yoga system has a elaborate methodology for achieving the spiritual perfection after removing the notion of Ego (*ahaṁkāra*).
124. *Cittaviśuddhi-prakaraṇa*, vv. 115, 117.
125. The meaning is "thought of enlightenment." The mental attitude that aspires to Buddhahood. *Buddhist Hybrid Sanskrit Grammar and Dictionary*, p. 402.
126. *Cittaviśuddhi-prakaraṇa*, v. 116.
127. The term-wise person is used in most of the philosophical literature of the Indian tradition to show the exclusivity of enlightened persons, irrespective of their religio-philosophical affiliations. In the ancient literature of *Thirukkural* of Thiruvaḻḻuvar (Tamil), the term is often used as *Santhorkal* (*Thirukkuraḷ*, ed. and trans. Rev.W.H. Drew & Rev. Jhon Lazarus, reprint, 1989).
128. *Cittaviśuddhi-prakaraṇa*, v. 118.
129. Ibid., v. 119.
130. H.V. Guenther, *The Dawn of Tantra*, p. 66.
131. *Cittaviśuddhi-prakaraṇa*, v. 120.
132. The three precious gems for a Buddhist are the Buddham, Saṅgham, and Dhammam.

133. *Guru* in Tāntric tradition is equal to the gods or one's own personal God. *Guru*'s assistance is very necessary for the student until he finishes his training.
134. *Cittaviśuddhi-prakaraṇa*, v. 123.
135. Ibid., v. 121.
136. David J. Kalupahana, *A History of Buddhist Philosophy*, p. 72.
137. Ibid., v. 124.
138. The practice of *prāṇāyāma* in Yoga is exactly meant for this purpose, in the system of *Patañjali Yogasūtras*, the practice of *prāṇāyāma* comes in the fourth stage of the practice. (*Patañjali Yogasūtras*, ed. Swami Prabhananda, v. 29, p. 88.) In the case of Buddhist Yoga practices, it is the second stage; it is the part of the *samādhi* Ānāpānasatisuttas, ed. Ven. U. Vimalaraśmi, 1997, p. 15.
139. *Cittaviśuddhi-prakaraṇa*, v. 125.
140. Ibid., v. 126.
141. Ibid., v. 127.
142. *Cambridge Dictionary of Philosophy*, p. 194.
143. *Cittaviśuddhi-prakaraṇa*, v. 128.
144. The importance of selecting a *guru* is considered as the most important accomplishment in one's spiritual journey. The student must have enough respect for the *guru*, and the *guru* in turn should be concerned about the well-being of the student. Sir John Woodroff, *The Principles of Tantra*, Part II, 1990, p. 203.
145. *Cittaviśuddhi-prakaraṇa*, vv. 129-30.
146. Ibid., 131.
147. Ibid., 132.
148. In the case of *vipāśana* meditation, it is the second stage, *śīla* and *samādhi*. In the case of *Yogasūtra*, it is the last stage of the *aṣṭāṅga* yoga, but Patañjali says it is the first stage of one's journey in to the Kaivalya.
149. *Cittaviśuddhi-prakaraṇa*, v. 133.
150. Ibid., v. 134.

Chapter Five

Cittaviśuddhi—A Practical Method for Philosophical Realization

5.1 The Object of Experience

As discussed earlier, the main concern of early Mādhyamika philosophy is to analyze the objective phenomenal world of things that is a part of our day-to-day experience.[1] As a philosophical position, it neither accepts an ultimate object as the substratum of the apparent world or a transcended subjectivity that is discerned from the apparent objective reality; similarly, it does not reject the existence of object completely, or positions objectivity in co-existence with subjectivity. The attempt of the Mādhyamikas here, is not to deal with the purely objective phenomena which are always defined in relation to human experience.[2] We need to understand the Buddhist view on the ontology of the objective phenomenal world which is based on a complete dialectical understanding of the true nature of the conceived object and the mind.

The mind, according to the Buddha's analysis, is the faculty that accounts for the reflection or memory. In this sense, the mind is capable of sharing the objects conceived by the five sense faculties. Originally, the object of mind is referred to as phenomenon (*dharma*), which means idea or concept.[3] In short, the mind is considered as the faculty which reflects the objects perceived through the sense faculties. Mind is also the seat of ignorance because it receives new knowledge from the objects perceived but the lack of sufficient information for adequate knowledge could lead it to a very confusing situation. The mind seeks adequate knowledge to satiate its urge to know more. Until arriving at the correct knowledge the mind shows a tendency to cling to and crave for what is perceived through the sense faculties. The mind, all the time, is craving to attain the perfect or adamantine knowledge (*vajrajñāna*). When the mind identifies the right knowledge, the problem of ignorance, originating out of the seeking nature of mind would come to an end. The problem of conceptualization does not end here. The dispositional tendency of the mind is another important aspect that plays a significant role.

Because of the presence of ignorance and extreme dispositional tendencies, the unenlightened person develops cravings for pleasurable objects and ideas. The mind configures these things into real entities developing strong attachment.[4] But the real nature of the cognized phenomena is dependent on causes and conditions, just as a lamp depends on various causes and situations.[5] In other words, the nature of the mind is such that it gestalts the dependently-arisen and momentarily-ceasing nature of the world of things to be real and permanent causing sufferings with cascading effect. Actually, the real problem of suffering is created out of the object conceived and that is the cause for confusion. According to Kalupahana.

> The object cognized is not as problematic as the objects conceived because the cognized is generally confined to the six senses, even though the sixth sense of the mind is responsible for the conceptualizations. If the mind were to restrict itself to the ideas (*dharma*) formed on the basis of the information provided by the five senses, the object cognized would pose no problem.[6]

The mind even interacts with the five senses in the process of perception, so the cognized too can create problems. The earlier discussions clearly indicate the need for the elimination of the mind's attachment to the phenomena, or cleansing of the mind from all conceptualizations. This is effectively possible only if one understands both the aspects—the internal functioning of mind and the ontology of the objects perceived.

5.1.1 *The Truth-value of the Cognised Objects*

To see the real nature of the phenomena, one must look into the ontology of the objects perceived to see whether they are free from contradictions; or whether they have independent existence *per se*, or whether they are dependent on other phenomena on causal or non-causal relations. In order to substantiate the insubstantial nature of the conceptualizations, Āryadeva introduced the fourfold method of negation, in order to confute the realists' view that negation of the existent is the acceptance of non-existence or nihilism. He refused to accept the application of apagogic proof,[7] as the basis for understanding the phenomenal world and introduced fourfold method of negation. The absolute truth-value of cognized things is not acceptable to the Mādhyamikas because they are not independent entities to claim absolute truth-value.

> A thing cannot at all be a union without being an effect. That union which exists in the form of an effect is not union according to Sages.[8]

The existence of a lamp is a union of various causes and conditions, but when the conditions are removed, the lamp ceases to exist. In the same manner, the effect of the lamp is the union of various adjuncts and their union is discernable only though the effect; in that sense, one cannot say that it is a union. The effect of the perception of snake in the place of rope is a good example where the union of various adjuncts gives the effect of a non-existent snake. In case of snake the union of adjuncts like the rope in the process perception cannot be substantiated; similarly, when one perceives the rope, the union of the adjuncts like fibre cannot be substantiated. From this process of understanding the truth-value of the perception of objects of the world, we come to a conclusion that the object perceived cannot be substantiated in any manner.

The wrongly cognized snake implies the problem in ascertaining the truth-value of the perceived object. To address this problem Āryadeva introduces four possible alternatives "P;" "not P;" both "P," and "not P;" and neither "P" nor "not P."[9] The mind, because of its innate nature of clinging and ceasing to what is apprehended as real, ascribes truth-value to the cognized phenomenal proposition "P." On verification, one could understand the insubstantial and dependent nature of "P," thus introducing criticism on the truth validity. Rejecting the truth-value of "P" is not the acceptance of "not P," but the rejection of all premises that prove the existence of a valid thesis. Āryadeva clearly expressed this in the *Catuḥśataka* that, when we observe a thing closely, its intrinsic nature is found to be not existing the thing as one and as plural doesn't exist.[10] The problem of apagogic proof is rejected by the Mādhyamikas on which the normal mind functions, where the negation of something implies the acceptance of the opposing view. By introducing the fourfold method of negation, Mādhyamikas introduced a new method to analyze the phenomenal world.

5.2 Phenomena and the Psychophysical Personality

The explanation given for mind in the canonical texts of Buddhism is that it is pure in the beginning without any intrinsic nature (*svabhāva*);

it is unoriginated and pure like a gem unlike the objective world of things; moreover, the mind reflects the objects perceived by it as the way it appears before it, without configuring it in any manner.

The conflicting manifestations of the elements create confusion in the mind, which postulates the transmigration of the psychophysical personality. Buddha says that after examining the five constituents (*skandhas*) of the human person, the transmigrating personality is not discoverable.[11] If the transmigration of the psychophysical personality is not identifiable, then discerning the existence of a permanent self (*Ātman*) pertaining to time (*kāla*) also is impossible.[12] Thus, if one can remove the dichotomies created by the phenomena then he can be free from the confusion created by the world of things. The Buddha says, "Monks, I do not conflict with the world; the world conflicts with me."[13] Incidentally, the meaning of this quote is very important with regard the discussions of the *Cittaviśuddhi-prakaraṇa*, in order that after the realization of the *Cittaviśuddhi*, with the help of his spiritual practices, a Yogi is able to see the world in its true manifestations, and his cognition about them will not create any confusion. For the Yogi, the confusion created by the world does not trouble, because his clear vision and sound judgement about the world makes it clear and certain to him.

Early Mādhyamikas accept the notion of selfhood at the mundane level. According to Nāgārjuna in *Mūlamādhyamikakārikā.*

> Subjectivity, the sense of unity and freedom intrinsic to selfhood, is the fulcrum on which personal life rests; it is an error to ignore this and try to explain away selfhood as an illusion and the person as a collocation of essentially separate elements.[14]

Mādhyamikas' view of rejection of the self should not be seen as an attempt to reject the existence of the human personality completely, but it only rejects the existence of an ultimate transcended eternal entity as the substratum of the apparent world. Accepting personality at the mundane experiential level is required for understanding the nature of the phenomenal world, as it is nonsensical to refuse the existence of personality, which is the fundamental basis for all our philosophical enquiries. In short, the Mādhyamikas criticize the notion of seeing the psychophysical personality as an eternally existing entity, or an extreme theorization of subjectivity.

5.2.1 *The Importance of Dispositions*

One of the criticisms against the Buddhists is that they purposely introduced the concept of aggregates to negate the existence of self, and it serves as a negative function; but a careful observation of this concept reveals that the aggregates are positive and explain the nature of empirical self.[15] Five aggregates are the only discernible entities that appear on analysis of the psychophysical personality, so the notion of an eternal self is merely an insubstantial illusion.

The feeling supports the emotive aspect of human personality, which is of two types, the pleasant and unpleasant. The perception is related to all other constituents of the human personality; each perception is a mixture of memories, concepts, dispositions, and material elements, and it is impossible to have pure precept. The disposition, forms the perspectives in a person, and it influences all other aggregates. It is the most important aspect of a personality and its surroundings. Consciousness explains the continuity of a person, individualized by dispositions; it is depending on the other aggregates especially form (*rūpa*). Consciousness according to the Buddhists is nothing more than the act of being conscious, it never forms a substratum.[16] But the dispositions formulate the way one views the world; it cogently determines the individualistic aspect of the human personality that an individual is not a part of an eternally existing universal soul. Specifically, the concept of dispositions explains the influence of *karma* on the individual and the unique particular nature of individuality. If an individual is under the influence of ignorance and the resultant craving and desires, he has to focus his spiritual training to appease the dispositions. According to Kalupahana,

> The elimination of dispositions is epistemological suicide. Dispositions determine our perspectives. Without such perspectives, we are unable to deal with the sensible world in any meaningful or fruitful manner. The Buddha realized that subdued dispositions are enlightened perspectives—hence his characterization of freedom (Nibbana) as the appeasement of dispositions.[17]

Āryadeva in the *Cittaviśuddhi-prakaraṇa* has highlighted this point by saying that a Yogi, after attaining the *Bodhicitta* is allowed to enjoy the objects of desire without getting attached to those objects.[18] When one gets control on the dispositional tendencies of the mind, his craving and desires to the objects of the world ceases. In that case the enjoyment of object of the world is just a pastime or making the consciousness to be aware of its existence. He never gets confused with the objects of the world. In explaining the process of perceptual experience, David Kalupahana writes:

> As long as a psychophysical personality exists and as long as its sense faculties are functioning, there will be contact or familiarity with the world and feeling or emotive response to that world. These are inevitable. However, because of the presence of ignorance and, therefore, of extreme dispositional tendencies, the unenlightened person can generate craving—or its opposite—for the object so experienced.[19]

The conceived phenomenon is certainly influenced by the ordinary human being's dispositional tendencies; consequently, it influences the dichotomous thoughts. The thoughts, thus, produced should be restructured by understanding the insubstantial nature of the phenomenon, through dialectical means with the help of *prajñā*, and then one should identify suitable means (*upāyas*), spiritual techniques, to change the dispositional tendencies of the psychophysical personality, gripped by the influence of ignorance. The path recommended by Āryadeva for attaining *Bodhicitta* (*nirvāṇa*), is to combine wisdom (*prajñā*) with suitable means (*upāya*). The process of removing ignorance and appeasing the dispositional tendencies through *prajñā* and *upāya*, is called *Cittaviśuddhi*.

5.3 The Dialectical Restructuring of Phenomena—Āryadeva's View

The Mādhyamikas' problem is not about accepting the conditioned personality, but considering the conditioned as separate from unconditioned, or conditioned as a mere illusion. This kind of segregation would lead to an enhancement of the clinging and ceasing aspect of the mind.[20] The true nature of mind is not clearly explained here, but explains the nature of mind formulated based on the thought-process. Āryadeva says in the *Cittaviśuddhi-prakaraṇa* that the mind by its very nature is like a gem, devoid of any taint in the form of thought process. It is pure, beginningless, without any taint, and has no self-nature (*svabhāva*).[21] Being devoid of any self-nature, the mind imbibes the nature of the objects conceived (phenomena), like a pure crystal imbibes the colour of the object placed beside it.[22] It is not just the world of objects alone that creates problems in the mind, but the conception of them as concepts and ideas is the main cause of confusion because the mind has the innate nature to cease to what has been apprehended and gestalt them as real and permanent entities.

According to the gestalt psychologists, the human experience is of organized wholes (gestalten) and not of collection of elements.[23] The formulation of concepts and ideas can be interpreted as the mind's innate urge to know more and in that process it latches on to any phenomena appears before it. In the Buddhist context, it can be explained as that when one attains perfect vision (*vajrajñāna*) his mind will not latch on to any knowledge comes its way but understands that every knowledge is subservient to this superior knowledge.

We may review the nature of conceived objects; the experience of the conceived object is not based on the constituent parts but on the whole object gestalt by the mind based on its dispositional tendencies. The gestalten of the mind suddenly falls into the process of associating (confusing) unreal, insubstantial, and dependent entities with real, substantial, and independent entities, and it is the cause for perpetual suffering in the world of existence. On the other hand, if the mind views the details of the elements of gestalten then, it will never fall into trap of confusion and suffering.

Buddhist philosophy opines that *tṛṣṇā* is the root of clinging and seizing and that is the origin of *kleśa*, the painful state of emotional conflict, which comes from the failure to fulfil the *tṛṣṇā* and the disparity between the expected and the realized. Ignorance, again functioning through *tṛṣṇā,* gives rise to *dṛṣṭi* (theories), which is to seize the specific concepts and conceptual systems that embody themselves as absolute and limitless.[24] The mind, having the habit of conceptualizing ideas conceived through the sense faculties falls further into the trap of confusion arising due to ignorance; and the person is drawn completely into the grab of illusory existence. The redemption involves two activities; the first one removes ignorance by using knowledge (*prajñā*); secondly, by understanding the true nature of mind and the influence of the world of phenomena on the mind, one finds suitable means (*upāya*). The first aspect involves removal of the ignorance using knowledge, while the second involves changing the mental faculties that generate cravings and clinging.

Tāntric Buddhism says that the *prajñā* and *upāya* form the dual principles of Tantra, and one attains spiritual maturity by commingling these two entities, where the *prajñā* shows the way and the *upāya* articulates it properly. Probably, the early Mādhyamikas pioneered the concept of associating intellectual knowledge perfectly with the actual functioning of the phenomenal world for attaining liberation. Therefore, they highlighted the importance of dialectical reconstruction of the objectively experienced phenomena or ideas as the purport of philosophical attainments.

After observing keenly the experienced world, Āryadeva introduces the spiritual practices in the text that is meant to redeem a practitioner from the illusory manifestations about the things in the phenomenal world of appearance; the practices never envisage seclusion of the individual from the world of objects, but equip him to develop harmonious interaction with them. Violence, death, fear, or the sufferings of the worst kind never affect a Yogi who has attained spiritual maturity. On the contrary, as a result of his spiritual practices, he can suggest suitable means (*upāyas*) to people who are under the influence of such sufferings.[25] The purity of the mind and the activity of the phenomenon can be compared to the illustration of a monk and the old man. According to Āryadeva:

> If the old man is asked by the monk to run fast and, as a result, if he falls down and injures himself or tortures himself and dies, the monk who has asked him to run would not be responsible.[26]

When the monk suggested the old man to run fast, he did with a good intention of, maybe, saving the old man from a disaster, but in the process of running if the man get into more problems or confronts a disaster, the monk is not responsible for homicide. Here, the emphasis is given for the purity of mind, the earnestness of purpose is important than the result of that action.

In fact the mind is endowed with purity, yet it is of the tendency to form concepts and views, which cause confusions and sufferings in the existent life; but if the mind is pure then it is remaining unaffected by such concepts and views that confuse.[27] Like a crystal, the mind imbibes the colour and nature of the object placed before it, yet unlike the crystal, the mind gestalts the perceived object into ideas and concepts (phenomenon). There are *sūtras* in the *Vinayapiṭaka* which say that if a person is associated with those phenomena and inflicts pain upon himself, then such a person accrues sin.[28] Furthermore, the crystal regains its purity when the object is removed, but the mind creates a world of its own even if the conceptions are proven wrong. Thus, it is not the conceived phenomena that are the problem for the sufferings, but the association with them. The conceived phenomena are susceptible to errors due to various reasons, and, thus, the truth-value of the objects conceived does not have any substantiation value. Āryadeva's advice is that one needs to review the phenomena with a cleansed mind with the certainty and precision of a physician who cures poisoning with help of the same poison.[29] By analyzing the insubstantial nature of the phenomena, one can remove the corruptive influences that the world of phenomena could formulate on a personality. It is not the understanding of the insubstantial nature of the phenomena, but the cleansed mind devoid of all dichotomous conceptualization that is the significant aspect of one's spiritual attainment.

5.3.1 *Dialectical Analysis of Phenomena—Philosophical Methodology of Early Mādhyamikas*

Unlike many philosophical systems of the world, the Mādhyamikas formulated their philosophical positions though dialectics, with the analysis of the conceived and cognized phenomena.

> The objects known or experienced often appear in a list of three and four (1) the seen (*diṭṭha*), (2) the heard (*suta*), (3) the conceived (*muta*), and (4) the cognized (*viññata*).[30]

The first two, the seen and the heard, act together with the other three sense faculties, the nose, tongue, and body; the seen and heard are susceptible to error, but subject to correction by physical verification. The conceived phenomena are coloured by the nature of the psycho-physical personality, as the mind reflects the phenomena and shares this cognized knowledge with other sense faculties, which again forms a chain. If it were to restrict itself to the phenomena (*dharma*) formed on the basis of the information provided by the five senses, the object cognized would pose no problems.[31] The reasoning through phenomenal analysis and establishing its authenticity, is extremely necessary for the mind to cognize the real nature of the objective world. The dialectics of Mādhyamika, discussing the nature of phenomena in which some appear as real and some unreal, tries to point out the insubstantial nature of each phenomenon to establish its truth-value. The *Vigrahavyāvartinī* explains that the Mādhyamika dialectics not just negate the intrinsic nature of the phenomena, but explains with the help of the same logical method of the substantialists (the *svabhāvavādins*) to clarify how difficult it is to accept the intrinsic nature (*svabhāva*) of things. The *svabhāva* of things, in essence, should be explaining the truth-value of things. But the *svabhāva* of things is apparent only, not real, because the mind configures the conceived phenomena into a reality; similar to the case of the crystal and the object placed before it, the crystal gives the appearance of the colour of the object near it. The nature of spiritual practice suggested is to separate not only the crystal and the object placed near it, but also the impression the object had on the mind, thereby removing the apparent influence of the conceived object.

Āryadeva agrees with the logical method introduced by Nāgārjuna in the *Vigrahavyāvartinī* that is based on the understanding of the insubstantial nature of the phenomena by analyzing it with dialectical arguments. He explains this aspect further in the *Cittaviśuddhi-prakaraṇa*; here, instead of dialectical arguments, he uses meditative methods and practices through which the conceptualization process and the insubstantial nature of phenomena are discerned fully. Like the snake poisoning is cured using poison,[32] the influence of phenomena (ideas) on the mind can be removed using the same phenomena (ideas). This can also be compared to the case of washer-man using dirt to clean the soiled cloths.[33] In the same way, the influence of anger, a basic instinct, on the mind can be removed by understanding the dispositions of the mind that creates anger. The removal is not the destruction of the innate instinct of anger, but the appeasing of the dispositions that generate anger (in the destructive mode). During the training period the *guru* suggests suitable methods (such as practising martial art, etc.) to control such instincts. Eventually, after becoming a Bodhisattva, the Yogi suggests suitable means to the uninitiated ones suitable means to practise to control the influence of such instincts on his personality.

The substantiality of the world of phenomena is compared to that of a mirage or it is like a city of illusions (*gandharvanagara*). The illusion of the mirage arises in the mind of a person who goes in the desert wishing to find water, it instigates him to find a solution to quench his thirst, and ultimately the apparent mirage ceases to be an oasis with water.[34] The strong desire (*tṛṣṇā*) in him to quench thirst manifests in the appearance of a mirage as a real oasis. On closer examination, the existence of the oasis is dithered. There are indeterminable numbers of phenomena that are apparent before the mind, but only those phenomena that are favourable to the mind controlled by craving and desires would be perceived by the mind and it tries hard to reflect them as real. The imaginative nature of mind configures the city of illusion (*gandharvanagara*), which is evidently unreal; similarly, the conceived phenomena coloured by imaginations of varying degrees create a notion of a real and eternal world.

In the *Vigrahavyāvartinī*, Nāgārjuna questions the truth-value of phenomena by citing the inconsistencies in accepting various epistemic processes for valid knowledge.

> If I apprehend something with the help of perception etc, then I would either affirm or deny. (But) since that thing does not exist, I am not to blame. If such and such objects are established for you through the *pramāṇas*, tell me how those *pramāṇas* are established for you.[35]

When the validity of perception is not established beyond doubt, how is it possible to substantiate the validity of the phenomena that are apprehended through them? Thus, Nāgārjuna contends that the intrinsic nature of all phenomena cannot be established perfectly and that the *śūnyatā* of the things is proven without doubt. It is said that

> if that perception were by its own nature, it would not be dependently originated. That perception, however, which comes into existence dependently, is *śūnyatā* indeed.[36]

If perception is *śūnya* then the perceived objects should also be *śūnya* and that we cannot attribute any permanence to them. The position of Mādhyamika is extremely difficult to explain, where a definition is required. We can say Mādhyamikas accept perception (*pratyakṣa*), inference (*anumāna*), comparison (*upamāna*), and testimony (*śabda*),[37] because using all the available means to understand thoroughly the apparent phenomena, these *pramāṇas* are the only dependent source. Whereas looking critically at the very validity of these *pramāṇas,* it is very evident that they themselves are not substantial. The question *Mādhyamikas* ask realists is how inherently insubstantial *pramāṇas* can reveal the real truth about the nature of phenomena? The self-nature of *pramāṇas* is void since it cannot be substantiated individually or collectively. Mādhyamikas' void is different from the Nihilistic void. Here, it is used as a tool to analyze the nature of everything that appears in the world of things, while the Nihilists' notion of void is a philosophical position against the realists.

5.3.2 *Meaning of Śūnyatā—Some New Perspectives*

The subtle difference between a positive statement and a negative statement is that in the positive statement we exclude things other than what have been stated. When we say "cat" we exclude all (animals) except cat; while, in case of negative statements we include more (things), viz., when we say "not this not that" the statement includes more things. When the statement about a truth is made, it is implied that the untruth, middle truth, etc. are discarded.[38] Therefore, in affirming something as existent, we are also falling into the same trap. Precisely at this point, the idea of *śūnyatā* as openness enters. The concept of *śūnyatā* includes everything in contrast with the truth statements, which exclude everything except what is being stated. *Śūnyatā* is a positive term in a negative form.[39] Mādhyamikas are successful in solving almost all philosophical problems using the conception of *śūnyatā;* on the other hand, the realists have to use too many theories and constants, in explaining the nature of life in the world.[40] As we know, the reasons for conflicts in theories are the constants. A constant is true to certain causes and conditions, but it may not be true in another condition or situation. The problem of too many constants and theories are chronic to philosophy. Mādhyamikas never exclude any phenomena that appear as a part of our experience, nor are they adverse to seek help from constants to understand the nature of the world. In short, the Mādhyamika's *śūnyatā* is one of the most effective epistemological tools to understand the objective world.

Mādhyamikas criticize the theories formulated on the basis of Abhidharma categories and also the theoretical positions of Sāṅkhyans and Vaiśeṣikas, to explain the phenomenal world. About the Abhidharma, the Hīnayāna schools of Buddhism analyze the psycho-physical personality into three broad categories: the *skandha*, the *dhātu*, and the *āyatana*. Based on these categories, they analyze the phenomenal existence and process (*saṁskṛta*), and also analyze the individual into number of states of psychological and physical elements.[41] The purpose of such categorization is meant to show that apart from these categories, there is no eternal *Ātman*. The collocation of *skandha* and *āyatana* may be termed the subjective, since the interest is mainly directed to sentient experience to the individual and his components. An objective classification irrespective of these moulds of thought came to be formulated in the later stages. The number of the subclasses of the objective phenomena varies from time to time.[42] This view, according to early Mādhyamikas, is a diversion from the original teachings of Buddhism, and also restricting human perspective about the phenomenal world. In fact, in the view of Āryadeva, the cleansed *citta* enables one to assail the notion of an eternally existing *Ātman* and the Abhidharma categories. It is the main theme of discussion in the *Cittaviśuddhi-prakaraṇa*.

As we have discussed, if the mind is able to conceive the real nature of the objective world, then according to the text, the mind is pure from the beginning, non-originated, not having any nature of its own, not having any stain whatsoever; and by perceiving such an entity as the world one is neither bound nor liberated.[43] When the illusory adjuncts of the phenomena are removed, and the mind attains purity through spiritual practices, there would not be any *vikalpas* to confuse the mind. Naturally, the mind realizes the real nature of elements that constitute the objective world without any confusion, the *dharmadhātu* realized to free the mind from confusion, and the *Bodhicitta* blossomed in the mind to steady it.

5.4 Dharmadhātu—The Elemental Composition of the Cognized Objects

The elements (*dhātus*) according to Buddhist canonical texts are six: *pṛthvīdhātu*, *āpodhātu*, *tejodhātu*, *vāyodhātu*, *ākāsadhātu*, and *viññāna-dhātu*.[44] These six elements are further classified by the Abhidharma schools into eighteen elements. These components are considered the reason for the things of existence. The *Puruṣa-pudgala* (human being) is made of six basic components, the physical and conscious aspect and analysable into these six elements. The phenomenal things (*saṁskṛta*) are composed of *dhātus*, which are irreducible. Two notions are involved in this conception: the first, fixing up of the number and nature of the components and second, the way in which these components are compounded to form things in the phenomenal sphere.[45] The conception of *dharmadhātu* is that the world of things including living beings is nothing but the combination of these components and there is no intrinsic value or any such permanently existing entity controlling them. On the whole, the *dhātus* are compounded in a definitive manner to form things, and these things can be created in the same manner on another occasion. We can explain the nature of the world with the help of these *dhātus*, in a satisfactory manner, but such explanation is not ultimate or independent. T.R.V. Murti says:

> We can also ask questions like the definitum is prior to the definition or not. If the definitum could exist without its specific property, then it is nondescript itself; and non descript entity is a non-entity; such a thing is not an object of experience.[46]

The idea is that we could discern material objects in relation to many aspects and adjuncts, and it could not be ascertained by analyzing any single component. The realm of *dharmadhātu* is more close to the concept of cognized objects,[47] but this is not a definitive position of the early Mādhyamikas, as they differ with the concepts of early Buddhism. We can view this concept in a different perspective to elaborate on the position of early Mādhyamikas.

Modern analytical science also faces a similar problem in understanding the nature of the analyzed objective world. The inability to determine the position and velocity of a subatomic particle in modern physics is a very interesting corollary to establishing the aspect of independent analysis of any single entity to assertion truth. Stephen Hawking cites the most important problem confronting modern physics:

> One can never be exactly sure of both the position and velocity of a particle; the more accurately one knows the one, the less accurately one can know the other. [48]

The predictability of the components of the material and way in which they are compounded cannot be predicted with absolute certainty; nevertheless, the world of objects offers a relative certainty and clarity. In actual experience, the world of things that are perceived as objects are not the collocations of the basic elements of things, but a superimposed entity like in the case of the snake seen on a rope. In the parlance of the gestalt psychologists, the whole is perceived instead of elements; here, the whole is influenced by the mental stages of cravings and desires. In other words, the inability to apprehend the real nature of phenomena can be explained that since the *skandha* and *āyatana*, etc. are not functioning properly, one perceives the objects of the world partially; but at the empirical level of actual error free perception, one could see the rope, not the snake. This form of perception can be interpreted as *dharmadhātu*.

The elements of existence can be discerned from the analysis of the objective reality, the rope, which is free from the superimposition of the illusion, the snake. Both the desert traveller visualizing the mirage like water, and the onlooker out of his craving (fear) visualizing the rope as snake, are under the influence of dispositions, strong feelings and the ignorance. Internal notions of the mind influence the objects experienced, and it might be possible to understand the possible real nature of the objects of perception by removing the ignorance. This illusion created by ignorance can be removed by knowledge (*vijñāna*), one of the aggregates (*skandhas*). Naturally, if a person attains spiritual maturity through spiritual practices, he always will be able to see the rope, the *dharmadhātu* of the phenomena, without the corruption of illusions. The *vajrajñāna*, originates after spiritual practice and acts as a shield to protect the mind from any conceptualization. He will never be attracted to the illusions superimposed in the objects, like a fried seed never germinates again.[49] The gestalten of the objects with illusions never deny the existence of the basic elements of existence, for one is able to understand the object as a combination of elements. According to the early Mādhyamikas, neither the illusory objects nor the ultimate elements of existence are substantial. One can discern only the rope; it is impossible to assess the truth-value of the snake or the subatomic particles of the rope.

The prevalent opinion about the nature of *dharmadhātu* is that it is in the form of a transcended entity with eternal existence grounded on pure consciousness; the *tathāgata*, the *bhūtakoṭi*, the *paramārtha*, the *animitta*, and the *dharmadhātu* denote the same transcended entity. This view is basically a Yogācāra view.[50] The real as the immanent as well as the transcendent *dharmadhātu* is a reference to the ultimate reality, *nirvāṇa*, the ultimate nature of all that is conditioned and contingent. In *dharmadhātu*, "dharma" stands for *nirvāṇa*. It stands also for *prajñā-pāramitā*, which is the ultimate reality, the same as *nirvāṇa*. *Dhātu* conveys the sense of the essential, intrinsic, inmost nature, the fundamental ultimate essence.[51]

This view is very difficult for Mādhyamikas to accept. If Mādhyamikas are to accept an ultimate reality at the trans-mundane level of existence, then it ceases to be the Mādhyamika philosophy of Nāgārjuna and Āryadeva. As Āryadeva has written in *Cittaviśuddhi-prakaraṇa*:

> The one who transcends the faculties of mind, such people there is no Saṁsāra or Nirvāṇa. The duality of Saṁsāra and Nirvāṇa are existing for those who are ignorant.[52]

Nirvāṇa is not a realization or an attainment at a different level, but it is the revelation when the ignorance and the afflictions thereof are removed from the mind, which is pure, beginningless and devoid of any intrinsic nature. The characterized (intrinsic) nature of the mind is due to its association with objects of the world; the duality of everything is removed when the phenomenalization process ceases. For the ignorant person, both *saṁsāra* and *nirvāṇa* are real, so that he tries hard to achieve the *nirvāṇa*; but to a Mahāyānist Yogi, it is not the achievement of *nirvāṇa*, he travelled from the world of phenomena (*saṁsāra*) to neither *saṁsāra* nor *nirvāṇa*.[53] The *dharmadhātu* can be interpreted as the essence of conceived objective phenomena without the *vikalpa* (dichotomous conceptualizations). This understanding helps one to know the unconditioned nature of the conditioned phenomena. Mādhyamikas use the unique dialectics to redeem the general conception that these elements of existence (*dhātus*) described in the canonical text are not substantial by nature, but they are named (earth, fire, etc.) merely for identification and conventional understanding. Mādhyamikas also are not in agreement of the concept of thing in themselves, for it is concerned only with the experienced objective world.[54]

5.4.1 *Āryadeva's View on Dharmadhātu and Dharma-nairātmya*

In the *Hastavālanāma-prakaraṇavṛtti*, Āryadeva opines that "Since something without parts cannot be imagined, the last part also is similar to inexistent."[55] Again, he says,

> Whoever with subtle mind knows that all the things are only dependent, that intelligent man easily throws out desire, etc., as (the man who knows that there is no snake but only a rope, throws out) the fear (produced) by the snake.[56]

Before dismantling the rope into parts, it is absolutely necessary for one to understand the nature of rope that it is substantial and at the same time insubstantial. On realization of the non-intrinsic nature of the basic elements of existence, the notion of rope also disappears like the snake.[57] Compared with the existent rope, the parts do not hold any intrinsic nature; the apparently existing rope is also dismantled into parts without any definable characteristics. The essence of rope is like the snake, erroneous and illusory. The concept of *Ātman* (essential nature) of the rope is not established; the concept of *nairātmya* (non-essential nature) of the rope is, thus, established.

The knowledge inferred through dialectical understanding is effective in interpreting the non-essential and insubstantial nature of the world of things, but to use this knowledge for the spiritual development requires proper situation for application. Integrating knowledge (*prajñā*) with right means (*upāya*) is the solution suggested in the *Cittaviśuddhi-prakaraṇa*. The yoking of *prajñā* and *upāya* is the means for acquiring *Cittaviśuddhi* and the blossoming of *Bodhicitta*, a stage of mind through which one could see the world of things properly without any misconceptions, as it is revealing the *dharma-dhātu* of all phenomena.

Turmeric powder, having the quality to change the colour of the substance it is added with, is similar to the yoking of *prajñā* and *upāya*. The *prajñā* is of the nature of the turmeric powder; the *upāyas* are similar to the substances added to the turmeric. Even though the means (*upāya*) provided by the phenomenal world exists irrespective of *prajñā*, it is the *prajñā* that transforms with the support of the suitable means transforms the phenomena (*dharma*) into the essence of phenomena (*dharmadhātu*).[58]

Irrespective of culture or tradition they belong to, philosophical schools all over the world accept, one way or another, the supremacy of knowledge and wisdom in discerning the world of phenomena, life, the moral principles, etc. They also agree that one should adopt right means for executing that knowledge. Mādhyamikas, introducing meditative practices based on the knowledge (*prajñā*) and the right means (*upāya*), might be the first philosophical school that developed an ethical system solely based on the development of the purity of *citta* or *Cittaviśuddhi*. In interpreting the world of phenomena, the Buddhist dialectician formulates his arguments cleverly that he desists from taking any position about the conflicting questions about the true nature of the existent world. Besides the Buddhist goal of spiritual enlightenment trainings are not meant to equip the mind to view this real nature of phenomena as permanence and certainty but of impermanence and uncertainty. To sum up this view: the mind should acquire the internal strength to understand the flux of the arising and ceasing nature of the phenomena. The speculative philosophers, who believe in the permanence of the entities of existence, postulate the results of the spiritual practices. For example the Mīmaṁsakas postulate the results of most of their karmic based spiritual practices. Āryadeva says, "In order to see a bracelet in one's hand one doesn't need a mirror [...]"[59] which means that one must have the spiritual strength to view the bracelet in the hand without the help of another theory or concept, because it is directly perceivable, immediate, and all the sense faculties are active in cognizing the object of bracelet. In fact, this is contrary to the view of the Mīmāṁsakas who try to explain the nature of bracelet with the help of textual knowledge (the Vedas) and other forms of knowledge that the bracelet reflects the existence of a different entity.

The conceived objects of the world at the normal level of apprehension are tarnished by subjective interpretations; either erroneous like the snake in the rope or the rope, both are insubstantial ultimately. Āryadeva, in order to transcend the illusory nature of the phenomena, suggests the acquirement of knowledge from, texts, learned people, etc. In the opinion of Āryadeva, "one has to learn about *prajñā* by churning the *Āgamas* and *Adhigamas*."[60] Knowledge acquired through texts and the knowledge acquired through spiritual practices is extremely important. Of course for the early Mādhyamikas, combining the knowledge with suitable means (*upāyas*) drawn from the actual functioning of life is the most important aspect. And, thus, the *upāya* forms an important aspect in Mahāyāna spiritual tradition, for it necessitated the introduction of Mahāyāna into Tantrism. An apt definition for *upāya* is difficult to discern. The possible explanation can be drawn from the whole continuum of the phenomenal world. The expanse of *upāya* ranges from the experiential world as predictable, understandable, and certain for the apparent phenomena; to the conception of the experiential world which does not have certainty, predictability, and understandability, by manifesting itself as unpredictable uncertain and non-understandable; thus, the realm of *upāya* comprises the whole spectrum of the observed world of phenomena. It takes care of the notion of certainty, uncertainty, certainty and uncertainty, neither certainty nor uncertainty aspects of phenomenal existence. One needs to commingle the knowledge (*prajñā*) acquired through various means of knowledge with suitable means (*upāyas*) that life offers. It is possible to create a pot from the mud and many forms of things from clay, but it is not plausible to create a square circle or finding a square circle. In other words, the wisdom is that the knowledge directed towards the impossible would be abortive; the knowledge that brings to the realm of the possible would be creative, generating *Bodhicitta*, removing misconceptions and revealing the *dharmadhātu* of each phenomena.

The *Bodhicitta*, after removing all the *vikalpas* from the mind with the help of Tāntric spiritual practices, blossoms in the minds of a Yogi, and makes him aware of the essence of the phenomena immediately. As per the object of a yogic perception, it is said:

> Just as one's image is reflected limpid and clear on a clean mirror, if one has clear eyesight; similarly the mind, cleared from the gamut of imagination and the distractions generated from the number of imaginations, is acting like a mirror reflecting the objects perceived limpid and clear.[61]

The mind acquires pure subjective nature and reflects the objects without any interference of subjectivity. The problem can be interpreted in another manner that the subject-object dichotomy, a problem that remains unresolved in philosophy, has been addressed here properly. The cognized objects of the world have to be independent of the mind, as one should conceive the essence of phenomena (*dharmadhātu*) which is free from mind's cravings and afflictions. The cleansing of mind (*cittaviśuddhi*) is achieved through spiritual practices, and the mind retains its purity like that of a gem. It is a big question in philosophy whether such a stage of complete segregation of the mind and matter is possible. Especially in western philosophy, this problem is discussed extensively.

> The dichotomy is an inter-implicative distinction between thinkers and what they think about. In which each presupposes the other. If there are no subjects, then neither are there objects in the true sense, and conversely.[62]

5.5 *Cittaviśuddhi*, *Dharmadhātu*, and the Tāntric Spiritual Techniques

The dialectics of Mādhyamikas addresses these problems from the beginning, as they criticize the validity of the premises of knowledge to adduce logically consistent arguments that can substantiate the truth-value of the concept. It is because of the inherent nature of the mind that we perceive things as real, eternal, and true. When the mind is freed from this affliction (*cittaviśuddhi*), it can see the world as the way it appears. The *dharmadhātu* is the object independent of the illusory configuration of the mind.

Thus, the *cittaviśuddhi* can be achieved through Tāntric spiritual practices, which is doctrinally possible by commingling the *prajñā* and *upāya*. The practical methods adopted by Mādhyamikas are particularly pertinent to Buddhist schools of philosophy. It is through *cittaviśuddhi*, cleansing the mind from the dichotomous thought activity, one is able to have complete realization of what has been taught in the philosophical discourses. *Cittaviśuddhi* is not the destruction of the individuality of a person, but it is practically achievable by appeasing the dispositions of the individual personality. Thus, the craving and clinging remains in the mind without harming the individuality. Āryadeva says in this regard that,

> Since there is no fear about the liberation (*mukti*), one can enjoy all the pleasures of the world; there is no sin attached with these activities, because one has to pass the time properly.[63]

Mostly, western philosophical systems engage in active dialectical arguments on the basis of conceptual formulations; the dialectics is the formulation of another theory or concept that is more close to reality, as it is a modified, ratified new synthesis of various thesis and counter thesis. Mādhyamika, on the other hand, questions the truth validation of the premises of the true instruments of cognition, not they question much on the validity of the concepts, but ascribe practical utility for those concepts. For them the concepts are in the realm of *samvṛti satya*. The nature of subjective mind, as the epicentre of human knowledge, is important in differentiating the subjective interference on the object; cleansing the mind from all the adjuncts that could create illusions with the object, is the answer to solve this problem. Whatever may be the method of practice; the mind should be endowed with apt concentration and attention: "As a gem called Udakamaṇi cleanses the impure water, the *śraddhā* (concentration) cleanses the mind from the impressions, concepts, and the craving and clinging tendencies."[64] Buddhist thinkers analyze this problem from the root and suggest a method of practice to achieve internal strength of the mind in case of a Bodhisattva.

References

1. Buddhism doesn't accept the thing in themselves or real entities. Instead, Buddhism is concerned with a state of being, thus, a term originally referred to form or becoming and not to matter. Junjiro Takakusu, *The Essentials of Buddhist Philosophy*, 1947, p. 204.

2. David J. Kalupahana, *A History of Buddhist Philosophy*, p. 73.
3. Ibid., p. 79.
4. Ibid., p. 76.
5. Human personality is beyond description, the middle way of describing it is explained as dependent arising. In positive terms, this represents an explanation of a person in bondage, while the negative terms explains the process of freedom. Ibid., p. 74.
6. Ibid., p. 81.
7. By introducing opposing view to counter the substantialists' position, Mādhyamika is not introducing a thesis of their own based on the "apagogic" proof that an assertion of a position indirectly by disapproving the opposite of that position. T.R.V. Murti, *The Central Philosophy of Buddhism*, p. 131.
8. *Catuḥśataka of Āryadeva*, XIV. 23.
9. Ibid., XIV. 21.
10. Ibid., XIV. 19.
11. David J.Kalupahana, *A History of Buddhist Philosophy*, p. 166.
12. Ibid., p. 167.
13. David J.Kalupahana, *Mūla-Mādhyamikakārikā*, XV. 7.
14. Ibid., XXVII. 8.
15. David J.Kalupahana, *A History of Buddhist Philosophy*, p. 70.
16. Ibid., p. 72.
17. Ibid., p. 75.
18. *Cittaviśuddhi-prakaraṇa*, vv. 41–43.
19. David J. Kalupahana, *A History of Buddhist Philosophy*, p. 76.
20. K. Venkata Ramanan, *Nagarjuna's Philosophy*, p. 66.
21. *Cittaviśuddhi-prakaraṇa*, v. 27.
22. Ibid., v. 26.
23. "Sensing and Perceiving," *Encyclopaedia Britannica*, CD99.
24. K. Venkata Ramanan, op. cit., p. 110.
25. *Cittaviśuddhi-prakaraṇa*, v. 133.
26. Ibid., vv. 11-12.
27. Ibid., v. 11.
28. Ibid., v. 13.
29. Ibid., v. 17.
30. David J. Kalupahana, *A History of Buddhist Philosophy*, p. 78.
31. Ibid., p. 79.
32. *Cittaviśuddhi-prakaraṇa*, V. 17.
33. Ibid., v. 37.
34. Ibid., v. 19.
35. Kamaleswar Bhattacharya, E.H. Johnston and Arnold Kunst, *The Dialectical Method of Nāgārjuna Vigrahavyāvartinī*, p. 115, vv. 31-32.
36. Ibid., p. 133.
37. T.R.V. Murti, op. cit., p. 230.
38. This is one of the problems with modern science; it is made on the premises of a certain number of truths where the untruth, semi-truth, etc. are discarded.

39. Herbert V. Guenther, *The Dawn of Tantra*, p. 68.
40. David J. Chalmers, "The Content and Epistemology of Phenomenal Belief," http://www. paradox.ucsc.edu.
41. David J. Kalupahana, *A History of Buddhist Philosophy*, p. 145.
42. T.R.V. Murti, op. cit., p. 185.
43. *Cittaviśuddhi-prakaraṇa*, v. 33.
44. T.R.V. Murti, op. cit., p. 189.
45. Ibid.
46. Ibid., p. 190.
47. David J. Kalupahana, *A History of Buddhist Philosophy*, p. 81.
48. Stephen W. Hawking, *A Brief History of Time*, p. 199.
49. *Cittaviśuddhi-prakaraṇa*, v. 68.
50. Harish Narain, *The Mādhyamika Mind*, 1997, p. 78.
51. K. Venkata Ramanan, op. cit., p. 261.
52. *Cittaviśuddhi-prakaraṇa*, vv. 22, 23.
53. Ibid., v. 22.
54. David J. Kalupahana, *A History of Buddhist Philosophy*, p. 78.
55. Āryadeva, *Hastavālanāma-prakaraṇavṛtti*, 3a-b, (ed. and trans. F. Tola and C. Dragonetti, *On Voidness*, p. 11).
56. Ibid., 5a-d, (ibid., p. 12).
57. Ibid., 1c-d, (ibid., p. 10).
58. *Cittaviśuddhi-prakaraṇa*, v. 48.
59. Ibid., v. 95.
60. Ibid., v. 130.
61. Ibid., vv. 89, 90.
62. *Cambridge Dictionary of Philosophy*, p. 773.
63. *Cittaviśuddhi-prakaraṇa*, v. 112.
64. Ibid., v. 130.

Chapter Six

Tāntric Indoctrination and Esoteric Practices—Ethical Dimension of *Cittaviśuddhi-prakaraṇa*

6.1 *Cittaviśuddhi* and the Conception of *Yuganaddha*

The awakening of *Bodhicitta* after the interaction of *prajñā* and *upāya*, results in the mind retaining the original nature (*sahaja*-nature)[1] as the mind acts like a mirror reflecting the *dharmadhātu* of every phenomenal appearance without being attached to them. The *sahaja*-nature can be interpreted as the real nature of mind devoid of any form of thought constructions, conceptual formulations, or theoretical postulations. It is an embodiment of ultimate compassion, beginningless and endless; of the nature of quietude; without any reference; and having no manifestations (*saṁskṛta*). It can be compared to the Buddha nature.[2] The *sahaja*-nature in fact is the state of *Bodhicitta*, achieved after the cleansing of mind (*cittaviśuddhi*). To achieve the *cittaviśuddhi*, or the *sahaja*-nature of mind, one needs to practise suitable spiritual disciplines. The introduction of Tantrism as a spiritual discipline into the philosophical findings of Mādhyamika is a perfect union of two systems, since both are set to achieve the harmonious settlement of human life. As we have seen earlier, the *Bodhicitta* comes into existence when *prajñā* and *upāya* are commingled perfectly, removing all the *vikalpas* and conceptualizations. In Tantrism, the bringing together of duality is called *Yuganaddha*. S.B. Dasgupta describes it:

> The synthesis or rather the unification of all duality in an absolute unity is the real principle of union, which has been termed as *Yuganaddha*. Textually the term is mentioned in the fifth chapter of the *Pañca-krama* as: When a state of unity is reached through the purging of the notions of the creative process (Saṁsāra) and absolute cessation (*nirvṛtti*) it is called *Yuganaddha*.[3]

Again, the real principle of *Yuganaddha* is the absence of the notion of duality as the perceivable and perceiver and their perfect synthesis in a unity. It is also the absence of the notions of eternity and limitations and their synthesis in a unity. Where there is no notion for extinction without any residuum (*anupādhi śeṣaḥ*) i.e., no notion of the non-essentialness of the *dharmas* (*dharma-nairātmya*) or the self (*pudgala-nairātmya*), that is called *Yuganaddha*, for the very nature of *Yuganaddha* implies freedom from all kinds of thought constructions.[4] The extinction of all duality-bound practices is meant to inculcate uniformity in the mind. It does not mean that the practitioner vanishes into the uniformity of a singularity, but he would be able to free himself from the confusion of duality, as in the case of, "the reflection of moon inside the water doesn't get defiled by the water."[5] The mind becomes pure and clear without any sort of defilement that would cause confusion and play of duality. Removing the play of duality is the spiritual purport of the Mādhyamikas.

6.2 The Dualism of Masculinity and Femininity

The conceptualization of the nature of duality is done based on the observations made on the internal system that is operative in a human being. The transcendence of this duality is the basis of the Tāntric spirituality. As *Yuganaddha* involves practices that remove the notions of duality existing in the human system. As H.V. Guenther says:

> We know that the bisexual constitution exists potentially in equal male-female ratios in conjugating reproductive protoplasm. It definitely exists in more or less unequal male-female ratios or female-male ratios in the chromosome and cytoplasm of zygotes of unfertile, hetero-sexual metazoa and in their gonads, germ cells, gametes, and other cells of the organism.[6]

The complex function of genes and endocrine glands determines the functioning of the physical body and the mental balance; it can be the reason for having masculinity in females and femininity in males. It is clear that the human system has duality in many forms: the matter and mind duality, masculine and feminine duality, etc. Such dualities are internal and inherent to the life in the world.

> To him who has been brought up in a strict dualism of body and soul, the Indian conception of man's highest aim as two in one, that is inseparability of body and soul as well as of masculinity and femininity as an integral whole is almost incomprehensible.[7]

Describing the complex internal activity as the cause of the mind's illusory formulations, *Sekoddeśaṭīkā* of Naḍapād (Nāropā), writes:

> The Experience of pure bliss and the body schema (*kāya*) that is still undifferentiated like the *rohita* fish are instantaneous comprehension. They

are that unique moment when in pre-natal growth the *ālayavijñāna* is about to enter upon its course of development and transformation within the maternal uterus, because the female ovum and the male spermatozoon (*bindu*) have met and become united.

But when the latent energies of the five receptive patterns that have been constellated by the residua of former experiences of visible objects and other sense objects (*vāsanā*) become active within the foetus on the same way as a turtle puts forward its five limbs, then there is fivefold comprehension.

When the foetus becomes differentiated and acquires the twenty functional factors, because the five receptive patterns each in its own proper place act on and are modified by the four elements of earth and so on then there is twenty-fold comprehensions.

When the newborn child encounters and experiences innumerable forms of existence, which are like a net of illusory ascriptions (*māyājālābhisaṁbodhi*).[8]

6.2.1 *The Subtle Dynamics of Mind*

There are very obscure and subtle happenings in the development of a human embryo into a human being, which are not easily explainable, but they go on absolutely based on the laws of nature without the knowledge of the individual. The inner constitution determines the final form of response; the hereditary factors can only be acquired in response to an environment; the acquired factors can only be secured by a modification of already existing structure and the human being is a conglomeration of all these factors taken together.

> The generic and external factors operate in the whole of life. This complicated interaction is hinted by the *niṣyanda-vāsanā* those factors which reproduce only special type of uniform unicellular organisms or masses of cells of one type, and by the *karma-vāsanā*, the environmental qualification of chromosomal cytoplasm. Both factors together form and differentiate the living organism.[9]

The internal mental activities, the reason for the mind to be attached to things of the world are actually controlled by the subtle bio-chemical functions. The spiritual practices are meant to transcend the mind's inherent attachment to things of the world. The intrinsic factors that are determined by the internal activities and the extrinsic activity characterized by the receptive sensory factors, are nothing but the two aspects of one unitary principle called energy or God.[10] The energy in the cell of a living organism is polarized into anabolism and catabolism, the former tending to conserve and the latter to change the tissue. The assimilation and building of energy, anabolism, is the opposite of breaking down and releasing energy. According to H.V. Guenther.

> The living cell's bio dynamics is important for the development of the two sexes, inasmuch as by increase of heat over the equilibratory mean a differentiation in the male-female direction sets in, whereas by decrease of heat under the equilibrating mean differentiation in the female-male direction sets in.[11]

The internal functioning of life in a living organism and the externally identifiable expression has very subtle activities, which are discernible only through very active meditation. Buddhist thinkers, by their unbiased attitude, are able to understand the actual nature of life's functioning through curious observations. It is not possible to identify complete femininity in females and masculinity in males, as the human mind is a complicated mixture of these two aspects of life. Even though the life energy is manifested in many forms, it is identifiable as a singular unit and that can be expressed as the universal life energy or God.

6.2.2 *The Bio-dynamics of Sexuality and the Dispositions*

The mind, because of its internal urge to manifest in the internal energy at the lower level of existence, tries to latch on to the apparent realities of the world. This clinging nature can be removed only by piercing through the veil of phenomenal flow. One will see that the world of phenomena is enslaving him with its magical spells, but when he goes behind the veil of appearance and understands them, he becomes free. One way to approach this problem is to break the barrier between the masculine and feminine energies. Tāntric meditations are developed from this basis.

> The problem of masculinity and femininity is not the idle play of an intellectual mind, it affects our life deeply and we have to come to an understanding of what is operating in us. The Tantras may help us in our present difficulty if they are understood correctly.[12]

The oneness of the energies is otherwise interpreted as *tathatā* or "thatness." According to S.B. Dasgupta:

> To enter into the final abode of thatness in body, word, and mind, thence again to rise up and turn to the miseries is called *Yuganaddha*. Where the mind doesn't lose itself in the absolute "thatness" nor does it rise up in the world of activity; here there is neither affirmation nor denial; neither existence nor non-existence; neither non-remembering through the absence of the *vāsanās* nor remembering; neither affection nor non-affection; neither the cause nor the effect; neither the production nor the produced; neither purity

> nor impurity, the synthesis of all these dualities is what meant by the principle of *Yuganaddha*.[13]

It is very difficult for the mind to rise above the distinctions to identify the unifying energy that exists in the human system. The Tāntric practices set the adept to move in that direction and venture like fearless warriors to conquer the world of dualities or rise above the dualities.

6.3 The Transcendence of Dualism: the Tāntric Way

A living cell or a singular cell organism is a highly complex being with an intricate demonstration of dualism. It functions in a particular way to fulfil the purpose of living the life and procreating or multiplying. Bio-chemically, it is proved that the cell stores up energy anabolically in the protein structures that is catabolically broken down for energy release in work.[14] However, if there is a deficiency in the energy levels, then it must be compensated by other cells; every living cell uses energy catabolically and constructs in a special way through anabolism, in order that to ensure a counter balance. It is a very subtle happening inside the organism. This formation is very important for the sustenance of life, whether they are single-cell units or multi-cellular units. The cell chemically works out the deficiency by chemically driving to anabolize adequate quantities of nutritional substance. In the case of singular cell organisms, when imbalances in the cell's constitution set in, the cell multiplies. A similar process happens in the case of advanced form of life too: the individual predominantly male or predominantly female would be driven to seek the opposite type to find a balance within. The duality existing in the psychophysical personality is extremely disturbing, yet strictly an internal activity.

> A man will seek the woman as well a woman the man. Such selective deficiencies or needs and cravings prove that every partial aspect is in want of its complement.[15]

The sexual intercourse that happens between a man and woman is a process of fulfilling this internal urge by suitably identifying each other's imbalanced masculinity or femininity.

The sexo-yogic practice is a very accepted method to bring unity in the imbalanced polarities. Based on the difference in the energies humanity has been divided into the community of men and women.

> The nature and spirit are basically one and that only thus we can get a glimpse of the blissful unity. In the same way as salt dissolves in water, so also the spirit that takes its proper spouse (transcends all boundaries). It penetrates into the essential, emotional moving unity (Saṁsāra) (of what seems to be separate and distinct), if it is constantly united with her.[16]

Thus, when the unification of the energies takes place, human consciousness would enter a different realm, and when constant meditative practice would enable the Yogi to transcend all notions of dualities permanently, he would find the object of his mind's craving and he would transcend the constantly retarding sexual instinct, his whole nature rising to the maximum expression. When viewed from the cellular analogy it is said:

> Mating behaviour is produced by a deficiency of anabolism or catabolism in a cell exciting chemical affinities, sensitivities, and motivates for union with another cell that complementary opposite ratios of counterbalancing properties. The anabolic-catabolic re-equilibrium brought about either through ingesting other cells of fitting qualities and qualities of nutritional substances, or through conjugation between two cells. In the same way as the fusion of cells in the biological field results in a rejuvenescent viability so also the re-equilibration or fusion of what we call man-ness and female-ness has the same effect in an individual.[17]

This union of two principles is highly regarded in the Tāntric tradition that the Lord Supreme and his Śakti are in deep union in the nature of *sahaja*-bliss through the affection of intense emotion, as in the tradition of Śaiva-Tantras. According to S.B. Dasgupta:

> In justification of the sexo-yogic practice in esoteric Buddhism it has often been said that man is bound through emotion or attachment and he is again liberated through that very emotion. It is further discussed, if perfect knowledge is attainable through the emotion of intense attachment, then all beings attached to worldly objects and sex-emotions are freed.[18]

It is said that the attainment of *cittaviśuddhi* or the *sahaja*-nature of the mind is attainable through sexo-yogic practices.

In the esoteric practices of the Buddhists, the application of *prajñā* and *upāya* represent femininity and masculinity respectively; in other words, all men and women are *upāya* and *prajñā* respectively in their ultimate nature. S.B. Dasgupta explains that the *prajñā* is feminine principle, the *Bhagavatī* or as the *mudrā* (the woman chosen for the sexual *sādhana*). In the *Hevajra Tantra, prajñā* is called the mother, the sister, the washer-woman, the danseuse, the daughter, the Ḍoma-girl, etc.[19]

Most of the Tāntric texts gives reverence to the woman, who is a personification of *prajñā*; the male aspect is called the *upāya*. In the *Śrīcakrasambhāratantra*, the appearance, the method, and the great compassion represent the male deity, while the void, tranquillity and great compassion symbolize the female deity.[20] There are various manifestations of the same principle in different Tāntric schools. The sexo-yogic practices of the Tāntrics are aimed at transforming the sex pleasure into the realization of infinite bliss in which the self and the world around are lost in the all-pervading oneness, the oneness of energy realized instantaneously.[21]

The esoteric Yogic practices of the Tāntric follow definite phases of development, as *sādhana* inculcates intense bliss in the practitioners, and the *Bodhicitta* is flourished as a result, or the *cittaviśuddhi* is performed, or the *sahaja*-nature of the mind is retained. S.B. Dasgupta remarks:

> The Bodhicitta is considered to be originated in the lowest part of the *Śarīra* (trunk part of the Body), moving upward in stages; with the help of breath control and other psychophysical practices such as *Bandhas* and *Kriyās*. The energy move in the body in stages: first the *maṇipūraṇa chakra*, near the navel region (the stage is denoted by *cakra*); then the *dharma chakra*, near the heart; the *sambhoga chakra*, situated near the throat; and finally the *uṣṇīṣa-kamala*, the lotus of the head, where the Bodhicitta is produced. The Bodhicitta produced through Yogic practice is the ultimate substance of the nature of five elements (earth, fire, air, water, and ether). In *Kunhapāda*, the Bodhicitta has been spoken of as the seed of five elements.[22]

The awakening of the *Bodhicitta* is the highest spiritual attainment of the Mahāyānistic Yogi. He has attained the *sahaja*-nature of the mind, has perceived the *dharmadhātu* of the phenomena in the form of five elements and has realized the true nature of the elements essenceless.

6.3.1 *Martial Art as a Tāntric Discipline*

As discussed earlier, in the spiritual practices of the Buddhists, martial arts play an important role. This tradition is followed even today in the East Asian countries where Buddhism is a practising religion. When we try to analyze the rationale of these practices on the basis of Tāntric tradition, we can see that anger is also one of the basic instincts like sexuality, which causes the origin of conceptualizations (*vikalpas*). This is one impediment that one has to control or cajole to attain *Bodhicitta*. The practice is similar to the instance of converting a metallic ball which naturally sinks in water, but when converted into a vessel floats on water and helps one traverse across a river.[23] The basic instinct of anger or the tendency to fight actually works as a protective means for human beings to live and survive in this world. We find that the function of anger and the tendencies to fight have both positive and negative effects. The positive aspect is that it cautions one from falling into the whimsical influence of the existent world or helps one to fight the negative influences of his mind. But at the same time, such instincts, on the negative side, working together with dichotomous conceptualizations due to the influence of one's dispositions and feelings, damage his personality. So, a Yogi has to acquire the technique and knowledge to clear the mind from such influences. Like in the case of *viṣa-vaidya*, a Tāntric Yogi, purges out the negative effects of such instincts, by using the same instincts in a disciplined manner.[24] A Tāntric Yogi, through his right visualizations, understands the function of negative instincts in the human personality, especially with regard to feelings and dispositions and identifies suitable techniques (*upāyas*) to remove them.

In case of martial arts practices, the focus is on the enhancement of the reflexive action of the mind. The mind in, its original nature, is pure and reflects the objects the way they appear before it.[25] Most of the practices of martial arts are conducted in a much disciplined atmosphere. The whole structure of practice is meant to remove fear, sloth, and ignorance. It aims at promoting mental equanimity, patience, concentration, and positive attitude.[26] In martial art practices, normally, actual weapons are used but guided by stylized methods of practice. These war weapons are, in fact, very dangerous; a moment of falling concentration could kill a person or give him a bad injury. So this training would equip one with quick reflexes and apt concentration, which he may not acquire from any other spiritual training. The practitioner involuntarily teaches his mind not to fall into laziness, sloth, dichotomous thoughts, and misconceptions. A martial artist is not only learning the technique of using the weapons but also training the mind to meditate at apt concentration. We can look into the practical method of one of the most ancient martial arts of the world, the Indian martial art tradition of Kalarippayat.[27]

The basic tenets of Kalarippayat are based on Tāntric traditions. The main training centre, Kalari, is built on the principles of Tantra, an architectural technique called *Tatchuśāstra* (the local dialect for

Vāstuśāstra). The same technique is used in the construction of temples in Kerala region, where Kalarippayat is popular. Normally, the architectural technique suggests the front gate or *Siṁhayoni* facing to the east with a width of 64/12; opposite to the front gate on the west-end is the place for the main deity of the martial art Kalarippayat, the Goddess, which is called Pū-thara. The interior area of the training ground is of the measurement of 42 ft × 21 ft. There are 21 deities consecrated in the Kalari. Next to the main Goddess is the place for Gaṇapathy, and the place next is for the *guru* or the chief instructor of the Kalari. The other main deities of importance are: on the right side of the west end is for the God called Antima-kālan, the right side of the eastend is the place for Goddess Bhadrakālī, and the north side of the centre is the place for the God Veṭṭekorumakan. In the centre, there is a place reserved for *homakuṇḍa*, where Śatṛsaṁhāra *homa* is conducted.[28] There is a place in front of the main deity, reserved for the students to practise meditation. One of the interesting aspects of the main deity of Kalarippayat is that it is not the representation of an idol, but it looks like a cone embedded on the westend corner having seven steps. These seven steps represent seven constituent elements of human body, or Seven Goddesses (*Sapta-mātṛkās*), or seven *cakras* of the Śakta-Tantra.[29] We can see here that the practice of Kalarippayat is a part of the Tāntric spiritual tradition, in content and spirit.

An aspirant (*sādhaka*) of the Kalari tradition is initiated into the system by a competent *guru*, considered as the human form of the Goddess, and he occupies a special consecrated place in the Kalari. The student, from the day of initiation is under the patronage of the Kalari system: his patent deity is the Goddess of Kalari and his preceptor is the *guru* of the Kalari, also, he should abide by the tenets of Kalarippayat. The training is conducted in a strictly disciplined atmosphere under the effective guidance of a *guru*. And he takes vow to not use the martial technique to harm anybody; however, if he is forced to use this technique, it is only used for protecting the weak and needy from the hands of evil and wretched, which is specifically explained in the canons of Kalarippayat. The practices we discussed are meant for attaining spiritual maturity and mental equanimity for a person otherwise deluded by the false notion of animosity and anger. The originated anger and hatred as part of the dispositional tendency of the human personality, are what the Tāntric practice of Kalarippayat tries to conquer and not the fear and weakness of the weaker folks. These are coded principles laid down as part of the Kalarippayat practices which act as the knowledge (*prajñā*) aspect; and the method of practice of this martial art is the best means (*upāya*) for attaining perfection in the functioning of the *Bodhicitta* and the human personality, liberating the mind from falling into the trap of misconceptions.[30]

6.4 Bodhidharma and the Indian Tradition of Martial Arts

The origin of martial arts as a spiritual practice is said to have originated in India and later migrated to China through trade and Buddhism. The Father of Zen (Chi-an in Chinese), Bodhidharma, an Indian Buddhist monk from Kāñcīpuram, is believed to have introduced this particular system of meditation into the spiritual tradition of Buddhism, together with his mission to preach the Mahāyāna doctrines. This south Indian monk, a missionary of the Mahāyāna schools is instrumental in introducing the teachings of the *Laṅkāvatārasūtra* in China, and he is also respected as the father of Chi-an and martial art, which has given as a spiritual practice for the Buddhist monks.[31] Bodhidharma is the first Buddhist monk who used martial art as a meditative technique. His name, as the most important missionary, spread beyond China to all other East Asian countries. The supporting evidence to this effect can be seen in, Shoalin Temple in southern China, where there is a series of mural paintings which shows the dark-skinned Indian monks teaching fair skinned Chinese the art of fighting.[32] Bodhidharma's country of origin and his authority on the *Laṅkāvatārasūtra* are clearly stated in the Taoyuan's *Record of the Transmission of the Lamp*:

> The Master further said, I have the *Laṅkāvatāra* in four fascicules, which is handed over to you, and in this is disclosed the essential teaching of the Tathāgata concerning his mental ground. It will lead all sentient beings to spiritual openings and enlightenment. Since I came to this country, I was poisoned about five times and each time I took out this sūtra and tried its miraculous power by putting it on a stone, which were spilt into pieces. I have come from South India to this eastern land and have observed that in this country of China the people are pre-disposed to Mahāyāna Buddhism.[33]

The narration by Bodhidharma himself provides enough evidence that these traditions have a common origin and collective development in the socio-philosophical field of India and its Asian neighbours. Bodhidharma as the patent saint of Chi-an (Zen) is respected in almost all East Asian countries. In Japan, he is known as Daruma, his importance not less than that of St Peter to the Catholic Church. In Korea, he is considered as the most important monk, and the Father of all martial arts. There is a saying in southern China which goes thus:

> Prior to the arrival of Bodhidharma, Chinese martial artists trained primarily to fight and were fond of bullying weaker folk. Bodhidharma brought *Wute*[34] from India, which taught that the martial arts are really meant to promote spiritual development and health, not fighting.[35]

It is clear from the Chinese and other sources that the martial art tradition is an accepted meditative technique.

6.5 The Tāntric Spiritual Practices of *Cittaviśuddhi-prakaraṇa*

The main discussion of the *Cittaviśuddhi-prakaraṇa* is to highlight the merits of Tāntric spiritual practices over the spiritual practices of the Brāhmanical schools, especially the Mīmāṁsakas. There are various aspects common to the systems of the Mādhyamika philosophy and the Tantric spiritual practices. Mādhyamika advocates the middle position as the basis of philosophical arguments while Tantrism propounds non-theoretical, non-conceptual, and observation-based methods of spiritual practices. Both the systems have many commonalities in the way they view life and the existence of the universe. According to Mādhyamikas, the *prajñā* (knowledge or wisdom) and the *upāya* are the two fundamental aspects that could help a human being to redeem himself from the world of illusions, as he realizes the essence of all phenomena and the essencelessness of the elements of phenomena. In other words, when *prajñā* and *upāya* are perfectly united in the meditative mind, one would be able to see the *dharmadhātu* of the *dharmas*; and from the *dharmadhātu* the non-intrinsic and non-cognisable nature of the elements of the *dharmas*, the *dharma-nairātmya*. In the case of Tantrism, various spiritual meditative techniques are used in order to awake the *Bodhicitta* or to bring back the mind to *sahaja*-nature. Because of the bio-dynamics of the incompletely balanced energies in the human body, which attempts to restore the internal and external equilibrium, the sexo-yogic practices are considered as the methodology for the equilibrium and counter-balancing of these energies into one. To sum up, with the blossoming of *Bodhicitta*, the mind accomplishes the strength to transcend all the dualities.

Āryadeva says that when the mind is influenced by the phenomena (*dharmas*), it is drawn into the ocean of existence, the *dharma* dragging the mind like a crocodile and conceptualizing the apparent as real and eternal.[36] The influence of phenomena on the mind is strong and it drags the mind to configure the apparent as real. It can be the result of the biodynamic activity of the mind, where the mind has the internal urge to seek perfection and in that process it works with the apprehended phenomena. According to Āryadeva, the only way to release from the shackles created by the *saṁsāra* (existence), is by using the same aspects that causes bondage in a different way, since the causes of bondage have the inherent power to release too.[37]

> In order to cure from the dangerous effect of poisoning, a physician uses poison expeditiously in the right quantity, the expertise of the physician playing an important role.[38]

Like the causes of bondage, the poison also has an adverse effect on an individual, but the correct and expeditious use of such things (poison or the causes of bondage) can release a person from all the ill-effects. The reasoning to this effect can be understood in the Mādhyamika way, such that the mind falls into the trap of existence and so on, because of its inherent notion of finding perfect knowledge from the apparent world of phenomena. So the use of spiritual techniques drawn from those causes which manifested bondage could be more effective than any other methods that purposely ignore the importance of such aspects. The imbalanced bio-dynamics of the mind, that is an internal activity on which an individual has not much control can create a very difficult problem for the individual.

One of the most important spiritual practices of the Tāntrics is commingling the masculinity and femininity in order to equilibrate the imbalanced bisexuality existing in each individual, as each one of them searches for the counterbalancing energy; a man looking for his counterpart, the woman; and the woman searching for the man. Understanding this aspect, the Tāntrics use the sexo-yogic techniques as one of the main spiritual practices. There are strict disciplines to be followed together with these practices, which are directed by the preceptor or the *guru*. Developing the spiritual virtue based on the tradition of Tāntric practices is the main methodology of the practice, as it comprises the development of each conscious centre ending in the *uṣṇīṣa-kamala* at the crown of the head. According to Āryadeva, it is not only the Yogi who practises this spiritual discipline, but also the woman who takes part in this practice, would be benefited:

> Damsels who are affected by the poison in the form of desire, by filling up the pure minds of the Yogis with the positive effects of the desire; they in fact enjoy the fruits of both desire and liberation.[39]

A Yogi never uses sexo-yogic practices for mere gratification of his basic instinct, but he uses it as a meditative practice, to reach the oneness. In that process, he helps the woman to receive the positive effects of desire, for she is liberated from the grip of desire. The sexo-yogic practices, done under the strict control of the *guru* and based on the directions described in various Tāntric texts, are meant to be practised by people who are properly initiated; and these practices are allowed for such initiated persons (Yogis) but censured for ordinary people, as it increases the poison of sexual urge, for the uninitiated.[40] These practices are highly sensitive.

Perfected with knowledge acquired from various Tāntric texts and performed under the competent supervision of an experienced preceptor who suggests proper deities and proper meditative practices, the Tāntric spiritual practices are efficient in redeeming a person from the whimsical grip of *saṁsāra*. The *Bodhicitta* awakens as the Yogi attains the highest stage of spiritual maturity that helps him to salvage the world.[41] The *Bodhicitta* is pure from the beginning, and devoid of any distinct nature; by receiving such an entity and viewing the world as the way it appears, a Yogi is neither bound nor liberated, and for him there is no distinction of *saṁsāra* or *nirvāṇa*.[42] *nirvāṇa* is real only if the man is living under the influence of *saṁsāra*. For one who has realized *Bodhicitta*, the distinction of both *nirvāṇa* and *saṁsāra* is redundant since he transcends all the distinctions, which are real only in the ordinary world of existence.

The desire, one of the adjuncts of the conditioned origination (*pratītyasamutpāda*) that reasons out the apparent world, is the cause for the mind's nature of clinging and ceasing and the suffering created by the world of appearance. By meditating on the phenomenal existence of the apparent world, the Yogi removes his attachment towards them. He enjoys the world of things, at the same time distancing himself from the attachments. Āryadeva says:

> The yogi by systematically thinking about the qualities of different Godheads with a mind full of desire will enjoy the world of things, at the same time liberating himself from the influence of the desired objects.[43]

The positive effects of the objects of desire are that they have the intrinsic power to redeem one from the influence of them. Knowing this aspect, a Yogi practises spiritual disciplines, getting himself distanced from the ill effects; consequently, he will be able to enjoy the objects of desire without getting attached to them. Most of the philosophical systems advocate abstinence from the objects of desire, knowing about their ill-effects. But Mādhyamika is the first philosophical system which propounds that it is not the objects of desire but the attachment towards them that is the problem. Mādhyamikas are in agreement with Tāntric systems that spiritual self-culture is the way to redeem one from the influence of the world of things.

> Like a physician who cures snake-bite, by sucking out the poison from the patient after meditating on the patent God Garuḍa; he, however, is not affected by the effect of poison even after drinking it straight.[44]

In order to counterbalance masculinity and femininity and to eradicate the influence of the disposition of sexuality from the human personality, sexo-yogic practices are recommended. The logic is:

> The water clogged in the ear or a thorn pierced inside the body, is removed by pouring more water into the ear or using another thorn to remove the thorn.[45]

Sex is one of the basic human instincts that have tremendous influence on the personality; it cannot be removed by abstinence or strict regime. Tantrism suggests that it can be removed by using the same instincts efficiently. It is well-known that the people who professes abstinence and self-denial suffer from the ill-effects of it severely. The desire can also be used as an *upāya.*

Modern biochemistry has proven that the cell's urge to find suitable nourishment leads it to behave in a particular manner. In the multicellular organism, this formulation is more complex. Each individual being is not distinctly differentiated based on sexual division, because of the intermixing of masculinity and femininity in the same individual. The bisexuality existing dormant in an individual is dangerous to the spiritual life when it is commingled with estrogens (hormone), driving the individual instinctively towards the opposite sex for the fulfilment of the femininity or masculinity. The practices of these techniques are extremely sensitive and even have the potential to plunge a person in to the abysmal depth of ignorance and bondage. However, when these are practised under proper guidance of a competent *guru*, they are effective in relieving a person from all the shackles of existence. According to the words of Āryadeva:

> The objects of desire and the involvement with them (sexo-yogic practices), done by an unwise person, will turn into a source of bondage; the same practices, if performed by a wise person (Yogi), become a source for liberation and enlightenment.[46]

One way of explaining the internal activity that happens in the human consciousness is that a person is internally seeking to find a fulfilment for the subdued femininity or masculinity dormant in him and which seeks manifestation. Based on this argument one can say that the perfect man or perfect woman may not seek the fulfilment of the dormant bipolarity, because they will not suffer from the subdued femininity or masculinity. Knowing this aspect, a Yogi engages in sexo-yogic techniques with the help of the patent God/Goddess and the *guru*; with the understanding of femininity he could transform his mind (*citta*) which is confused and deluded into *Bodhicitta* (perfected consciousness). The awakened *Bodhicitta* helps the individual to enjoy the things of the world without being attached to them. Āryadeva rightly exemplifies this aspect:

> Like the iron ball when thrown into the water drowns instantaneously, the mind too is drowned into the water of existence instantaneously; when the ball made into a vessel will float over the water, in the same way, the mind transformed like the vessel (into *Bodhicitta*) stays afloat over the world of existence.[47]

The practice of these spiritual disciplines is the continuance of a tradition, which is very ancient. A definite practical methodology is available for adaptation, in which the Yogi could discern the positive aspects:

> The wise swan drinks milk alone from the mixture of milk and water, similarly, in the objects of desire, a wise yogi uses only those aspects that could redeem from the world of existence.[48]

The mind that is purified by the auspicious means, the *upāyas*, transforms itself from dependence to independence retaining its pure form (*Prakṛti nirmalam*).[49] The mind shows certain characteristics because of its association with the world of things, but once the mind retains its original nature it becomes independent of all the influences and reflects the *dhamadhātu* of the perceived phenomena. It is similar to the instance:

> When the mercury (*rasa*) and the unallied copper are rubbed together, the copper turns into Gold; and as the knowledge aspect purifies the afflictions of the mind, it produces auspicious results.[50]

The knowledge that is stored in the mind and the knowledge which the mind is going to perceive would be pure and clear without the influence of *vikalpas* (conceptualizations). The innumerable thought chains which form in the mind as a result of the ceasing and clinging nature of the mind, cease to exist. Instead the mind would view the world of phenomena the way it appears before it. The wisdom, obtained from spiritual practices and meditations, would act like a bowstring, which could shoot an arrow of knowledge that could cleanse all false ascriptions (*vikalpas*).[51]

When the *dharma-nairātmya* of all phenomenally existing entities is realized, the notion of the existence of self is removed, similar to the notion of snake on the rope. When the existence of the rope is apprehended, the rope removed the notion of erroneous snake, and the snake vanished from the mind permanently. Perfection of knowledge (*vajrajñāna*) is originated after cleansing of the mind (*cittaviśuddhi*), revealing the *dharmadhātu* of things. It also protects the mind from further conceptualizations.[52] When the mind realizes the *dharma-nairātmya* of all the elements of existence, and its cosmic nature, which goes beyond the conceptual frame of mind, the apparently existing entities are not able to confuse the mind in any manner. The Yogi attains knowledge of *vajrajñāna*. The fundamental purport of Tantrism is to work on the dualistic principles and transcend the realm of dualism, so that dichotomy created by duality no longer troubles the Yogi. In order to transcend the web of dualism which craves innumerable contradictions, false ascription, and confusion, one needs to practise spiritual disciplines that would bring both the entities together.

> When two pieces of *Arani* wood are rubbed against each other, fire originates; it is pure in the beginning, middle, and end, illuminating the objects of the world. Similarly, when *prajñā* and *upāya* are brought together, the Yogic knowledge originates, which is unwavering, steady and pure always.[53]

The difference between Yogic knowledge and the ordinary knowledge is that ordinary knowledge is susceptible to verification, correction, and relates to the impulsive nature of an individual. On the other hand, Yogic knowledge is steady, devoid of confusion, enlightening, and pure and clear by nature. A Yogi is able to help another human being from his confusions. As we have discussed earlier, the internal mind's functioning cannot be explained properly with all its manifestations and articulations. One needs to be following certain convictions and practices which are traditionally articulated; otherwise he may damage his personality or fall into the grip of lunacy.

The *mantras*, which relieve the mind from the grip of thought-constructs, are an important aspect of Tāntric spiritual practices. They could elevate the mind from lower level of consciousness to higher level of consciousness, protecting it from further conceptualizations, keeping the mind's purity intact. Āryadeva clarifies this aspect further:

> The bracelet in one's hand is direct and certain, a mirror is not required to show it; similarly, in Mahāyāna one can find enlightenment through the efficacy of Mantras, which are clear and certain.[54]

The use of *mantras* is a part of Indian spiritual tradition, but the Mādhyamikas use *mantras* to direct the mind in the direction of *śūnyatā*. The syllables used mean nothing, keeping the mind detached from the meanings of the world of things. The *mantra* is the most effective spiritual technique that can reveal the insubstantial (real) nature of the things in the world very quickly, as the manifestations of the five basic elements, or the *dharmadhātu*. Mastery of *mantras* would break the conceptual frame of mind, going beyond the realm of the phenomena, and disclosing the fundamental cosmic elements of earth, fire, water, air, and ether and consciousness.[55] It professed non-injury to all living beings, it taught the principles of three *ratnas*, it brought mental quietude, it revealed the *Bodhicitta*, it highlighted the rule of the teaching of the Master, that the power of *mantras* is superior to all spiritual disciplines.[56]

The purpose of all spiritual practices is to redeem the mind from the bondage of worldly existence. The mind is actually like a gem defiled or muddied by the association of beginningless *vāsanās* (impressions); once cleansed with the help of *prajñā* and *upāya*, it will shine in its original nature of purity.

6.6 *Pudgala-nairātmya* (Essencelessness of the Self) as the Manifestation of God

The expression of God as the manifestation of male and female forms in Śaiva-Tantra is the most profound expression of this idea. A human being experiences the nature of maleness and femaleness because of the expression of this energy.

> To the imperfect eye, to the spirit still toiling through the lower planes of time, space, and causation, the whole process of becoming is tending to appear and this appearance is taken for reality.[57]

The spiritual development of an individual in the Tāntric sense, transcends the play of duality and leads to the perfection of internal subtle energy which is in the form of universal life energy, the Vajrapāṇi for the Mahāyāna Buddhist or Maheśvara for the Śaiva schools. In case of Mahāyāna Buddhists, the conception of Vajrapāṇi is different from the Maheśvara of the Śaivaites.[58] As for Śaivaites, the God form of Maheśvara is the perfected absolute of all the mysteries involved in the imperfect human life; but the Buddhists won't accept the mysterious something behind the five aggregates that comprise the subjective stage of mind as such representation is irrelevant. For the Mahāyānists, each of the five aggregates is represented by a God with specific functions. As we have seen, the Buddhists decline to accept any mysterious entity beyond the conception of the five aggregates.[59] Tāntric conception of the Gods relating to human personality are:

1. Body (*rūpa*)—*Vairocana*—ethics
2. Feelings (*vedanā*)—*Ratnasambhava*—concentration
3. Perception (*saṁjñā*)—*Amitābha*—appreciation
4. Dispositions (*saṁskāra*)—*Amoghasiddhi*—freedom
5. Consciousness (*vijñāna*)—*Akṣobhya*—vision in freedom[60]

The representation of Gods relating to the functions of the human personality is meant to help the mind liberated from all substantive manifestations. According to Kalupahana,

> The symbolism is not meaningless doctrinally, for it represents a non-substantialist interpretation of the relationship between Saṃsāra and Nirvāṇa.[61]

To quote from Nāgārjuna in this regard from *Mūlamādhyamikakārikā*:

> The life process has nothing that distinguishes it from freedom. Freedom has nothing that distinguishes from the life process.[62]

From the above discussions it is clear that the conception of Vajrapāṇi as the supreme God is to denote the freedom an individual can attain in this life, and not to denote or manifesting a supreme conscious entity as the controller of the universe.

References

1. S.B. Dasgupta. op. cit., p. 145.
2. *Cittaviśuddhi-prakaraṇa*, vv. 4-6.
3. S.B. Dasgupta. op. cit., p. 113.
4. Ibid.
5. *Cittaviśuddhi-prakaraṇa*, v. 110.
6. H.V. Guenther, *Tantric View of Life*, p. 3.
7. Ibid., p. 7.
8. Ibid., p. 8.
9. Ibid., p. 9.
10. Ibid.
11. Ibid., p. 11.
12. Ibid., p. 13.
13. S.B. Dasgupta, op.cit., p. 114.
14. H.V. Guenther, *Tāntric View of Life*, p. 30.
15. Ibid., p. 31.
16. Ibid., p. 33.
17. Ibid., p. 34.
18. S.B. Dasgupta, op. cit., p. 123.
19. Ibid., p. 102.
20. Ibid., p. 106.
21. Ibid., p. 146.
22. Ibid., p. 144.
23. *Cittaviśuddhi-prakaraṇa*, v. 40.
24. Ibid., v. 31.
25. Ibid., v. 90.
26. Taisen Deshimaru, *The Zen Way to the Martial Arts*, p. 30.
27. Michael Croucher, *The Way of the Warrior*, 1986, p. 24.
28. Interview with Vimalan Gurikkal and Bhaskaran Gurukkal at Mahe, northern part of Kerala, by the author, June 24, 1998.
29. The representation of the deity is very important in the practice of Kalarippayat. As per traditional Indian physiology the human body is constituted of seven *dhātus*, see, Vasant Lad, *Ayurveda, the Science of Self-Healing*, 1943, p. 40. The representation of the seven steps and the light at the top can be the representation of the various aspects of human consciousness and the light is the enlightenment attained. It can be also the Goddess represented by *Sapta-mātṛkās*.

30. In case of Śākta-Tantra practice the same attainments are accomplished, instead of *Bodhicitta*, it could be the supreme Goddess.
31. Michael Croucher is a well-known B.B.C. television producer who produced a serial on martial arts and later published a book. His observations were path-breaking and paved a new avenue and light to the whole tradition of martial arts, its Indian origin, etc. His studies show that the tradition of martial arts is a contribution of Indians, and Buddhists popularized it throughout the world. Michael Croucher, *The Way of Warrior*, pp. 8-24.
32. Ibid., p. 4.
33. D.T. Suzuki, *Studies in the Laṅkāvatārasūtra*, p. 45.
34. *Wu-Te*, in Chinese means the virtue of martial arts or the meditative power one receives by practising martial arts. Michael Croucher, op. cit., p. 43.
35. Ibid.
36. *Cittaviśudhi-prakaraṇa*, vv. 9, 10, 19.
37. Ibid., v. 6.
38. Ibid., v. 17.
39. Ibid., v. 29.
40. Ibid., v. 28.
41. Ibid., v. 32.
42. Ibid., v. 33.
43. Ibid., v. 35.
44. Ibid., v. 30.
45. Ibid., v. 36.
46. Ibid., v. 42.
47. Ibid., v. 38.
48. Ibid., v. 43.
49. Ibid., v. 45.
50. Ibid., v. 50.
51. Ibid., v. 52.
52. Ibid., vv. 66-68.
53. Ibid., v. 89.
54. Ibid., v. 96.
55. David J. Kalupahana, *A History of Buddhist Philosophy*, p. 72.
56. *Cittaviśudhi-prakaraṇa*, vv. 96, 115-16.
57. H.V. Guenther, *Tāntric View of Life*, p. 11.
58. David J. Kalupahana, *A History of Buddhist Philosophy*, p. 220.
59. Ibid., p. 69.
60. Ibid., p. 223.
61. Ibid.
62. Ibid.

Chapter Seven

Śūnyatā and Tantra: The Innate Relationship

The philosophical contributions of early Mādhyamikas have a timeless appeal to thinkers all over the world. Their contribution can be considered as one of the most philosophical thoughts that have influenced thinkers of Indian and Eastern philosophy, especially the interpretation given by them to the conception of *śūnya.* The methodology of philosophy of Nāgārjuna and Āryadeva have an everlasting influence as they have persuaded the philosophical thought for centuries in India; especially, the dialectical method propounded by them, captured the attention of many leading thinkers. The conception of *śūnyatā* introduced as a result of this dialectical method representing the essence of their teachings. However, many critics as well as the scholars misinterpreted *śūnya* according to their individual perspectives and contextual compulsions. In the case of orthodox schools of Indian philosophy, the term *śūnya* denotes the nihilistic interpretation of the existent world. On the other hand, the Yogācāra school of Mahāyāna Buddhism theorizes it as an absolutistic entity, connoted by the relative terminology like the *mahāśūnya* (the emptiness of the highest degree), *asvabhāva* (no self substance), *advaya* (non-duel), and *bhūtakoṭi* (ultimate limit).[1] The later Mādhyamika schools struggle hard to interpret the meaning of *śūnya* to bring out its original interpretation. In that process, the Svatantra School accepts the partial existence of entities and the Prasaṅga School engages in active and strong dialectical arguments, which created more misconceptions than clear understanding.[2] All these views seem to be at divergence from the original position of the early Mādhyamikas. Modern academics are not quite impressed by this concept in the way it required to be considered. Most of them take it as a useless concept or as something which has gone out of bounds giving no practical results.

We have seen already from our discussions that these concepts have immense potentiality in remaking a man from the very complicated and troublesome existence that he is destined to go through in the phenomenal world. We also have seen that the remade man is not a new creature but a simple human being who reacts to life naturally and intuitively without confusing himself with the bewildering effect of the world. He takes decisions appropriately, with the healthy continuance of life as the goal in mind.

As pointed out earlier, the verbal interpretation of *śūnya* is indeed an extremely difficult task. Nāgārjuna and Āryadeva have a special purpose in introducing this term such as to make the concepts of *dharma-nairātmya* and *pudgala-nairātmya* easily understandable. *Śūnyatā* can be interpreted as an implicit entity existing in each phenomenon of the objective world, and it is realizable after purification of mind (*cittaviśuddhi*). The phenomenal world appears as real and the notion of reality is a big question in philosophy. This, according to Mādhyamika, is due to the human mind's internal inherent tendency to cling to each conceived and cognized phenomenon and configure it as real and eternal, and to substantiate both the cognized object and the cognizing subject as real and eternal. In other words, the subject configures the object as a real entity to prove its own existence.

Contrary to the views of the other systems of philosophy, the Buddhist philosophy is concerned with the object experienced rather than the object itself or the thing in itself. Instead of a subjective self, the concern is about the composition of the human personality, which is manifested as five aggregates (*pañcaskandha*). Like the human personality divided into five aggregates, the objects of experience are also divided into two divisions, the objects known and the objects of knowledge. The objects known are further divided into: (1) the objects seen, (2) the objects heard, (3) the objects conceived, and (4) the objects cognized.[3] The objects conceived and the objects cognized are important as far as the human perceptive faculties are concerned. The objects conceived are susceptible to greater amount of confusion and conceptualization than the objects cognized, as the cognized objects are generally confined to the six senses. The mind is responsible for conceptualization as it reflects the objects conceived by it. If the objects cognized are there to be restricted by the other five senses then the objects cognized do not create much problem of conceptualization and confusion.[4]

The objects of knowledge are the objects that can be a part of the experience with the gateways (*āyatana*). These are: material form (*rūpa*), sound, smell, taste, touch, and concept (*dharma*) and these are experienced through the eyes, ear, nose, tongue, body, and mind.[5] This division of objects of knowledge indirectly signifies an important truth that there are objects beyond our sense faculties, and, therefore, the deterministic attitude towards objects of the phenomenal world would be inconclusive. Thus, Buddhism is not concerned with the existence of objects *per se* or the things in themselves, but the focus is on the objects experienced and their insubstantiality. As discussed earlier, the tendency of the mind to crave, cling, and grasp for things apprehended, is actually controlled by strong feelings, dispositions and ignorance; and it is suggested that the way to freedom is possible by appeasing the dispositions.

The substantiation of the objects as entities having intrinsic nature is supported first by problems created by the conceived objects and then by the dispositional tendencies of the human personality to configure those things as real and eternal. So, when there is a clear and certain dialectical understanding of the non-intrinsic nature of the objects conceived, the substantiation arguments leading to the intrinsic nature of the objects would be removed. Similarly, when the subjective human personality that apprehends the phenomenon attempts for a qualitative shift in the dispositional tendencies, then the mind would be able to apprehend the things the way they appear before it.

In our effort to find the real position of the Mādhyamikas, we should first deconstruct the notion that the things of the world are not eternal and real. Their existence in the world is supported by various adjuncts whose existence also insubstantial. This aspect is reviewed with the help of dialectical arguments set by Nāgārjuna in the *Vigrahavyāvartinī*, where the non-intrinsic nature of the things and the intrinsic nature of the things are put into regressive analysis to introduce the philosophy of Mādhyamika. The *Vigrahavyāvartinī* discusses the problems of rejecting the intrinsic nature of the objective experience as an epistemological fallacy; at the same time, it accepts that accepting the intrinsic nature of the objects experienced creates logical confusion. The former argument is the refutation to the Abhidharma School of Satyasiddhi and Sautrāntika, and the later argument is against the Abhidharma School of Vaibhāṣika or

Sarvāstivāda, because both these schools accept either the subjective stage or the objective stage of experience as substantial. This, according to early Mādhyamikas, is a diversion from the original teachings of Buddhism, where the *dharma-nairātmya* and *pudgala-nairātmya* are equally important. To interpret it in strict Buddhistic terms, the non-substantiality of the elements and the non-substantiality of the subtle personality that transmigrates from one life to another life until the attainment of freedom, are unacceptable due to epistemological and logical discordance.[6] Mādhyamikas use the concept of *śūnyatā* in order to substantiate their arguments relating to the insubstantiality of the elements and that of the subtle personality, which may fall into the dialectical trap of apagogic proof in which we prove an assertion indirectly by disproving the opposite.[7]

With the introduction of the *śūnyatā* as a property of the phenomenal existence, Nāgārjuna evades the dialectical trap that is set against his arguments leading to the insubstantiality of both the elements and the subtle personality. As he cleverly mentioned in the last verse of the *Vigrahavyāvartinī*, everything prevails for one who is in agreement with the concept of *śūnyatā*, and nothing prevails for one who is not in agreement with the concept of *śūnyatā.*[8]

The objects of the world are there for our experience and understanding. It is not possible to discard their existence, but Mādhyamikas never accept their eternal existence. Here, the arguments are based on a text written by Āryadeva, the *Hastavālanāma-prakaraṇavṛtti*, which explains the *śūnyatā* as existing in each stage of the experience with the object conceived. In the case of the conceived object like the snake apprehended on a rope, the text says that the proper cognition of the object namely, the rope removes the illusory notion of snake that has originally apprehended. At the first stage of perception, the phenomena (*dharma*) or idea of the conceived object is obtained; in the second stage of perception the phenomena is verified with the six sense faculties to obtain essence of phenomena (*dharmadhātu*), or the cognized object is obtained; in the third stage of perception, the essencelessness of phenomena (*dharma-nairātmya*), the object as neither snake nor rope is discerned. In short, the conceived object is equal to phenomenon (*dharma*) like the snake, creating confusion in the mind about the object. At the same time, the object cognized is equal to the essence of the phenomena (*dharmadhātu*) as it gives relative certainty about the object, which is verified by the six senses.

But the experienced object's ultimate nature is unknown and insubstantial. The experienced object, when subjected through regressive analysis, turns out to be insubstantial; or on close examination of the constituent elements, ontological existence of the objects becomes uncertain and unpredictable. Taking the conceived object as the basis and developing it in various stages of experiential process, we can see that in the ultimate analysis the object's existence is insubstantial and uncertain. Therefore, it can be concluded that the *śūnytā* or *dharma-nairātmya* is a property of the experienced world of objects. Another way of putting the concept of *śūnyatā* is that it is an analytical tool that helps one to see the emptiness implicit in each phenomenon, or works like a panacea that cures the disease of dichotomous conceptualizations (*vikalpas*).

Modern science, in its effort to understand the truth through the analysis of the experiential world objects, suggests that the objects experienced possess only relative and not absolute existence. The analysis of the ultimate particle is not conclusively revealing a singular element or a group of elements that are substantial, but a world of chaotic manifestations, proving the dependent nature of the world of things. The concept of *dharma-nairātmya* is not the complete negation of the world of things, but rather stating the dependent nature of them.[9] Modern analytical science is also in agreement with the early Mādhyamikas that the experienced world exists relatively on an uncertain and indeterminable foundation. In other words, the experienced things do not leave an ultimate particle as a characteristic substance of the substratum of the experienced things. Even though this knowledge is important, it is not sufficient to redeem one from the world of suffering, for redemption requires a method to appease the dispositional tendency of the mind, which gestalts the phenomenal world as real and eternal. The discussion in the *Cittaviśuddhi-prakaraṇa* focuses on the ways and means to achieve change in the human personality. The *Cittaviśuddhi-prakaraṇa* goes on to say this aspect:

> The realization of the *Nairātmya* (essencelessness of subjective and objective entities), removes the notion of self, so also the erroneous perception of shell as silver is removed after the realization of shell.[10]

Here, it is clear that through dialectical knowledge one could discern the insubstantial nature of the phenomenal world. But for realizing the real nature of the world, one should practise required spiritual disciplines that could appease or change the dispositional tendencies and remove the causes of attachment and suffering. On the real reason for suffering, Kalupahana writes:

> His (the Buddha's) first priority, then, was to recognize the fact of suffering. Human beings are guided by the dispositions that can transform themselves into wishes and desires of the extreme sort, bringing them into conflict with the very constitution of the universe, namely, arising and ceasing (=dependent arising); in the case of the human universe, this constitution represents birth, old age, sickness, and death.[11]

When one attempts to remove the craving and clinging nature of the perceiving subject, dispositional tendency turns out to be the most important aspect, because the mind tends to latch on to the phenomenon (the conceived object). So it is clear that the dispositional tendencies become preponderant in determining a subjective stage of the personality, impelling one to accept the existence of metaphysical entities such as self that could influence the objective experience, and compelling one to look for mysterious substances. Thus, the solidified dispositional tendencies find their expression in the form of greed, lust, craving, or hatred, and these are referred as the cause of suffering.[12] Clarifying this view further, the *Cittaviśuddhi-prakaraṇa* says:

> With the perception of the rope, the notion of the snake in the rope is removed, for the notion of snake (in rope) is not coming back in this birth.[13]

When the human subject (the Yogi) attains control on the dispositional tendencies, he no longer sees the snake in a rope. The solidified dispositional tendencies are removed from the perception so that he would be able to view the rope as a rope. Viewing this problem in another way, the conceived object that could create dichotomous conceptualizations would change to cognized object, which is relatively clear and certain as the rope in the rope-snake anecdote. When one understands the relative existence of the rope, one is perfectly in harmony with the world of existence.

The conception of duality is absolutely essential for understanding the nature of life in the world; at the same time, the problem of duality should be transcended for cognizing the phenomenal world without the problem of dichotomous conceptualizations (*vikalpas*). Most of the philosophical systems reflected extensively on this problem. The

Sāṅkhya philosophy envisages the *Kaivalyamukti* as a stage of perfect understanding of the functioning of *Puruṣa* and that of *Prakṛti*, doubting the functioning of both entities is considered as the cause of dichotomous conceptualization. According to Sāṅkhyans, *vikalpas* are due to misconception of *buddhi* as *Puruṣa*. So, the removal of misconceptions is achieved through pure intellectual activity. In the case of Advaita philosophy, the *vikalpas* are due to the delusions manifested by *māyā*, which create a characteristic *jīva*; the *jīva* under the influence of *vikalpa* falsely identifies with the phenomenal realities (*vyāvahārika satya*) as the Brahman (*Paramārtha-satya*). In all these cases the transcendence of *vikalpas* is possible only with the removal of the play of duality by experiencing the reality of the entities the way they appear before us.

In the case of the early Mādhyamikas, they identified that the problem of *vikalpas* is due to the incessant thought that formulates in the mind and the mind's natural tendency to latch on to such thought constructs. It has been observed in the canonical texts of Buddhism that the problems of misconceptions are due to the human dispositions (*saṁskāras*), which must be changed or appeased through spiritual practices. The Yoga philosophy also takes a similar position that it is only through changing the influence of *saṁskāras* with the help of *buddhi*, one is able to attain *Kaivalyamukti*. If the problem of *saṁskāras* is not addressed properly, there is a serious problem of maintaining the spiritual perfection that the person acquired through spiritual practices. The *Cittaviśuddhi-prakarṇa* mainly addresses the problem that spiritual practices should be aimed at acquiring a change in the dispositions of the human personality. Its emphasis is not on the destruction of the dispositions or desire, but on achieving a change in the formulation of dispositions or desire. Here, the dialectics adopted is not the regressive analytical methodology discussed in the *Vigrahavyāvartinī* or the systematic analytical methodology; but the progressive method of analysis adopted in the *Hastavālanāma-prakaraṇavṛtti*. In this analytical methodology, one can see the rational reconstruction of phenomena (*dharma*) with the essence of phenomena (*dharmadhātu*).

The reading from the text is an important aspect of the discussion, where the focus is on the rational reconstruction of phenomena (*dharma*) with the essence of phenomena (*dharmadhātu*), the relatively actual nature of the world of things. This is possible only with a proper union of knowledge (*prajñā*) with suitable means (*upāya*). The meaning of knowledge is the dialectical knowledge; the *upāya* is the means through which one could attain the *cittaviśuddhi*, a stage at which one's dispositions would not interfere with the way he conceives the world of objects. Naturally, one would be able to see the world "as it is" without searching for a "mysterious something" as the true nature of the world. At the stage of *Bodhicitta*, when *prajñā* and *upāya* are commingled, one is able to see the *dharmadhātu* of things, knowing that the things themselves are insubstantial.

The text is very explicit in its introduction of Tantrism into the background of Mādhyamika philosophy. The Tāntric spiritual techniques are used as a method to appease the dispositional tendencies of the mind. The efficacy of Tāntric spiritual techniques in realizing the desired spiritual merit is pointed out through them so that one could attain the Bodhisattvahood in this life itself. The attainment of *cittaviśuddhi* means the realization of *pudgala-nairātmya*. Thus, when the notion of self is removed by removing ignorance, using knowledge (*prajñā*), and the dispositions are appeased or changed using Tāntric spiritual techniques (*upāya*), one realizes the true insubstantial nature of subjectivity and objectivity proving the conception of *dharma-nairātmya* and *pudgala-nairātmya*.

When we examine the ethical dimension of the Tāntric practices from the philosophical position of the Mādhyamikas, we can see that the Tāntric system, with its various types of techniques, agrees with those positions. Here, it is argued that the ethics of Mādhyamika is not a set of coded rules or a manifesto, but a set of well-designed spiritual practices that substantiate the doctrinal positions. What is introduced in the Mādhyamika teachings can be realized only through the practices of Tantra-Yoga, especially with the help of *mantra sādhana*. *Mantras* are considered as one of the most important spiritual technique to change the dispositional tendency of the mind and through them the desired *cittaviśuddhi* can be achieved directly. As S.B. Dasgupta writes:

> On the whole it seems that most of the Mantras and *Dhāraṇīs* are composed of a string of syllables which have lost their etymological meaning. Vasubandhu says in his *Bodhisattvabhūmi* that this absolute meaninglessness is the real significance of the Mantras. A *Sādhaka* is to meditate on these Mantras as something absolutely meaningless and this constant meditation on the

> meaninglessness of the Mantras will gradually lead to a state of mind where it will be very easy for him to meditate on the ultimate nature of the *dharmas* as absolutely meaningless; this meaninglessness is the void nature of the *dharmas* and, thus, the meditation on the Mantras will gradually lead a *Sādhaka* to the realization of the void nature of the *dharmas*.[14]

The *mantras* not only lead the mind to the realization of *śūnya*, but also protect the mind from falling into the trap of conceptualization (*vikalpas*). Thus, the use of *mantras* leads a *sādhaka* to the absolute meaninglessness of the dharmas and protects him from falling into conceptual formulations. *cittaviśuddhi-prakaraṇa* reiterates the function of *mantra* with the example of a person who need not use a mirror to see the bracelet in his own hand. Besides this, it also discusses the meaning of adopting sexo-yogic practices as a part of the *sādhana* for a Yogi as sex is one of the strongest human dispositions. It is inevitable for a Yogi to transcend the inherent craving tendency towards sex, for attaining *cittaviśuddhi*, otherwise, the *prajñā* obtained through dialectical knowledge would be absurd. Another spiritual practice discussed here is the use of martial arts as a spiritual training; this is also aimed at removing another important disposition of the human mind, that of anger and fighting. Though there are various spiritual techniques used by Tāntrics, the *mantra-sādhana*, the sexo-yogic *sādhana* and the martial arts practices, explain the rationale of such practices. The last verse of the text is a testimony to what has been discussed in this thesis. Āryadeva says:

> With the purification of the mind, I have obtained *Cittaviśuddhi* and immense happiness; let that happiness be attained by everyone through *Cittaviśuddhi*.[15]

On the question of providing an ethical foundation to the philosophical system of Mādhyamika, the responsibility is given to the Bodhisattva, who works with the people having intellectual acumen (*prajñā*) and spiritual maturity attained through suitable means (*upāya*), to provide spiritual and intellectual support, because it is impossible for each and every human being to practise these strenuous Tāntric spiritual disciplines. To quote again from the text in this regard, Āryadeva says:

> A wise person who is endowed with the natural compassion by nature, having *Śraddhā*, and well read, he alone can suggest the suitable *upāyas* to destroy sufferings of the Mankind, and he could also suggest suitable *upāyas* for obtaining happiness.[16]

Here, the methodology I have adopted is the same philosophical methodology introduced by the early Mādhyamikas which is in complete agreement with the original teachings of the Buddha. The attempt here is to understand the meaning of the conception of *dharma-nairātmya* and *pudgala-nairātmya*, because Buddhistic teachings are not in support of an eternally-existing subject or an eternally-existing object as the substratum of human experience. Buddha's silence relating to questions about the most subjective subject or the most objective object is the foundation of the discussions.

Our understanding of the world is mostly coloured by our expectations rather than the actual occurrences in the world of phenomena. It can also be the case that the human cognitive faculties are limited in many ways and it is absolutely impossible for it to adduce truth about the world of phenomena. We can see that the discussion in the *Vigrahavyāvartinī* exactly focuses on this aspect: it is not the *prameyas* that are undependable and insubstantial but it is the *pramāṇas* that reveal the *prameyas* that are insubstantial. The instruments of true cognition (*pramāṇas*) are not able to reveal the truth about the phenomenal world, and the premises of *pramāṇas* are logically inconsistent. So, the truth revealed by them also is not consistent and true.

Mādhyamikas contend that the logically inconsistent *pramāṇas* cannot reveal truths that are consistent and true though they can be conventionally true. They cannot be true even verifying with the experiences of the world of phenomena; the phenomena are dependent and insubstantial, the essential intrinsic nature of which is *śūnya*. The substantiation of the phenomenal world is the most important question that Buddhist philosophy tries to address. The findings of the Buddha as well as the later interpreters of Mādhyamika philosophy are that it is the dispositions and the feelings of the human personality configuring the notion of an eternal self. The notion of the eternal self, in turn, configures the things of the external world as real and existing, for substantiating its own existence. Most of the other schools of philosophy try to formulate theories based on the insubstantial self or insubstantial phenomenon. Mādhyamikas and other Buddhist schools criticize this aspect.

There is another interesting problem that we can observe in the modern world. The problem of theoretical frameworks which are actually meant to solve a problem are turning to be source of new frameworks or paradigms. This way of understanding the phenomenal world creates more problem than the problem of *pramāṇas*. Most of our understanding about the world is similar to or even less substantial than the case of theories formulated out of the information from *pramāṇas*. Our expectations of a world that works perfectly based on scientific principles are basically formulated out of insubstantial data.

Thomas Kuhn has discussed the problem of theoretical frameworks (paradigms). Most of the theoretical frameworks are considered as a reconciliation of certain diverse discussions on the same problem. The scientific community and society consider these paradigms as perfectly verified truth, since the truth value of such discussions are based on identifiable and provable evidences based on scientific reasoning. Ironically, many of these theoretical frameworks change characteristically when a more acceptable theory replaces them or questions the foundations of the existing theoretical frameworks. According to Kuhn:

> How are paradigms created, and how do scientific revolutions take place? Inquiry begins with a random collection of "mere facts" (although, often, a body of beliefs is already implicit in the collection). During these early stages of inquiry, different researchers confronting the same phenomena describe and interpret them in different ways. In time, these descriptions and interpretations entirely disappear. A pre-paradigmatic school appears. Such a school often emphasises a special part of the collection of facts. Often, these schools vie for pre-eminence. From the competition of these pre-paradigmatic schools, one paradigm emerges—To be accepted as a paradigm, a theory must seem better than its competitors, but it need not, and in fact never does, explain all the facts with which it can be confronted, thus making research possible. As a paradigm grows in strength and in the number of advocates, the other pre-paradigmatic schools or the previous paradigm fade.[17]

The problem discussed here is relevant to our observations about objective phenomena. The conceived or cognized phenomena are not certain and clear for the formulation of a theory, but the formulation of theoretical frameworks is an internal activity of man, irrespective of its ultimate truth validation. When a new framework, which is close to most of the observations, emerges with the acceptability of the scientific community, the old frameworks shift. What we observe in this situation is that the *pramāṇas* are not efficient enough to explain the *prameyas* with absolute certainty. The problem is not with the ontology of the phenomena (*prameyas*), but the inability of the cognitive faculties and the instruments of true cognition to find absolute truth about the world.

Buddhist philosophy is less concerned with the truth-value of the objective entities of the apparent world; it is more concerned with the truth-value of the conceived or cognized objects of the phenomenal world. The ontological nature of the conceived and cognized phenomena are insubstantial or *śūnya*. This aspect can be discernible through independent and impartial intellectual understanding. The problem introduced by Thomas Kuhn is one of such understanding that one and the same truth when analyzed by different people (the pre-paradigmatic discussions) produces different scientific truths. Whereas, when a theoretical framework (paradigm) is accepted by many scientists based on its utility all other pre-paradigmatic discussions stops and the framework assume acceptability. Similarly, our knowledge about the phenomenal world too is not based on actual analysis of the phenomenal realities, but on paradigms created by most acceptable observations. According to Buddhist philosophy, finding a proposition about the apparent world and the subsequent formulations of theoretical frameworks are due to an inherent nature of the mind, which originates from the dispositions and feelings of the human personality and ignorance. Knowledge is instrumental in removing ignorance, which is the state of unenlightened mind; but the dispositions can only be changed by suitable practices. Tāntric systems provide suitable techniques to appease the dispositions that create the notion of permanence.

Introduction of *śūnya* for a philosophical understanding of the existence of the world is not introduced by the early Mādhyamikas or the Buddhist thinkers. This concept was a part of a discussion on classical Indian philosophy even before the Buddha. The pre-Buddhistic non-Brāhmanical thinkers have introduced the conception of *śūnya* and interpreted in various dimensions: Some of the materialistic schools introduced it from the perspective of the voidness of the existent world and what is experienced or seen as similar to a dream; for some other it is the emptiness of the subjective self as they proclaim the existence only of the materialistic world; for the Upaniṣadic schools of Brāhmanical tradition, it is the insubstantial nature of the phenomenal world in relation to the eternally existing soul or self; for the schools like Ājīvikas, it is the emptiness of certainty of any logical position about the phenomenal world; the Sañjaya School or Amaravikṣepas (logical sceptics), it is a perfect example or construing negative premises for logical understanding as they engage in arguments with negative propositions as *śūnyatā* is the best way to understand the phenomenal world. The Mādhyamikas' understanding of the term is very different from all these views as they introduce very clear and specific limits for the conception of the phenomenal world with the introduction of two terms, the *pudgala-nairātmya* and the *dharma nairātmya*. It means that the *śūnyatā* is either the insubstantiality of phenomena or the insubstantiality of the substantial self, and not the apparent world.

Our discussion followed this logical method of understanding the phenomenal world, which agrees with almost all positions but at the same time disagrees with all the philosophical understandings. Firstly, understanding the elemental composition of the phenomena (*dharma*) that are cognized or conceived; secondly, the nature of the human-personality (*pudgala*) that cognizes the phenomena. Buddhist philosophy proves that the phenomenon appears as real, because the cognizing subjective faculties (human personality) configure them as real and eternal. Most of the philosophical systems accept the insubstantial nature of phenomenal realities, but posit a true and mysterious reality subsisting with them. Mādhyamikas, on the other hand, reject any mysterious reality behind the phenomena, and state that the human personality and the phenomena are equally insubstantial, introducing this with the conception of *pudgala-nairātmya* and *dharma-nairātmya*. Here, it is also argued that only through cleansing the mind (*cittaviśuddhi*) of the influence of dispositions on the human personality, one is able to realize the insubstantial nature of the phenomenal world. On the other hand, if the realization of *dharma-nairātmya* is only through knowledge, then it causes the formulation of a theory based on *dharma-nairātmya* or it remains as an entity in the realm of intellectual understanding. In short, the cleansed mind is able to experience the insubstantial nature of the phenomenal realities, and also see the arising and ceasing (dependent) nature of the phenomenal world.

References

1. D.T. Suzuki, *Studies in the Laṅkāvatārasūtra*, p. 288.
2. Peter Della Santania, *Mādhyamika Schools in India*, p. 154.
3. David J. Kalupahana, *A History of Buddhist Philosophy*, p. 78.
4. Ibid., pp. 80, 81.
5. Ibid., p. 83.
6. Ibid., p. 166.
7. T.R.V. Murti, op. cit., p. 131.
8. *Vigrahavyāvartinī*, v. 70.
9. David J. Kalupahana, *A History of Buddhist Philosophy*, pp. 162-65.
10. *Cittaviśuddhi-prakaraṇa*, v. 67.
11. David J. Kalupahana, *A History of Buddhist Philosophy*, p. 87.
12. Ibid., p. 89.
13. *Cittaviśuddhi-prakaraṇa*, v. 68.
14. Sashibhushan Dasgupta, *An Introduction to Tāntric Buddhism*, p. 59.
15. Ibid., v. 133.
16. Ibid., v. 100.
17. Thomas Kuhn, *The Structure of Scientific Revolutions*, synopsis by Frank Pajares, http:// www.philosophers.co.uk.

Appendix

आर्यदेवविरचित चित्तविशुद्धिप्रकरणम्
Āryadevaviracita Cittaviśuddhi-prakaraṇam
(The *Cittaviśuddhi-prakaraṇa* of Āryadeva with Sanskrit Text and English Translation)

अनादिनिधनं शान्तं भावाभावविवर्जितम्।
निर्विकल्पं निरालम्बमनवस्थितमद्वयम्॥१॥
अदृष्टान्तमनाख्यानमचिन्त्यमनिदर्शनम्।
अनाश्रयाप्रतिष्ठानं निर्विकारमसंस्कृतम्॥२॥
सर्वेषामाश्रयं बुद्धं करुणामयविग्रहम्।
नानाधिमुक्तसत्त्वानां नानोपायप्रदर्शकम्॥३॥
महारागं नमस्कृत्य पद्मनर्तेश्वरं प्रभुम्।
इह स्तोकं प्रवक्ष्यामि स्वचित्तप्रत्यवेक्षणात्॥४॥

anādinidhanaṁ śāntaṁ bhāvābhāvavivarjitam /
nirvikalpaṁ nirālambaṁ anavasthitaṁ advayam // 1 //
adṛṣṭāntaṁ anākhyānaṁ acintyaṁ anidarśanam /
anāśrayāpratiṣṭhānaṁ nirvikāraṁ asaṃskṛtam // 2 //
sarveṣāṁ āśrayaṁ buddhaṁ karuṇāmayavigrahaṁ /
nānādhīmuktasattvānām nānopāyapradarśakaṁ // 3 //
mahārāgaṁ namaskṛtya padmanarteśvaraṁ prabhum /
iha stokaṁ pravakṣyāmi svacittapratyavekṣaṇāt // 4 //

1-4. After offering my most respectful salutations to the Buddha, seated in the lotus posture, I explain in nutshell, with due respects, about him depending on my introspections: The great lord who is also an embodiment of quietude *(śāntham)*, who transcends existence and non-existence, unsupported; who is beginningless and endless; who doesn't have a specified existence, non-dual; who can't be perceived without a name, beyond thought and uninstanceable; who doesn't have a substratum, unestablished, without any modification and cannot be articulated (*saṁskṛta*). At the same time, everyone can depend on the Buddha, who is the centre for all beings to seek refuge, because he is an embodiment of compassion (*karuṇā*); he presents and offers manifold means (*upāya*) to the beings, who seeks liberation (aspiring to be Bodhisattvas).

योगाचारस्य नयतः सर्वमेव सुनिश्चितम् ।
तत्सर्वमिह वक्तव्यं तस्मादेतत्समाचरेत् ॥५॥
yogācārasya nayataḥ sarvameva suniścitam /
tatsarvamiha vaktavyaṁ tasmādetatsamācaret // 5 //

5. By the principle of Yogācāra everything (about the universe), indeed, has been established. All that have been stated and explained here.

येन येन हि बन्ध्यन्ते जन्तवो रौद्रकर्मणा ।
सोपायेन तु तेनैव मुच्यन्ते भवबन्धनात् ॥६॥
yena yena hi badhyante jantavo raudrakarmaṇā /
sopāyena tu tenaiva mucyante bhavabandhanāt // 6 //

6. All those forbidding actions (*raudrakarma*) which can bind a person to the world of existence; such forbidding actions, if used intelligently, can release the person from the shackles of those bondages that bind him to the *saṁsāra*.

विशुद्धेरेव सत्वस्य विशुद्धं जायते फलम् ।
महायाने सुविस्पष्टमुक्तमेतत्सुविस्तरम् ॥७॥
viśuddhereva satvasya viśuddhaṁ jāyate phalam /
mahāyāne suvispaṣṭamuktametatsuvistaram // 7 //

7. Pure results are obtained from the purity (of the mind) of beings like Bodhisattvas; the Mahāyāna school have clearly explained this aspect and elucidated it accordingly.

धर्मपुद्गलनैरात्म्यं[१] चित्तमात्रं जगौ मुनिः ।
ततोऽपि सर्वमुत्पन्नमागमात्यनुकूलकम्[२] ॥८॥
dharmapudgalanairātmyaṁ cittamātraṁ jagau muniḥ /
tato'pi sarvaṁ utpannaṁ āgamātyanukūlakaṁ // 8 //

[१] नैरात्म्यात् ।

[२] न्नं गमकं सुनीराकुलम् ।

[3] The conceived objective thing is called *citta-mātra*, the subjective aspect of

8. It is said by sages that the *cittamātra*[3] (the conceived phenomenon) is constituted of *pudgala-nairātmya* and *dharma-nairātmya*; everything originated from that; this is elaborately described in the Bauddhāgamas.

भावग्रहावेश[४] गृहीतान्प्रतिचोदितम् ।
आगमेऽपि हि सुव्यक्तो विस्तरः करुणात्मना ॥९ ॥
bhāvagrahāveśagṛhitānpraticoditam /
āgame'pi hi suvyakto vistaraḥ karuṇātmanā // 9 //

9. Holding on to existence is activated like the crocodile grab[5] (holding on to existence in this world is controlled by instincts similar to crocodile grab). The compassionate one (the Buddha) has explained elaborately and clearly about this aspect in the (Bauddha) Āgamic texts.

मनःपूर्वङ्गमा धर्मा मनःश्रेष्ठाः[६] मनोजवाः ।
मनसा[७] हि प्रसन्नेन भाषते वा करोतिवा ॥१० ॥
manaḥ pūrvaṅgamā dharmā manaḥśreṣṭhāḥ manojavāḥ/
manasā hi prasannena bhāṣate vā karoti vā // 10 //

10. The conceived phenomena (*dharma*) are born in the mind and also superior function of mind is born in the mind; without the mind is clear, how one could speak out or act on.

स्वपता भिक्षुणा[८] वृद्धः शीघ्रं गच्छति प्रेरितः[९] ।
पतनाच्च मृते तस्मिन्नान्तर्यैण युज्यते[१०] ॥११ ॥
svapatā bhikṣuṇā vṛddhaḥ śīghraṁ gacchati preritaḥ/
patanācca mṛte tasminnāntaryeṇa hi yujyate // 11 //

the object for mind, *caitta*, see Thomas A. Kochumuttom, *A Buddhist Doctrine of Experience*, p. 203. See also, David J. Kalupahana, *A History of Buddhist Philosophy*, p. 81.

[४]पभ्रावेश ।

[5]The crocodile grab is considered as a strong seizure from which freeing is a difficult task.

[६]श्रेष्ठं ।

[७]सा च प्रदुष्टेन ।

[८]णादिष्टः ।

[९]प्रेरितम् ।

[१०]गृह्यते ।

11. (Suppose) A monk instigate an old man, who has fallen, to walk fast, if the old man falls down and dies, it is said that the death does not happened because of the suggestion of the monk. In this example the old man represent the *dharma* (phenomena) and the sleeping monk is the mind (with its original nature) that the mind is not responsible, at this stage, all the actions of the individual.

स्वग्लनेनार्हतादिष्टः स्वगलं परिपीडितम् ।
उपस्थायकभिक्षुः स मृते तस्मिन्न दोषभाक् ॥१२॥
svaglānenārhatādiṣṭaḥ svagalaṁ paripīḍitam /
ūpasthāyakabhikṣuḥ sa mṛte tasminna doṣabhāk // 12 //

12. Because of one's sadness, one torments his voice from the throat.[11] Similarly if the old man dies, the sage is not responsible for the death of the old man.[12]

अन्यसंज्ञया[१३] नान्यास्तु[१४] मारयन्दोषमश्नुते ।
इत्युक्तं विनये व्यक्तं न दोषोऽदुष्टचेतसाम् ॥१३॥
anyasaṁjñayā nānyāstu mārayandoṣamaśrute /
ityuktaṁ vinaye vyaktaṁ na doṣo'duṣṭacetasām // 13 //

13. It is clearly said in the Vinaya that sin is not a product of cruelty, so also because of others' words or of the presence of others happening death is not heard.

न स्तूपखनने[१५] दोषस्तत्संस्कारधिया यतः[१६] ।
केवलं पुण्यराशिः [१७]स्यादुपानन्तर्यकारणात् ॥१४॥
na stūpakhanane doṣastatsaṁskāradhiyā yataḥ /
kevalaṁ puṇyarāśiḥ syādupānantaryakāraṇāt // 14 //

14. The persons, whose mind is with pure impressions, will not accrue any sin, even for digging up a stūpa. For those who have transcended sufferings (*duḥkha*), any actions result in acquisition of merit.

[11]*The Buddhist Hybrid Sanskrit Grammar and Dictionary* gives the meaning of *galitam* is "fluent voice."

[12]The intention of the *bhikṣu* was not to torture the old man.

[१३]अन्यसङ्गीनि ।

[१४]चाल्यास्तु ।

[१५] खल्णे ।

[१६]मतम् ।

[१७]स्यादुःइखानन्तर्य ।

उपानद्युगलं[१८] दत्त्वा मुनेर्मूर्ध्नि शुभाशयात्।
अपनीय तथा [१९]चान्यो राज्यं फलमवाप्नुतः॥१५॥
upānadyugalaṁ datvā munermūrdhni śubhāśayāt /
apanīya tathā cānyo rājyaṁ phalamavāpnutaḥ // 15 //

15. A person who places a pair of shoes on the head of a sage with good intention, and also another person, who removes them from there, both would acquire the merit equally to that of a kingdom. Here, it is made clear that all those actions which are meant for redeeming a person from suffering would benefit a person with a lot of merit; also if the mind is pure the highest of sins would not resulting to any demerit.

[२०]तस्मादाशयमूला हि पापपुण्यव्यवस्थितिः।
इत्युक्तमागमे यस्मान्नापत्तिः शुभचेतसाम्॥१६॥
tasmādāśayamūlā hi pāpapuṇyavyavasthitiḥ /
ityuktamāgame yasmānnāpattiḥ śubhacetasām // 16 //

16. Therefore, the scheme of merit (*puṇya*) and demerit (*pāpa*) is based on intention. Since it is said in the Āgamas that the auspicious minded people won't conflicts with this.

[२१]स्वाधिदैवतयोगात्मा जगदर्थकृतोद्यमः।
भुष्ठानो विषयान् योगी[२२] मुच्यते न [२३]च लिप्यते॥१७॥
svādhidaivatayogātmā jagadarthakṛtodyamaḥ /
bhuṣṭhāno viṣayān yogī mucyate na ca lipyate // 17 //

17. A Yogi, who's self is in association with the natural gods, while making efforts for world's wellbeing, is not tainted even while enjoying sense objects, but remains liberated.

यथैव विषतत्वज्ञो विषमालोक्य भक्षयन्।
केवलं मुह्यते नासौ रोगमुक्तश्च जायते॥१८॥
yathaiva viṣatattvajño viṣamālokya bhakṣayan /
kevalaṁ muhyate nāsau rogamuktaśca jāyate // 18 //

18. As a person who knows the alchemy of the poison sees and understands the poison, by consuming it not just falls unconscious, but is relieved of diseases. There are many

[१८]मयुगलं।
[१९]चान्यं।
[२०]दाश्रयं।
[२१]स्वाधिदेवत।
[२२]योगात्।
[२३]चलिस्यति।

medicines, which are made from poison, by people who know alchemy. Such medicines may make a person unconscious, but it has the power to cure diseases. Āyurveda have many such medicines.

मायामरीचिगन्धर्वनगरस्वप्नसन्निभम् ।
जगत्सर्वं समालोक्य किं कथं केन भुज्यते ॥१९ ॥
māyāmarīcigandharvanagarasvapnasannibham /
jagatsarvaṁ samālokya kim katham kena bhujyate // 19 //

19. The whole universe is like an illusory mirage, or a city of dreams (*gandharvanagara*), or similar to a dream (*swapna*); having seen such a world, "who" enjoy "what" by "whom."

बाला रज्यन्ति[२४] रूपेषु वैराग्यं यान्ति मध्यमाः ।
स्वभावज्ञा विमुच्यन्ते रूपस्योत्तमबुद्धयः ॥२० ॥
bālā rajyanti rūpeṣu vairāgyaṁ yānti madhyamāḥ /
svabhāvajñā vimucyante rūpasyottamabuddhayaḥ // 20 //

20. The inferior men (*bālā*),[25] get attracted to objects of forms (phenomena); the mediocre intelligent men go for renunciations; the superior ones who understands the true nature of the forms (phenomena)—the *dharmadhātu*—get liberated.

विचिन्त्य समयं सर्वं देवतापूजनाविधिम् ।
शुद्धमालोक्य निःशङ्कं भोक्तव्यं मन्त्रचोदितम् ॥२१ ॥
vicintya samayaṁ sarvaṁ devatāpūjanāvidhim /
śuddhamālokya niḥśaṅkaṁ bhoktavyaṁ mantracoditam
// 21 //

21. Such persons (the Mahāyānist Yogis) have to ponder over all the schools (of philosophy), all the methods of worshipping deities; after conforming the purity, he should do everything without any confusion but should be done it in accordance with the prescribed *mantras*.

[२४] मज्जन्ति ।

[25] The people who are with distorted dispositions and strong feelings (in the Buddhist's sense, an under cultivated personality).

शोध्यं बोध्यं तथा दीप्यमक्षरत्रययोगतः।
अङ्गुष्ठानामिकाग्राभ्यां प्रीणयेच्च तथागतान् ॥२२॥
śodhyaṁ bodhyaṁ tathā dīpyamakṣaratrayayogataḥ /
aṅguṣṭhānāmikāgrābhyāṁ prīṇayecca tathāgatān // 22 //

22. One should purify, understand and illumine, with the association of the three syllables (Bīja *mantras*), through the thumb, ring finger and forefinger so that he could please the Bodhisattvas. The *mantras* have the intrinsic power to cleanse the mind and protect the mind from any sort of conceptualisations. The three-syllable Bīja *mantra* is very important as for the Tāntric practices.

यत्सत्यमिति बालानां तन्मिथ्या खलु योगिनाम्।
[२६]गच्छन्नन्तमनेनैव न बद्धो न च मुच्यते ॥२३॥
yatsatyamiti bālānāṁ tanmithyā khalu yogināṁ /
gacchannantamanenaiva na baddho na ca mucyate // 23 //

23. The truth and reality for an average intelligent person is illusory and unreal for a Yogi; by transcending the faculties of mind, he is neither bound nor released. If one can envision the reality, there is neither *saṁsāra* nor *nirvāṇa*. The *nirvāṇa* is real for one who is under the whimsical influence of *saṁsāra*, but one who have transcended all the dualities there is neither *saṁsāra* nor *nirvāṇa*.

संसारं चैव निर्वाणं मन्यन्तेऽतत्वदर्शिनः।
न संसारं न निर्वाणं मन्यन्ते तत्वदर्शिनः ॥२४॥
saṁsāraṁ caiva nirvāṇaṁ manyante'tattvadarśinaḥ /
na saṁsāraṁ na nirvāṇaṁ manyante tattvadarśinaḥ // 24 //

24. *Saṁsāra* and *nirvāṇa* are real for one who is ignorant (*atattvadarśinaḥ*); *saṁsāra* and *nirvāṇa* are redundant for those who are enlightened (*tattvadarśinaḥ*).

विकल्पो हि महाग्राहः संसारोदधिपातकः।
अविकल्पा महात्मानो मुच्यन्ते भवबन्धनात् ॥२५॥
vikalpo hi mahāgrāhaḥ saṁsārodadhipātakaḥ /
avikalpā mahātmāno mucyante bhavabandhanāt // 25 //

[२६]कार्येनैव तु संप्राप्तम्।

25. Dichotomous conceptualisations (*vikalpa*) is like a big crocodile that pulls one into the ocean of *saṁsāra*; those great souls, freed from the notion of dichotomous conceptualisations (*vikalpa*), are released from the bondage of *saṁsāra.*

शङ्काविषेण बाध्यन्ते विषेणैव पृथग्जनाः ।
[२७]तमिवोत्खात्य निर्मूलं विचरेत्करुणात्मकः ॥२६ ॥

śaṅkāviṣeṇa bādhyante viṣeṇaiva pṛthagjanāḥ /
tamivotkhātya nirmūlam vicaret karuṇātmakaḥ // 26 //

26. The poison in the form of doubt ordinarily affects normal people; nevertheless, by digging it out, the compassionate one (Bodhisattva) moves forward, without being affected by such alternatives (*vikalpas*).

यथैव स्फटिकः स्वच्छः परागेण रज्यते ।
तथैव चित्तरत्नं तु कल्पनारागरञ्जितम् ॥२७ ॥

yathaiva sphaṭikaḥ svacchaḥ pararāgeṇa rajyate /
tathaiva cittaratnaṁ tu kalpanārāgarañjitam // 27 //

27. A colourless and clear crystal receives the colour of the objects placed near to it; the inherently pure mind gem, which is similar to a crystal, pure and untainted, gets affected by thought constructions.

[२८]प्रकृत्या कल्पनारागैर्विविक्तं चित्तरत्नकम् ।
आदिशुद्धमनुत्पन्नं [२९]निःस्वभावमनाविलम् ॥२८ ॥

prakṛtyā kalpanārāgairviviktaṁ cittaratnakam /
ādiśuddhamanutpannaṁ niḥsvabhāvamanāvilam // 28 //

28. The original nature of mind-gem[30] is devoid of any thought construction; it is pure without any taints, beginnigless, and of non-intrinsic nature (*nis-svabhāva*).

तत्तद्यत्नेन कर्तव्यं [३१]यद्यद्बालैर्विगर्हितम् ।
स्वाधिदैवतयोगेन चित्तनिर्मलकारणात् ॥२९ ॥

[२७]तामे ।

[२८]प्रकृते ।

[२९]निजरूप ।

[30]The gem is considered as a pure thing, which is untainted originally.

[३१]द्बालविगर्हितम् ।

tattadyatnena kartavyaṁ yadyadvālairvigarhitam /
svādhidaivatayogena cittanirmalakāraṇāt // 29 //

29. In order to purify the mind, many things, which are censured by ordinary people, are to be performed by the Yogis, carefully, with dedication to one's personal God. The Tāntric practices permit certain privileges that are not permitted to ordinary people, but it should be performed with the directions of the traditionally accepted practices.

रागाग्निविषसंमुग्धा योगिनां [३२]शुभचेतसा।
कामिताः खलु कामिन्यः [३३]काममोक्षफलावहाः ॥३०॥
rāgāgniviṣasaṁmugdhā yogināṁ śubhacetasā /
kāmitāḥ khalu kāminyaḥ kāmamokṣaphalāvahāḥ // 30 //

30. The damsels, filled up with desire, in the form of poison and fire of passion, will fill the pure minds of the Yogis with desire; indeed, they (the damsels) acquire the fruits of both the desire and the liberation. The sexo-yogic practice is a part of certain Tāntric practices. It says that a woman would be benefited by such practices that she fill up the mind of the Yogi with desire and help him to remove that desire.

यथा स्वगरुडं ध्यात्वा [३४]विषमाकृष्य संपिवन्।
करोति [३५]निर्विषं साध्यं न विषेणाभिभूयते ॥३१॥
yathā svagaruḍaṁ dhyātvā viṣamākṛṣya saṁpivan /
karoti nirviṣaṁ sādhyaṁ na viṣeṇābhibhūyate // 31 //

31. This is similar to the instance of a physician who cures poisoning (*Viṣa-vaidya*), bringing out the poison under control, by meditating on the Lord Garuḍa, and by drinking it; he won't be affected by the negative effect of the poison. Here it is high lighted the merits of the spiritual practices of Tantra, because if such practices that are detrimental, practised according to the right method, could bring very positive results.

द्वादशयोजनव्यासं चत्रं वैशिरसि भ्रमन्।
बोधिचित्तंा समुत्पाद्य अपनीतमिति श्रुतिः ॥३२॥

[३२]शुद्धचेतसा।
[३३]काममोच्य।
[३४]गारुडिको विषं पिवन्।
[३५]हि विषम्।

dvādaśayojanavyāsaṁ cakraṁ vai śirasi bhraman /
bodhicittāṁ samutpādya apanītamiti śrutiḥ // 32 //

32. As we have heard that there is a wheel having diameter of twelve *yojanas* moving in the head producing *Bodhicitta* and recedes by itself. This might be the testimonial declaration of some Yogis or referred from some texts.

बोधिचित्तं समुत्पाद्य सम्बोधौ कृतचेतसा।
तन्नास्ति यन्न कर्तव्यं जगदुद्धरणाशया॥३३॥
bodhicittaṁ samutpādya sambodhau kṛtacetasā /
tannāsti yanna kartavyaṁ jagaduddharaṇāśayā // 33 //

33. With the production of *Bodhicitta*, the mind is centred on *saṁbhodhi* (the perfect realisation); there is nothing more one should do in order to salvage the world.

आदिशुद्धमनुत्पन्नं निःस्वभावमनाविलम्।
जगद्भावेन सम्पथ्यन्न बद्धो न च मुच्यते॥३४॥
ādiśuddhamanutpannaṁ niḥsvabhāvamanāvilaṁ /
jagadbhāvena sampathyanna baddho na ca mucyate // 34 //

34. The real nature of the world is pure from the beginning, non-originated, not having a nature of its own whatsoever. Conceiving such a world one is neither bound nor released.

विचिन्त्य विधिवद्योगी देवतागुणविस्तरम्।
[३६]रज्यते रागचित्तेन रागभोगेण मुच्यते॥३५॥
vicintya vidhivadyogī devatāguṇavistaram /
rajyate rāgacittena rāgabhogeṇa mucyate // 35 //

35. A Yogi systematically meditating upon the qualities of different Godheads with a mind full of desire, is getting liberated by the objects of desire, at the same time enjoying the objects of desire.

किं कुर्मः [३७]कुत्र वैलभ्या विचित्रा भावशक्तयः।
[३८]विषात्क्रान्तो यथा कश्चिद्विषेणैव तु निर्विषः॥३६॥
kim kurmaḥ kutra vai labhyā vicitrā bhāvaśaktayaḥ /
viṣākrānto yathā kaścidviṣeṇaiva tu nirviṣaḥ // 36 //

[३६]रागयेत् रागचितेन रज्यते न च मुज्यते।
[३७]कालाय लभ्या।
[३८]विषाज्जा(घ्रा)तो।

36. The power of existence is indeed confusing, especially with regard to what to do and where to obtain (liberation), yet it is like somebody who is affected by poison can be de-poisoned by poison alone. The nature of the world of existence is very confusing that one cannot seek any proper direction independently, but one can see from the world of experience that the effect of poison can be removed by poison alone.

कर्णाज्जलं जलेनैव कण्टकेनैव कण्टकम् ।
रागेणैव तथारागमुद्धरन्ति मनीषिणः ॥३७॥
karṇājjalaṁ jalenaiva kaṇṭakenaiva kaṇṭakam /
rāgeṇaiva tathārāgamuddharanti manīṣiṇaḥ // 37 //

37. The clogged water in the ear is removed by pouring more water; the pierced thorn is removed by another thorn, similarly, the wise people transcend the effect of desire by desire alone. Except the Tāntrics, most of the spiritual disciplines advocates abstinence from desire; Tāntrics are practical people who believe in the actual development of spiritual merit.

यथैव रजको वस्त्रं मलेनैव तु निर्मलम् ।
कुर्य्याद्विज्ञस्तथात्मानं मलेनैव तु निर्मलम् ॥३८॥
yathaiva rajako vastraṁ malenaiva tu nirmalam /
kuryyādvijñastathātmānaṁ malenaiva tu nirmalam // 38 //

38. A washerman uses dirt (of mud and ash) to cleanse the cloth from dirt; in the same way a wise man uses desire to cleanse the mind (from desire).

यथा भवति संशुद्धो रजोनिर्घृष्टदर्पणः ।
सेवितस्तु तथा विज्ञैर्दोषो दोषविनाशनः ॥३९॥
yathā bhavati saṁśuddho rajonirghṛṣṭadarpaṇaḥ /
sevitastu tathā vijñairdoṣo doṣavināśanaḥ // 39 //

39. By accepting the defects, wise people destroy the defects in them, as a dusted mirror is cleansed when rubbed with (the same type of) dust.

लोहपिण्डो जले क्षिप्तो मज्जत्येव तु केवलम् ।
पात्रीकृतं तदेवान्यं तारयेत्तरति स्वयम् ॥४०॥
lohapiṇḍo jale kṣipto majjatyeva tu kevalam /
pātrīkṛtaṁ tad evānyaṁ tārayettarati svayam // 40 //

40. An iron ball in water drowns naturally; but when made into a vessel, it floats and takes another person across the water.

तद्वत्पात्रीकृतं चित्तं प्रज्ञोपायविधानतः ।
भुञ्जानो मुच्यते कामो मोचयत्यपरानपि ॥४१ ॥
tadvatpātrīkṛtaṁ cittaṁ prajñopāyavidhānataḥ /
bhuñjāno mucyate kāmo mocayatyaparānapi // 41 //

41. Similarly, by converting the mind into a vessel through the union of *prajñā* and *upāya*, the wise man gets liberated from the desires through the enjoyment, and he helps others to redeem.

दुर्विज्ञैः सेवितः कामः कामो भवति बन्धनम् ।
स एव सेवितो विज्ञैः कामो मोक्षप्रसाधकः ॥४२ ॥
durvijñaiḥ sevitaḥ kāmaḥ kāmo bhavati bandhanam /
sa eva sevito vijñaiḥ kāmo mokṣaprasādhakaḥ // 42 //

42. The objects of desire and its enjoyment, for an unwise person, could become a source of bondage (*bandhanam*); the same object of desire and its enjoyment, for a wise person, becomes a source of liberation. All the spiritual practices of Tantrism should be practised under the guidance of a *guru* and the prescribed texts; otherwise the same practices that are meant to redeem a person could turn out be a source of bondage.

प्रसिद्धं [३९]सकले लोके [४०]क्षीरं विषविनाशनम् ।
तदेव फणिभिः पीतं सुतरां विषवर्धनम् ॥४३ ॥
prasiddhaṁ sakale loke kṣīraṁ viṣavināśanam /
tadeva phaṇibhiḥ pītaṁ sutarāṁ viṣavardhanam // 43 //

43. It is well-known in the world that milk has the capacity to neutralise poison (and is used as a medicine against poisoning); at the same time, the same milk consumed by a snake increases the poison in it.

जले क्षीरं यथाविष्टं हंसो पिवति पण्डितः ।
सविषान् विषयांस्तद्वदुभुक्त्वा मुत्तरुश्च पण्डितः ॥४४ ॥

[३९]सहसाल्लोक्य ।
[४०]क्षारं ।

jale kṣīraṁ yathāviṣṭaṁ haṁso pibati paṇḍitaḥ /
saviṣān viṣayāṁstadvadubhuktvā muktaśca paṇḍitaḥ // 44 //

44. Like a swan, drinking the milk alone from a mixture of milk and water, a wise person enjoys the world of objects and becomes liberated.

यथैव विधिवद्भुक्तं विषमप्यमृतायते ।
दुर्भुक्तं घृतपूरादि बालानान्तु विषायते ॥४५ ॥

yathaiva vidhivadbhuktaṁ viṣamapyamṛtāyate /
durbhuktaṁ ghṛtapūrādi bālānāntu viṣāyate // 45 //

45. Even the poison can turn into nectar (*amṛta*), if consumed according to the directive associated with it; whereas, the sweet made out of ghee can turn into a poison, if consumed improperly. As far as the world of objects are concerned one should find a fine and wise balance in its use; improper use by immature people would create more sufferings.

इदमेव हि यच्चित्तं शोधितं हेतुभिः शुभैः ।
निर्विकल्पं निरालम्बं भाति प्रकृतिनिर्मलम् ॥४६ ॥

idameva hi yaccittaṁ śodhitaṁ hetubhiḥ śubhaiḥ /
nirvikalpaṁ nirālambaṁ bhāti prakṛtinirmalam // 46 //

46. The mind, which is purified by auspicious means (*upāyas*) and which become independent (*nirālambam*) and freed from conceptualisations (*nirvikalpam)*; it will manifests in a naturally pure form (*prakṛtinirmalam*).

यथा वह्निः कृशोप्येष तैलवर्त्यादिसंस्कृतः ।
दीपो निर्मलनिष्कम्पः स्थिरस्तिमिरनाशनः ॥४७ ॥

yathā vahniḥ kṛśo'pyeṣa tailavartyādisaṁskṛtaḥ /
dīpo nirmalaniṣkampaḥ sthirastimiranāśanaḥ // 47 //

47. A thin flamed fire, when prepared with (*saṁskṛta*) oil, wick and suitable surroundings, becomes bright and still, and it destroys the pervading stillness of darkness.

वटबीजं यथा सूक्ष्मं सहकारसमन्वितम् ।
शाखामूलफलोपेतं महावृक्षविधायकम् ॥४८ ॥

vaṭabījam yathā sūkṣmaṁ sahakārasamanvitam /
śākhāmūlaphalopetaṁ mahāvṛkṣavidhāyakam // 48 //

48. A small and tiny seed of a banyan tree when associated with suitable means grows into a big tree with roots, fruits and branches. The suitable means (*upāyas*) are extremely important for any thing to find its way in this existent world.

हरिद्राचूर्णसंयोगाद्वर्णान्तरमिति स्मृतम् ।
प्रज्ञोपायसमायोगाद्धर्मधातुं तथा विदुः ॥४९ ॥
haridrācūrṇasaṁyogādvarṇāntaramiti smṛtam /
prajñopāyasamāyogāddharmadhātum tathā viduḥ // 49 //

49. Colours of substance change, when mixed with turmeric; in the same way the wisdom (*prajñā*) of a person change for revealing *dharmadhātu*, when properly associated with suitable means (*upāya*). It is important to develop and inculcate suitable spiritual techniques to realise *Bodhicitta* and *saṁbodhi.*

घृतञ्च मधुसंयुक्तं [४१]समांशं विषतां व्रजेत् ।
तदेव विधिवद्भुक्तमुत्कृष्टन्तु रासायनम् ॥५० ॥
ghṛtañ ca madhusaṁyuktaṁ samāṁśaṁ viṣatāṁ vrajet /
tadeva vidhivadbhuktamutkṛṣṭaṁ tu rasāyanam // 50 //

50. When an improper mix of honey, ghee and meat made into a compound, it can turn out to be a poison; but the same meat compound prepared properly, in accordance with the prescribed rules (*vidhi)*, it becomes the best rejuvenating tonic.

[४२]रसघृष्टं यथा ताम्रं निर्दोषं काञ्चनं भवेत् ।
[४३]ज्ञानशुद्धया तथा क्लेशाः सम्यक् कल्याणकारकाः ॥५१ ॥
rasaghṛṣtaṁ yathā tāmraṁ nirdośaṁ kāñcanaṁ bhavet /
jñānaśuddhayā tathā kleśāḥ samyak kalyāṇa-
kārakāḥ // 51 //

51. The unalloyed copper and mercury (*rasa*) when rubbed together, the copper changes into gold; auspicious results accrue (in the mind) when the afflictions are rubbed away by knowledge.

हीनयानाभिरूढानां मृत्युशङ्का पदे पदे ।
[४४]संग्रामजयचित्तस्तु दूर एव व्यवस्थितः ॥५२ ॥

[४१]समांसं ।
[४२]रासास्पृष्टं ।
[४३]ज्ञानावृत्दथा क्लेशः ।
[४४]संग्रमजयतुन्तेन ।

hīnayānābhirūḍhānāṁ mṛtyuśaṅkā pade pade /
saṁgrāmajayacittastu dūra eva vyavasthitaḥ // 52 //

52. The followers of the path of Hīnayāna, are afraid of death in every moment. A person, after winning a battle, should stay away from fighting. For the practitioners of the Hīnayāna school of Buddhism, *nirvāṇa* is considered as the ultimate reality to be realised. After realising *nirvāṇa* he strive hard to protect it, so he lives in the constant fear of death. For those Yogis who practise Mahāyāna *nirvāṇa*, are not in a stage of attainment, they transcend both *nirvāṇa* and *saṁsāra*.

महायानाभिरूढस्तु करुणाधर्मवर्मितः।
प्रज्ञातन्तुधनुर्बाणो जगदुद्धरणाशयः ॥५३॥
mahāyānābhirūḍhastu karuṇādharmavarmitaḥ /
prajñātantudhanurbāṇo jagaduddharaṇāśayaḥ // 53 //

53. The practitioners of Mahāyāna are protected by *karuṇā* and *dharma*,[45] and the wisdom (*prajñā*) is like the thread of the bow from where an arrow can be set off, in order that to redeem the world. The practitioners of Mahāyāna understand the real nature of the world of existence that they transcend the fear of everything, even death.

महासत्त्वो महोपायः स्थिरबुद्धिरतन्द्रितः।
जित्वा दुस्तरसङ्ग्रमं तारयेदपरानपि ॥५४॥
mahāsattvo mahopāyaḥ sthirabuddhiratandritaḥ /
jitvā dustarasaṅgramaṁ tārayedaparānapi // 54 //

54. A person, with enormous courage (*mahāsattva*); endowed with great many means (*mahopāya*); and firm intelligence (*sthirabuddhi*), and who is steady and unwavering, wins over the difficult world, and helps others to win over the difficulties of the world.

पशवोऽपि हि क्लिश्यन्ते स्वार्थमात्रपरायणः॥
जगदर्थविधातारो धन्यास्ते विरला जनाः॥५५॥
paśavo'pi hi kliśyante svārthamātraparāyaṇaḥ /
jagadarthavidhātāro dhanyāste viralā janaḥ // 55 //

[45]Here the meaning of *dharma* is the religious literature based on the teachings of the Buddha.

55. Taking care of the selfish ends alone, even animals are bound to suffer. The blessed ones are those who care for the welfare of the world, and they are very few.

शीतवातादिदुःखानि सहन्ते स्वार्थलम्पटाः ।
जगदर्थप्रवृत्तास्ते न सहन्ते कथं नु ते ॥५६॥

śītavātādiduḥkhāni sahante svārthalampaṭāḥ /
jagadarthapravṛttāste na sahante katham nu te // 56//

56. Selfish people are fools, because of selfishness they suffer from the problems of winter, rain, storm, and such natural happenings; the people who are dedicated after the welfare of the world, are not bothered about such problems.

नारकाण्यपि दुःखानि सोढव्यानि कृपालुभिः ।
शीतवातादिदुःखानि कस्तान्यपि विचारयेत् ॥५७॥

nārakāṇyapi duḥkhāni soḍhavyāni kṛpālubhiḥ /
śītavātādiduḥkhāni kastānyapi vicārayet // 57 /

57. The suffering caused by the changes in weather like heat, cold and storm, are immaterial to a compassionate Yogi who dedicated his life for the benefit of the world, is prepared even to face the suffering of the hell.

न [४६]कष्टकल्पनां कुर्यान्नोपवासेन न क्रियाम ।
स्नानं शौचं न चैवात्र ग्रामधर्मं विवर्जयेत् ॥५८॥

na kaṣṭakalpanām kuryānnopavāsena na kriyām /
snānam śaucam na caivātra grāmadharmam
vivarjayet // 58 //

58. One need not undergo penance, or undertake fasting as a part of his rituals or follow routine like bathing, cleaning and the like (the *grāmadharmas*), for attaining liberation.[47]

नखदन्तास्थिमज्जानः पितुः शुक्रविकारजाः ।
मांसशोणितकेशादि मातृ शोणितसम्भवम् ॥५९॥

nakhadantāsthimajjānaḥ pituḥ śukravikārajāḥ /
māṁsaśoṇitakeśādi matṛśoṇitasambhavam // 59 //

[४६]निष्टकल्पानां ।

[47]The text written in the back drop of the Brāhmanical (Mīmāṁsā) spiritual praxis, which according to Ārydeva, is having its own problems for the attainment of *mokṣa* (liberation).

59. In the constitution of the human body, the nail, the teeth, the bones and the marrow are the transformation of father's semen; the flesh, the blood, the hair, and the like, are originated from the blood of the mother.[48]

इत्थमशुचिसम्भूतः पिण्डो [४९]योऽशुचिपूरितः ।
कथं [५०]संस्तादृशः कायो गङ्गास्नानेन शुध्यति ॥६० ॥
itthamaśucisambhūtaḥ piṇḍo yo'śucipūritaḥ /
katham saṁstādṛśaḥ kāyo gaṅgāsnānena śuddhyati // 60 //

60. Thus the body is originated from impurities and is full of impurities. Will such a body be purified by bathing in Gaṅgā? Bathing in Gaṅgā is considered by the Brāhmanical systems as a secret *dharma* that can purify the body which contains the soul.

न ह्यशुचिर्घटस्तोय क्षालितोऽपि पुनः पुनः ।
तद्वदशुचिसम्पूर्णः पिण्डोऽपि न विशुद्ध्यति ॥६१ ॥
na hyaśucirghaṭastoya kṣālito'pi punaḥ punaḥ /
tadvadaśucisampūrṇaḥ piṇḍo'pi na viśuddhyati // 61 //

61. A pot which is inherently impure cannot be purified, even if it is washed repeatedly by water; so also the body which is filled with impurities, cannot be purified by washing (even in Gaṅgā water).[51]

प्रतरन्नपि गङ्गायां नैव श्वा शुद्धिमर्हति ।
तद्वधर्मधियां पुंसां तीर्थस्नानं तु निष्फलम् ॥६२ ॥
pratarannapi gaṅgāyāṁ naiva śvā śuddhimarhati /
tadvaddharmadhiyāṁ puṁsāṁ tīrthasnānaṁ tu
niṣphalam // 62 //

62. A dog which swam across Gaṅgā should get the purity suppose to have acquired by a Brāhman; similarly the Brāhman who practises bathing in holy places also like the dog, would not get any benefit of purity.

[48]This belief might have been existed at the time of Āryadeva.

[४९]य्होशुचिपूरितः ।

[५०]सन् तादृशः ।

[51]Purifying through washing is considered as ritual that has the intrinsic value of cleansing the mind or soul.

धर्मो यदि भवेत्स्नानातकैवर्तानां [52]कृतायति।
नक्तन्दिवं [53]जलस्नस्थानां मत्स्यादीनां तु का कथा॥६३॥
dharmo yadi bhavetsnānātakaivartānāṁ kṛtāyati /
naktandivaṁ jalasthānāṁ matsyādīnāṁ tu kā kathā // 63 //

63. If *dharma* accrues, by bathing in holy waters, then the fisher-folk will be the gainers, not to talk of the fish and other organisms which reside in such waters, day and night.

पापक्षयोऽपि स्नानेन नैव स्यादिति निश्चयः।
यतो रागादिवृद्धिस्तु दृश्यते तीर्थसेविनाम्॥६४॥
pāpakṣayo'pi snānena naiva syāditi niścayaḥ /
yato rāgādivṛddhistu dṛśyate tīrthasevinām // 64 //

64. It is widely seen that people who have taken holy bath are having more attachment (to things of the world), so it is definite that removal of sin is not possible by holy bath.

रागो द्वेषश्च मोहश्च ईर्ष्या तृष्णा च सर्वदा।
पापानां मूलमाख्यातं नैषां स्नानेन शोधनम्॥६५॥
rāgo dveṣaśca mohaśca īrṣyā tṛṣṇā ca sarvadā /
pāpānāṁ mūlamākhyātaṁ naiṣāṁ snānena
śodhanam // 65 //

65. The roots of sin are well-known to be attachment, aversion, delusion, jealousy, craving, ablution (washing away by water) cannot purify these things from the mind. Since the real nature of sin is not known to these Yogis, their Yogic practices won't earn them anything, that the negative notions are prevalent and due to lack of care they may be more active in them.

आत्मात्मीयग्रहादेते सम्भवन्ती जन्मिनः।
अविद्याहेतुकः सोऽपि साविद्या भ्रान्तिरिष्यते॥६६॥
ātmātmīyagrahādete sambhavantī janminaḥ /
avidyāhetukaḥ so'pi sāvidyā bhrāntiriṣyate // 66 //

66. Mistaking of non-self for self and vice versa is the reason for rebirth. This mistaking of non-self for self is due to *avidyā*, and that *avidyā* is known as delusion.

[52]कृतार्थता।
[53]प्रविष्टानां।

रौप्यबुद्धिर्यथा शुक्तौ शुक्तिदृष्टया निवर्तते ।
नैरात्म्यादर्शनात्सापि निर्मूलमवसीदति ॥६७ ॥

raupyabuddhiryathā śuktau śuktidṛṣṭaya nivartate /
nairātmyādarśanātsāpi nirmūlamavasīdati // 67 //

67. Just as the erroneous perception of shell as silver is removed after the realisation of shell, even the latter is uprooted by the realisation of the *nairātmya*. The things of the world are of non-intrinsic nature. It is doubted to be having intrinsic nature and that is the real reason for delusion. Delusion is the real reason for sin. It cannot be removed by ablution, that it is necessary to have definite spiritual practices to remove delusion.

सर्पबुद्धिर्यथा रज्जौ रज्जुदृष्टौ निवर्तते ।
सर्पबुद्धिः पुनस्तत्र नैव स्यादिह जन्मनि ॥६८ ॥

sarpabuddhiryathā rajjau rajjudṛṣṭau nivartate /
sarpabuddhiḥ punastatra naiva syādiha janmani // 68 //

68. With the perception of the rope, the notion of the snake in the rope is removed, for the notion of snake (in rope) does not return in this birth. When mind is free from conceptualisations after spiritual practices, it would be able to see the essence of phenomena (*dharmadhātu*) of each phenomena, it loosing its clinging to the phenomena of the apparent world.

सत्वबुद्धिस्तथात्रापि वज्रज्ञानान्निवर्तते ।
न भावः सम्भवेत्तत्र दग्धबीज इवाङ्कुरः ॥६९ ॥

sattvabuddhistathātrāpi vajrajñānānnivartate /
na bhāvaḥ sambhavettatra dagdhabīja ivāṅkuraḥ // 69 //

69. The notion of everything as existing is removed by the dawn of *vajrajñāna* in the mind. It is impossible to have the notion of everything as existing again in the mind, like the impossibility of a sprout to be germinated from a fried seed.

नैरात्म्याशुचिसंसृष्टः पिण्डः प्रकृतिनिर्मलः ।
तस्य सन्तापने धर्मः कथं बालैर्विकल्पितः ॥७० ॥

nairātmyāśucisaṁsṛṣṭaḥ piṇḍaḥ prakṛtinirmalaḥ /
tasya santāpane dharmaḥ kathaṁ bālairvikalpitaḥ // 70 //

70. With the discernment of *nairātmya*, the body become pure; people with average intelligence tormenting the body (as a part of spiritual practice), is very difficult to accept. As the Brāhmanical schools engage in dogmatic ritualistic practices as a part of their spiritual self-culture, the materialistic schools and the Jainas engage in spiritual practices that are similar to tormenting the body, which is indeed difficult for Mādhyamikas to accept.

चन्द्रोदयव्ययश्चापि अपेक्ष्य तिथिकल्पना ।
सूर्योदयव्ययेनापि दिवारात्रिव्यवस्थितिः ॥७१ ॥
पूर्वादिव्यवहारोऽपि कल्पनापेक्षया क्वतः ।
ग्रहनक्षत्रराश्यादि सर्वलोकैर्विकल्पितम् ॥७२ ॥

candrodayavyayañcāpi apekṣya tithikalpanā /
sūryodayavyayenāpi divārātrivyavasthitiḥ // 71 //
pūrvādivyavahāro'pi kalpanāpekṣayā kvataḥ /
grahanakṣatrarāśyādi sarvalokairvikalpitam // 72 //

71-72. The calendar is based on the rising and setting of moon. The rising and setting of sun decide the days and nights. The four directions like east, west, north, and south; and the astrological usage like planets (*graha*), *nakṣatra* (stars), constellation of stars (*rāśi*), etc., are merely verbal reference and imaginary innovations of human beings (*vikalpa*).[58] The usage of such things as direction and astrological predictions are a part of the dogmatic ritualistic Brāhmanical schools, which Āryadeva refutes.

शीतोष्णवर्षणापेक्षा तथैव ऋतुकल्पना ।
स्वकर्मफलभोगोऽयं शुभाशुभग्रहोदितः ॥७३ ॥

śītoṣṇavarṣaṇāpekṣā tathaiva ṛtukalpanā /
svakarmaphalabhogo'yaṁ śubhāśubhagrahoditaḥ // 73 //

73. The seasons such as summer, rain and winter and also the imagination about the seasons, that all these manifestations are for experiencing the results of one's own *karma*, which is arising from the position of auspicious and inauspicious planetary positions.

अविद्याकर्दमालिप्तं चित्तचिन्तामणिंः पुमान् ।
प्रवृत्तः क्षालितुं विद्वान् कोऽविद्यां बृंहयेत्पुनः ॥७४ ॥

avidyākardamāliptaṁ cittacintāmaṇiḥ pumān /
pravṛttaḥ kṣālituṁ vidvān ko'vidyāṁ brṁhayetpunaḥ // 74 //

74. The mind (*cittacintāmaṇi*) is like gem immersed in the mud of impurities, in the form of ignorance (*avidyā*). If a wise man endeavours to cleanse it up, who could make an effort to increase the volume of ignorance (*avidyā*). If a Yogi tries to cleanse his mind from all the afflictions, he can make great success in the effort; no one can stop him from attaining his end.

न [५४]ग्रहतिथिनक्षत्रदेशकालाद्यपेक्षणम् ।
विहरेन्निर्विकल्पस्तु निर्निमित्तमशङ्कितः ॥७५ ॥
na grahatithinakṣatradeśakālādyapekṣaṇam /
viharennirvikalpastu nirnimittamaśaṅkitaḥ // 75 //

75. When one decides to renounce the world, he can denounce the humanly manifested things like calendar, *nakṣatra*, time and place, as the renunciate is not going to suffer from the world of alternatives; he does not require any instruments for living and he can live without being in fear of losing anything from the world.

यद्यदिन्द्रियमार्गत्वं यायात्तत्तत्स्वभावतः ।
सुसमाहितयोगेन सर्वं बुद्धमयं वदेत् ॥७६ ॥
yadyadindriyamārgatvaṁ yāyāttattatsvabhāvataḥ /
susamāhitayogena sarvaṁ buddhamayaṁ vadet // 76 //

76. The (phenomena), originated out of sense organs, are having intrinsic nature in accordance with their activities; nevertheless a wise man, because of his control of mind, puts everything as in the form of Buddha (*Buddhamayam*).

चक्षुर्वैरोचनो बुद्धः श्रवणं वज्रसूर्यकः ।
घ्राणं च परमाश्वस्तु पद्मनर्तेश्वरो मुखम् ॥७७ ॥
कायः श्रीहेरुको राजा वज्रसत्त्वश्च मानसम् ।
एवं सम्यक् सदा योगी विचरेत्करुणात्मकः ॥७८ ॥
cukṣurvairocano buddhaḥ śravaṇaṁ vajrasūryakaḥ /
ghrāṇaṁ ca pramāśvastu padmanarteśvaro mukham // 77 //

[५४]वाराति ।

kāyaḥ śrīheruko rājā vajrasattvaśca mānasam /
evaṁ samyak sadā yogī vicaretkaruṇātmakaḥ // 78 //

77-78. Filled with full of compassion in the mind, the Yogi moves around with *Vairocana* Buddha as his eyes; *Vajrasūrya* Buddha as his ears; *Parameśvara* Buddha as his nose (sense to smell); *Padmanarteśwara* as his mouth; *Śrī Heruka* as his body; *Vajrasattva* as his mind.

[५५]सिद्धान्ती निर्विकल्पोऽसौ स्थिरकल्पस्तु धीधनः ।
यथेष्टचेष्टाव्यापारः[५६] सर्वभुक् सर्वकृत्तथा ॥७९ ॥

siddhāntī nirvikalpo'sau sthirakalpastu dhīdhanaḥ /
yatheṣṭaceṣṭāvyāpāraḥ sarvabhuk sarvakṛttathā // 79 //

79. All his contemplation and activities are done in accordance with his volition, hence he can enjoy anything and perform anything, his views determined about the world, being freed from the influence of all alternatives, with established intellect as his wealth.

सर्वकामक्रियाकारी यथारुचितचेष्टितः[५७] ।
उत्थितो वा निषण्णो वा चङ्क्र मन्वा स्वपंस्तथा ॥८० ॥

sarvakāmakriyākārī yathārucitaceṣṭitaḥ /
utthito vā niṣaṇṇo vā caṅkra manvā svapaṁstathā // 80 //

80. He is one who does all activities in order to satisfy his desire; he can be without any activities, if he desires so: he stands, sits, moves or sleeps. Here, it is clear that the attachment to desire is natural and a part of human life, but what is to be declined is the desire commingled with ignorance, which is dangerous to one's spiritual well being.

अमण्डलप्रविष्टो वा सर्वावरणवानपि ।
स्वाधिदैवतयोगात्मा मन्दपुण्योऽपि सिध्यति ॥८१ ॥

amaṇḍalapraviṣṭo vā sarvāvaraṇavānapi /
svādhidaivatayogātmā mandapuṇyo'pi sidhyati // 81 //

81. Even if he has to live in places where he is bounded (like a captive) or in places where he is absolutely free, without

[५५]सिद्धान्तो ।
[५६]व्यहारी ।
[५७]रुचिरचेष्टितम् ।

any boundaries, he enjoys his existence and his association with his duties, even though they are less meritorious.

अनेन सर्वसौरित्वं सर्वबुद्धत्वमेव वा।
जन्मनीहैव तत्त्वज्ञः सम्प्राप्नोति न संशयः ॥८२॥
anena sarvasauritvam sarva buddhatvameva vā /
janmanīhaiva tattvajñaḥ samprāpnoti na saṁśayaḥ // 82 //

82. There is no doubt about the fact that with the help of Yoga, an enlightened person, can attain the divine qualities, the Buddha nature, in this life itself. Mādhyamika always advocated the attainment of Enlightenment in this life itself; it rejects the notion of realisation of it in another world, in another birth, at pre-determined time, or of total nullity.

यथा [५८]प्राकृतलोकेन योगिलोको न बाध्यते।
बाध्यन्ते धीविशेषेण योगिनोऽप्युत्तरोत्तरैः ॥८३॥
yathā prākṛtalokena yogiloko na bādhyate /
bādhyante dhīviśeṣeṇa yogino'pyuttarottaraiḥ // 83 //

83. The world of Yogis doesn't get sublated by the ordinary world; the special mind of the Yogi sublates the influence of the ordinary world in course of time. The relationship with the existent world and the Yogis world are same, but the Yogi sees and experiences them differently.

महाप्रज्ञमहोपायमहाकृपाधिमोक्षतः।
महायानसमुद्दिष्टं महासत्त्वस्य गोचरम् ॥८४॥
mahāprajñamahopāyamahākṛpādhimokṣataḥ /
mahāyānasamuddiṣṭaṁ mahāsattvasya gocaram // 84 //

84. The path of a *Mahāsattva* (Bodhisattva) who follow Mahāyāna is filled with *Mahāprajñā, Mahopāya, Mahākṛpā,* and *Mahākaruṇā.*

यत्कल्पानामसंख्येयैर्न प्राप्तं बहुभिर्मतम्[५९]।
जन्मन्यत्रैव बुद्धत्वं प्राप्यते नात्र संशयः ॥८५॥
yatkalpānāmasaṁkhyeyairna prāptaṁ bahubhirmatam /
janmanyatraiva buddhatvaṁ prāpyate nātra saṁśayaḥ // 85 //

[५८]प्रकृतको लोको।
[५९]बहुभिर्मतैः।

85. The achievement that hasn't taken place in innumerable births, after following different school of philosophies, can be achieved in this life here. There is no doubt about this.

महायानस्य महात्म्यां पुण्यज्ञानेन[६०] सम्भृतम्[६१] ।
सर्वज्ञत्वं पदं रम्यं सद्योजन्मनि लभ्यते ॥८६ ॥
mahāyānasya mahātmyāṁ puṇyajñānena sambhṛtam /
sarvajñatvaṁ padaṁ ramyaṁ sadyo janmani labhyate // 86 //

86. The greatness of the Mahāyāna contains in the meritorious knowledge that the beautiful stage of being, the omniscience, can be achieved in this life itself.

आगमश्रुतिचिन्ता तु महायाने न गृह्यते ।
आशयानुशयाभेदाद् यानभेदः प्रकाश्यते ॥८७ ॥
āgamaśruticintā tu mahāyāne na gṛhyate /
āśayānuśayābhedād yānabhedaḥ prakāśyate // 87 //

87. The understanding of the Mahāyāna is not complete without the Āgamas (Bauddhāgamas); because of the different dispositions and attachments, there are different paths (*yāna*) introduced.

[६२]अन्य एवाधिमोक्षोऽयं तथान्या बोधिचरिका ।
अन्याचित्तविशुद्धिश्च फलमन्यदिहोच्यते ॥८८ ॥
anya evādhimokṣo'yaṁ tathānyā bodhicārikā /
anyācittaviśuddhiśca phalamanyadihocyate // 88 //

88. According to Mahāyāna, the theory relating to enlightenment, the practices for getting enlightenment, the mental purification (*cittaviśuddhi*), and the results to be spoken of, are different (from one another).

[६३]समीपे निर्मलादर्शे रूपं निर्मलचक्षुषः ।
यथा भाति सुविस्पष्टं स्वच्छप्रकृतिनिर्मलम् ॥८९ ॥
विधूतकल्पनाजालविस्पष्टशुद्धचेतसां ।
योगिनाञ्च तथा ज्ञानं प्रज्ञानिर्मलदर्पणैः ॥९० ॥

[६०]महात्म्यात् पुण्यज्ञनस्य ।

[६१]सम्भवः ।

[६२]अन्यत्र बोधि ।

[६३]समिपं निर्मलदर्शे चिरं ।

samīpe nirmalādarśe rūpaṁ nirmalacakṣuṣaḥ /
yathā bhāti suvispaṣṭaṁ svacchaprakṛtinirmalam // 89 //
vidhūtakalpanājālavispaṣṭaśuddhacetasām /
yogināñca tathā jñānaṁ prajñānirmaladarpaṇaiḥ // 90 //

89-90. The image of one standing in front of a mirror, is reflected clearly, if one's eyesight is clear and the mirror is limpid; similarly, for the Yogis whose minds are purified from the distractions of imaginations and the gamut of imaginations, knowledge arises clearly like in a mirror. The knowledge (about the external world) in the mind is getting immersed in the distractions of imaginations, once that is purified, the mind reflecting the knowledge like in a mirror.

सूर्यकान्तिसमाश्रिष्टसूर्यकान्तमणौ यथा ।
सहसा प्रज्वलत्यग्निः समथः स्वार्थसाधने ॥९१ ॥
अपास्तकल्पनाजालं सूर्यकान्तनिभं मनः ।
प्रज्ञासूर्यां सुसंश्लिष्टं तद्वज्ज्वलति योगिनाम् ॥९२ ॥
sūryakāntisamāśriṣṭasūryakāntamaṇau yathā /
sahasā prajvalatyagniḥ samarthaḥ svārthasādhane // 91 //
apāstakalpanājālaṁ sūryakāntanibhaṁ manaḥ /
prajñāsūryāṁsusaṁśliṣṭaṁ tadvajjvalati yoginām // 92 //

91-92. When the geṁ Sūryakāntamaṇi is associated with sunrays, is capable of achieving its own purpose (producing fire); similarly the mind-like the gem, in association with *prajñā*, is able to destroy the totality of imaginations, so that it illuminates from the mind of Yogis.

काष्ठद्वयनिघर्षेण यथा ज्वलति पावकः ।
आदिमध्यान्तसंशुद्धः सर्ववस्तुप्रकाशकः ।
प्रज्ञोपायसमायोगाद्योगिज्ञानं तथा विदुः ॥ ९३ ॥
kāṣṭhadvayanigharṣeṇa yathā jvalati pāvakaḥ /
ādimadhyāntasaṁśuddhaḥ sarvavastuprakāśakaḥ /
prajñopāyasamāyogādyogijñānaṁ tathā viduḥ // 93 //

93. When two pieces of wood rubbed against each other fire originates. It is pure in the beginning, in the middle and in the end, it illuminates the objects of the world; in the same manner, when *prajñā* and *upāya* are brought together they produce Yogic knowledge of pure nature.

यथौवैकःप्रदीपोऽयं वर्त्यन्तरसमाश्रितः ।
यथास्वार्थं यथास्थानं करोत्युच्चैः प्रकाशनम् ॥९४

yathauvaikaḥ pradīpo'yaṁ varttyantarasamāśritaḥ /
yathāsvārthaṁ yathāsthānaṁ karotyuccaiḥ
prakāśanaṁ // 94 //

94. As a lamp is lighted from the wick of another lamp, illuminating the objects around it, the knowledge arising from *prajñā* and *upāya* could illuminate and help others to receive the wisdom.

स्फुरणानन्तमूर्तिस्तु प्रज्ञोपायविभावनैः ।
नानाधिमुक्तसत्त्वनां यथाकृत्यमनुष्ठयेत् ॥९५॥

sphuraṇānantamūrtistu prajñopāyavibhāvanaiḥ /
nānādhimuktasattvanāṁ yathākṛtyamanuṣṭhayet // 95 //

95. Through the *prajñā* and *upāya* and meditations, one can destroy the multiplicity of minds, manifesting the omniscient at the highest stage.

विधिज्ञो हि यथा कश्चित्क्षीरादमृतमुद्धरेत् ।
निर्दोषं शीतलं हृद्यं सर्वव्याधिविनाशनम् ॥९६॥

vidhijño hi yathā kaścitkṣīrādamṛtamuddharet /
nirdoṣaṁ śītalaṁ hṛdyaṁ sarvavyādhivināśanam // 96 //

96. If a person knows the way (injunctions), he can extract nectar (*amṛta*) from the milk that is non-defective, cool, soothing of the heart, and panacea for all the diseases.

प्रज्ञाक्षीरमहोपायाद्विधिवन्मथनोत्थितः ।
विशुद्धधर्मधातुः स सुखासुखविनाशनः ॥९७॥

prajñākṣīramahopāyādvidhivanmathanotthitaḥ /
viśuddhadharmadhātuḥ sa sukhāsukhavināśanaḥ // 97 //

97. The milk of *prajñā* when churned by the great *upāyas* there arises the *dharmadhātu*, destroying all the pleasure (*sukha*) and pain (*duḥkha*). When the wisdom get associated with the adequate means (*upāya*), the churning effect of that association is revealing the *dharmadhātu* (the real nature of the phenomenal reality), which is transcending the realm of pleasure and pain.

यथा लता समुद्भूता फलपुष्पसमन्विता।
तथैकक्षणसम्बोधिः सम्भारद्वयसंयुता॥९८॥

yathā latā samudbhūtā phalapuṣpasamanvitā /
tathaikakṣaṇasambodhiḥ sambhāradvayasaṁyutā // 98 //

98. Just as a creeper coming up with beautiful flowers and fruits, the instantaneous enlightened state (*saṁbodhi*) originated with the association of the two accessories.

[वशद्वेषगतिस्तम्भ] [६४]घर्षणाकर्षणादिकम्।
मद्यमांसरती[६५] योगी कुर्वन्नाप्युपलिप्यते॥९९॥

[vaśadveṣagatistambha] gharṣaṇākarṣaṇādikam /
madyamāṁsaratī yogī kurvannāpyupalipyate // 99 //

99. A Yogi perfects his *sādhanas* with all the adjuncts of his practices like meat, alcoholic drinks, sexo-yogic practice and he acquires powers like controlling (*vāśikaraṇa*), creating jealousy (*dveṣa*), movement (*gati*), stoppage (*stambha*), making contact, and attracting things; he however is not influenced by any of these. The Tāntric practices as a system considered sexo-yogic practices together with the consumption of alcoholic drinks and eating of meat as a part of the spiritual discipline. A Yogi also attains certain powers because of his superior mental faculties, but he never be influenced by any of these, either the methods of practice or the results of such practices.

[हस्तकङ्कणबिम्बाय कि] मादर्शः समीक्ष्यते।
महायाने यतोऽद्यापि मन्त्रसामर्थ्यदर्शनम्[६६]॥१००॥

[hastakaṅkaṇabimbāya ki] mādarśaḥ samīkṣyate /
mahāyāne yato'dyāpi mantrasāmarthyadarśanam // 100 //

100. To see the bracelet in one's own hand, one need not use a mirror; similarly in Mahāyāna, it is certain and clear that through the efficacy of *mantras* one can attain enlightenment.

मातृदुहितृसम्बन्ध [स्तत्त्वतोऽथ न कल्पयते।
भग्नायोधूपवर्त्तीव] जगदाह तथागतः॥ १०१॥

[६४]वर्षणाकर्षणा।

[६५]मद्यमांसरतो।

[६६]मन्त्रसामर्ध्यदर्शनत्।

mātṛduhitṛsambandha [*stattvato'tha na kalpayet* /
bhagnāyodhūpavarttīva] *jagadāha tathāgataḥ* // 101 //

101. According to the Tathāgata, there is no such relationship with one's mother, daughter, etc.; in reality, it is like broken armour or an extinguished lamp. A Yogi should himself transcend the restrictions of relationships even with own mother, sister and daughter, etc.

पञ्चभूतात्मकं शुक्रं शोणितञ्चापि तादृशम् ।
तन्मयः खलु पिण्डोऽयं को विप्रः कश्च वान्त्यव्रजः ॥१०२॥

pañcabhūtātmakaṁ śukraṁ śoṇitañcāpi tādṛśam /
tanmayaḥ khalu piṇḍo'yaṁ ko vipraḥ kaśca vāntyavrajaḥ // 102 //

102. Semen is made up of the five elements (*pañcabhūtas*), and the blood is also made of same *pañcabhūtas*; the body in its totality is a manifestation of all these; therefore what is the difference between a Brāhman and a Caṇḍāla.

[पञ्चस्कन्धात्मकम् सर्वं] शरीरं खलु भिक्षवः ।
अनित्यं दुःखशून्यञ्च न जातिर्न च जातिमान्[६७] ॥१०३॥

[*pañcaskandhātmakaṁ sarvaṁ*] *śarīraṁ khalu bhikṣavaḥ* /
anityaṁ duḥkhaśūnyañca na jātirna ca jātimān // 103 //

103. Oh Bhikṣus! Indeed the physical body consists of *pañcaskandhas* and it is ephemeral in nature and thus devoid of any sorrow (*duḥkha-śūnya*). Because of this reason, it cannot belong to (*jāti*) or represent any (*jāti*).[68]

कैवर्त्तीगर्भसम्भूतः कश्चिच्चाण्डालजातिमान् ।
तपसा ब्राह्मणो जातस्तस्माज्ज्ञातिरकारणम् ॥१०४॥

kaivarttīgarbhasambhūtaḥ kaściccāṇḍālajātimān /
tapasā brāhmaṇo jātastasmājjātirakāraṇam // 104 //

104. Some person born to a fisherwoman, or somebody who belong to the caste of the Caṇḍāla can be reborn as a Brāhman

[६७] जातिवान् ।

[68] The mention of *pañcaskandha* is the mention of the editor (as he had included in the place of the missing words). It could be *pañcabhūta*, which normally meant to express the physical body, but the *skandhas* are representing the subjective stage or the mind. One belongs to a particular caste claim greatness because of his birth, which cannot be accepted.

through his penance, thus the question of caste itself stands unsubstantiated. The importance of caste hegemony in the spiritual practices says that a person born in a certain caste is born with certain karmic purity that cannot be changed, but the examples shown are sound and clear that such claims are unsubstantiated.

स्वसारं मातरं श्वशुरं स्वपुत्रीं भागिनेयिकाम् ।
ब्राह्मणीं क्षत्रियां वैश्यां विधिज्ञानेन शूद्रिकाम् ॥१०५॥
एकाङ्गविकलां हीनां गर्हितामन्त्यजामपि ।
योषितं पूजयेन्नित्यं ज्ञानवज्रप्रभावनैः ॥१०६॥

svasāraṁ mātaraṁ śvaśuraṁ svaputrīṁ bhāgineyikām /
brāhmaṇīṁ kṣatriyāṁ vaiśyāṁ vidhijñānena śūdrikām // 105 //
ekāṅgavikalāṁ hīnāṁ garhitāmantyajāmapi /
yoṣitaṁ pūjayennityaṁ jñānavajraprabhāvanaiḥ // 106 //

105-6. Because of the perfect knowledge and the influence of *Vajrasattva*, a person (Yogi) would worship the mother, the sister, the mother-in-law, the daughter, the niece, and the sister's daughter; or a lady belonging to the Brāhman caste, the Kṣatriya caste, the Vaiśya caste, or the Śūdra caste; or somebody handicapped, one condemned by the society, or one belonging to the lowest strata of society.

सर्वदा स्मितवक्त्रेण मन्त्रविस्तृतचक्षुषा ।
सम्बोधौ चित्तमुत्पाद्य स्वाधिदैवतभावतः ॥१०७॥
पश्येदृश्यं क्षणं किञ्चिच्छ्रोतव्यं शृणुयात्तथा ।
सत्यासत्यवियुक्तं तु वदेद्वाक्यमतन्द्रितः ॥१०८॥

sarvadā smitavaktreṇa mantravistṛtacakṣuṣā /
sambodhau cittamutpādya svādhidaivatabhāvataḥ // 107 //
paśyedṛśyaṁ kṣaṇaṁ kiñcicchrotavyaṁ śṛṇuyāttathā /
satyāsatyaviyuktaṁ tu vadedvākyamatandritaḥ // 108 //

107-8. After opening his mind to the *saṁbodhi* with the help of the *mantras* and the patent deity, the Yogi will be keeping a smiling face with pleasant appearance and broad vision. The Yogi listens only what to be listened perceives only what is to be perceived. He remains quiet, and speaks a little that is neither true nor false.

स्नानाभ्यञ्जनवस्त्रादिखानपानादियन्ततः ।
स्वाधिदैवतयोगेन चिन्तयेत्पूजनाविधिम् ॥ १०९ ॥
[गीतं] वाद्यं तथा नृत्यं सोपायेन व्रत भजेत् ।
अकुर्वन्निह भावेषु सर्वेष्वभिनिवेशनम् ॥ ११० ॥

snānābhyañjanavastrādikhānapānādiyantataḥ /
svādhidaivatayogena cintayetpūjanāvidhim // 109 //
[*gītaṁ*] *vādyaṁ tathā nṛtyaṁ sopāyena vrata bhajet /*
akurvanniha bhāveṣu sarveṣvabhiniveśanaṁ // 110 //

109-10. One should take care of his spiritual practices in a prescribed way such as meditating on one's personal God; ensures personal cleanliness like smearing of oil, clothing, eating, drinking, etc. Such a person, a *sādhaka* would practise music both instrumental and vocal, and also the dance, without developing any attachment towards them.

स्वात्मभावप्रहाणेन तापयेन्न तपस्यया ।
सुखाद्यथा सुखं ध्यायेत्सम्बुद्धोऽयमनागतः ॥ १११ ॥

svātmabhāvaprahāṇena tāpayenna tapasyayā /
sukhādyathā sukhaṁ dhyāyetsambuddho'yamanā-
gataḥ // 111 //

111. The austerity and spiritual practices are meant for the destruction of the notion of self, and it should not be by tormenting the body, because happiness comes out of happiness and the enlightenment doesn't have an origin at all. The *sādhaka* should develop healthy methods of spiritual practices, and it is not advisable to make such practices which are based on tormenting the body. This argument is against some of the heterodox schools which promote tormenting of the body as a spiritual method.

सर्वकामोपभोगैस्तु रमथ मुक्तितोऽभयात् ।
मा भैष्ट नास्ति वइ पापं समयो दुरतिक्रमः ॥ ११२ ॥

sarvakāmopabhogaistu ramatha muktito'bhayāt /
mā bhaiṣṭa nāsti vai pāpaṁ samayo duratikramaḥ // 112 //

112. Since there is no fear about the liberation (*mukti*), one can enjoy all the pleasures of the world; there is no sin attached with these activities, but one has to pass the time properly. A Yogi is not striving for liberation after death or aiming at a

different stage of existence, for him the liberation happen with the awaking of *saṁbodhi*. There is no sin attached with the enjoyment of one's desired objects, because it is absolutely necessary to pass one's life in this world, happily.

मन्त्रसंस्कृतकाष्ठादि देवत्वमधिगच्छति ।
किं पुनः ज्ञानवान् कायः कष्टं मोहविचेष्टितम् ॥ ११३ ॥
mantrasaṁskṛtakāṣṭhādi devatvamadhigacchati /
kiṁ punaḥ jñānavān kāyaḥ kaṣṭaṁ mohaviceṣṭitam // 113 //

113. Even a piece of wood when consecrated (*Mantra-saṁskṛtam*), attains the state of God; what to speak of the body which is endowed with knowledge. One caught in delusion is to be pitied.

प्राकृतत्वमहङ्कारं परित्यज्य समाहितः ।
प्रज्ञोपायविधानेन [69]क्रियामेतां समाचरेत् ॥ ११४ ॥
prākṛtatvamahaṅkāraṁ parityajya samāhitaḥ /
prajñopāyavidhānena kriyāmetāṁ samācaret // 114 //

114. One can be free from the influence of one's own natural ego, by being composed and by following the acts of Buddha through *prajñā* and *upāya*.

पंकजातं यथा पद्मं पङ्कदोषैर्न लिप्यते ।
विकल्पवासनादोषैस्तथा [70]योगो न लिप्यते ॥ ११५ ॥
paṅkajātaṁ yathā padmaṁ paṅkadoṣairna lipyate /
vikalpavāsanādoṣaistathā yogo na lipyate // 115 //

115. The mud never taints the lotus originated in the mud; similarly a Yogi, living in the world of pluralities of the impression of the world, is never tainted by these defects. The Yogi's mind is cleansed of all those dichotomies which confuses and attaches his mind to the world of things.

[विकल्पो बिम्बसङ्काशो दृष्टिदोषैर्न लिप्यते ।
अम्भसा लिप्यते नैव यद्वदुदकचन्द्रमाः] ॥ ११६ ॥
[*vikalpo bimbasaṅkāśo dṛṣṭidoṣairna lipyate /*
ambhasā lipyate naiva yadvadudakacandramāḥ] //116 //

[69]क्रियामिमांङ्गसमाचरेत् ।
[70]योगी ।

116. As the moon reflected inside the water is not defiled by the water; the defects of the sight never defile the objects of the world, which are like reflected images.

अनादिवासनापङ्कैर्विलिप्तं चित्तरत्नकम् ।
प्रज्ञोपायजलेनैव [क्षालितं सम्प्रकाशते] ॥ ११७ ॥
anādivāsanāpaṅkairviliptaṁ cittaratnakaṁ /
prajñopāyajalenaiva [kṣālitaṁ samprakāśate] // 117 //

117. Because of its association with the mud of beginningless *vāsanās* (impressions), the mind, which is like a gem, is defiled. When it is cleansed with *prajñā* and *upāya*, it will shine in its original nature.

स्वाधिदैवतयोगस्य स्थिरचित्तस्य धीमतः ।
मुक्तः कुदृष्टिमेघैश्च् भासते चित्तभास्करः ॥ ११८ ॥
svādhidaivatayogasya sthiracittasya dhīmataḥ /
muktaḥ kudṛṣṭimeghaiśca bhāsate cittabhāskaraḥ // 118 //

118. To a wise person, associated with the personal God, having a steady mind, and the clouds of maligned vision are removed, the sun of *citta* shines forth.

प्रज्ञालक्ष्मपरिच्छेदे भूतार्थस्य विनिश्चयात् ।
धर्मधातुरुपादेयोऽविद्याव्यत्ययवर्जनात् ॥ ११९ ॥
prajñālakṣmaparicchede bhūtārthasya viniścayāt /
dharmadhāturupādeyo'vidyāvyatyayavarjanāt // 119 //

119. When the mind is delimited with a delimited object, there arises the certitude about an existing object. In order to remove the mass of ignorance (*avidya*), one has to accept the *dharmadhātu*. The mind is having the inherent notion of getting attached to things on its apprehension, and that it is getting limited by the objects that gestalt it as real and eternal. To transcend this problem one has to realise the *dharmadhātu* of things.

प्रज्ञामुद्गरविध्वस्ते सहसा कल्पनाघटे ।
प्रकृत्या निर्मलः स्वच्छो ज्ञानदीपः प्रकाशते ॥ १२० ॥ ।
prajñāmudgaravidhvaste sahasā kalpanāghaṭe /
prakṛtyā nirmalaḥ svaccho jñānadīpaḥ prakāśate // 120 //

120. The hammer in the form of *prajñā* can destroy the pot (the illusory world of objects); the knowledge, like a lamp pure,

transparent and clear by nature, shines forth. The knowledge here is the knowledge acquired after the *prajñā* and *upāya* are commingled, the *vajrajñāna*.

सुप्रसिद्धानि भूतानि क्षित्यग्निजलवायवः।
क्रियन्ते ह्यन्यथा विज्ञैर्मन्त्रसामर्थ्ययोगतः॥ १२१ ॥

suprasiddhāni bhūtāni kṣityagnijalavāyavaḥ /
kriyante hyanyathā vijñairmantrasāmarthyayogataḥ // 121 //

121. It is well-known that the existent world is made of the elements like earth, fire, water and air; the wise man, with the mastery of *mantras*, could be able to creatively transform them.

सर्ववादं परित्यज्य मन्त्रवादं समाचरेत्।
यस्य मन्त्रस्य सामर्थ्यात्सौख्यभावोऽपि सिद्ध्यति॥ १२२ ॥

sarvavādaṁ parityajya mantravādaṁ samācaret /
yasya mantrasya sāmarthyātsaukhyabhāvo'pi siddhyati // 122 //

122. One has to resort to the efficacy of Mantravāda, which is superior to all other practices, and it helps one to attain mental quietude.

[७१]त्रिरत्नं न परित्याज्यं बोधिचित्तं तथा [७२]गुरुः।
न [७३]वध्याः प्राणिनः केऽपि समयान्यप्यधिष्ठयेत्॥ १२३ ॥

triratnaṁ na parityājyaṁ bodhicittaṁ tathā guruḥ /
na vadhyāḥ prāṇinaḥ ke'pi samayānyapyadhiṣṭhayet // 123 //

123. The three gems, Buddham, Dharmam, and Saṅgham; the *guru*, and the *Boddhicitta*; the principles of no-harm no-injury to other living beings, one should follow these cardinal principles that are ruled by teachings. The Ethical teaching of Buddhism is cosmopolitan and they are devised according to the teachings of the Buddha.

[७४]मधु रक्तं सकर्पूरं रक्तचन्दनयोजितम्।
[७५]मुनिवज्रोदकं चैव पञ्चैतान्यप्यधिष्ठयेत्॥ १२४ ॥

[७१]स्त्री रत्नं।
[७२]गुरुम्।
[७३]ह्यत्मा।
[७४]महारत्न।
[७५]अलि वज्रादिकश्चैव।

madhu raktaṁ sakarpūraṁ raktacandanayojitam /
munivajrodakaṁ caiva pañcaitānyapyadhiṣṭhayet // 124 //

124. The materials like liquor (*madhu*), blood (*raktam*), and pure camphor (*karpūram*), red sandal, and *munivajrodakaṁ* are the five adjuncts which are important.

अन्यश्च [७६]समयैर्दिव्यैश्चित्तस्योत्कर्षकारकैः ।
मारुतक्षोभशान्तार्थं प्रोणयेच्चित्तवज्रकम् ॥१२५॥
anyaiśca samayairdivyaiścittasyotkarṣakārakaiḥ /
mārutakṣobhaśāntārthaṁ proṇayeccittavajrakam // 125 //

125. In other times, to keep the *citta* elevated and to keep the vital airs under control, one should depend on the *cittavajrakam*. This is perfectly denoting the importance of spiritual practices and observance of certain subtle aspects like controlling the vital airs in the body should be performed some other time than one realises the *Bodhicitta*, where one has to give full attention and concentration.

[नाशुचिभाव आशङ्क्योऽविकल्पयोगलीलया ।
समायुक्तेऽन चित्तेन मन्त्रो सर्वं समाचरेत्] ॥१२६॥
nāśucibhāva āśaṅkyo'vikalpayogalīlayā /
samāyuktena cittena mantro sarvaṁ samācaret // 126 //

126. Because of the operation of the confused thoughts (*vikalpas*), one should not think that he is impure; the one who mastered the *mantras* and having an equipoise mind shall perform everything in the world.

मक्षिकापदमात्रेण विषेणाप्यभिभूयते
अणुमात्रा घृणा [७७]शङ्का मृत्युकष्टेन संयुता ॥१२७॥
makṣikāpadamātreṇa viṣeṇāpyabhibhūyate /
aṇumātrā ghṛṇā śaṅkā mṛtyukaṣṭena saṁyutā // 127 //

127. The poison generated by the fall of a fly (in food) can create poisoning and the difficulties thereof; an iota of doubt can create suffering equal to death. It is the nature of the mind to gestalt anything that come as a part of the thought chain;

[७६]समयैर्द्रव्यै ।
[७७]घृणां लज्जां दूरतः परिवर्ज्जयेत् ।

the doubt can be configured into pain equal to that of the hell.

सुयुद्धं वाचरेद्विज्ञः सुपलायनमेव वा।
आन्तरालिकभावस्तु व्यर्थो वै पतनं भवेत्॥१२८॥

suyuddhaṁ vācaredvijñaḥ supalāyanameva vā /
āntarālikabhāvastu vyartho vai patanaṁ bhavet // 128 //

128. Either a wise man fights a battle, or he make an honourable exit; the stage in between is dangerous that it can lead one to fall.

गुरोराज्ञाञ्च मुद्राञ्च छायामपि न लङ्घयेत्।
गुणास्तस्य परं ग्राह्या दोषा नैव कदाचन॥१२९॥

gurorājñāñca mudrāñca chāyāmapi na laṅghayet /
guṇāstasya paraṁ grāhyā doṣā naiva kadācana // 129 //

129. One should not transgress the commands of one's preceptor, nor one should not forget his *mudrās*, or even his shadow; the preceptor's merits and good qualities have to be followed, not his bad qualities.

आचार्यः परमो देवः पूजनीयः प्रयत्नतः।
स्वयं वज्रधरो राजा साक्षाद्रूपेण संस्थितः॥१३०॥

ācāryaḥ paramo devaḥ pūjanīyaḥ prayatnataḥ /
svayaṁ vajradharo rājā sākṣādrūpeṇa saṁsthitaḥ // 130 //

130. The preceptor is the supreme deity for an adept, has to be worshipped, as he is none other than the King of the *vajra* (the *vajradhara rājā*) who can be directly perceived.

यथोदकमणिः शुद्धः कलुषोदकशोधकः।
श्रद्धामणिस्तथा प्रोक्तथित्तरत्नविशोधकः॥१३१॥

yathodakamaṇiḥ śuddhaḥ kaluṣodakaśodhakaḥ /
śraddhāmaṇistathā proktathittaratnaviśodhakaḥ // 131 //

131. The gem called Udhakamaṇi cleanses the impure water; in the same manner, the gem in the form of *śraddhā* can clean the mind. The Tāntric spiritual practices requires a substantial amount of concentration and attention from the part of the adept that only through the perfection of concentration one could achieve *cittaviśuddhi*.

श्रद्धावान् मुह्यते[७८] कोऽपि प्रज्ञाचक्षुर्विवर्जितः।
उत्पादयेदतः प्रज्ञामागमाधिगमात्मिकाम्॥१३२॥

śraddhāvānmuhyate ko'pi prajñācakṣurvivarjitaḥ /
utpādayedataḥ prajñāmāgamādhigamātmikāṁ // 132 //

132. Having *śraddhā* and because of the lack of vision in the form of *prajñā,* some aspirants get deluded, and hence, one has to create the *prajñā* by churning the Āgamas and Adhigamas. The Mādhyamikas are not against the authority of text, as they support the use of text as a reference material to know about the experiences of the Yogis who have gone through such practices. The knowledge should be received from any reliable source; at the same time they object the authority of the texts as the only source of knowledge.

श्राद्धो बहुश्रुतः प्राज्ञः प्रकृत्या करुणात्मकः ।
जगद्दुःखविनाशाय सुखोपायं स विन्दति ॥ १३३ ॥

śrāddho bahuśrutaḥ prājñaḥ prakṛtyā karuṇātmakaḥ /
jagadduḥkhavināśāya sukhopāyaṁ sa vindati // 133 //

133. A wise person who is endowed with the natural compassion by nature, having *śraddhā*, and well read, he alone can suggest the suitable *upāyas* to destroy sufferings of the mankind, and he could also suggest suitable *upāyas* for obtaining happiness· A Bodhisattva through his practice of spiritual disciplines suggests suitable *upāyas* to the normal human beings transform themselves from the sufferings of the world.

चित्तविशुद्धिमाधाय यन्मयोपार्जितं [७९]सुखम् ।
चित्तविशुद्धिमाधाय तेनास्तु सुखितो जनः ॥ १३४ ॥

cittaviśuddhimādhāya yanmayopārjitaṁ sukham /
cittaviśuddhimādhāya tenāstu sukhito janaḥ // 134 //

134. With the purification of the mind, I have obtained *cittaviśuddhi* and immense happiness; let that happiness be attained by everyone through *cittaviśuddhi.*

॥कृतिरियमार्यदेवपादानामिति ॥

kṛtiriyamāryadevapādānāmiti //

Colophon: This work has been written by the venerable Āryadeva.

[78]The *guru* in Tāntric tradition is considered as the embodiment of the supreme deity; the human form of the one who can redeem him from the world of suffering.

[७९]पूज्यते ।

Bibliography

1. *Important (Source) Texts by the Early Mādhyamikas*

Āryadeva, *Cittaviśuddhi-prakaraṇa*, compiled with an Introduction by Haraprasad Śāstrī, *Journal of Asiatic Society of Bengal*, 1898.

—, *Cittaviśuddhi-prakaraṇa*, edited from Tibetan and Sanskrit sources with Introduction and the Full text in Sanskrit by Prabhubhai Bhikhabhai Patel, *Viśva-Bhāratī*, 1949.

—, *Hastavālanāma-prakaraṇavṛtti*, edited from Tibetan sources with Verse to Verse translation, Interpretations, Commentary, and Notes by Fernando Tola and Carmen Dragonetti, in *On Voidness*. Delhi: Motilal Banarsidass, 1995.

—, *Catuḥśataka*, edited from Sanskrit and Tibetan sources with Introduction, Verse to Verse explanation, Commentary, and Notes by Karen C. Lang. Copenhagen: Akademisk Forlag, 1986.

—, *Akṣaraśataka and Ṭīkā*, edited from Tibetan and Chinese sources with English translation and Commentary by Karen C. Lang, *Buddhist Philosophy form100 to 350 AD*, in *Encyclopedia of Indian Philosophies*, VIII, ed. Karl H. Potter. Delhi: Motilal Banarsidass, 1999.

—, *Śataka*, edited from Kumārajīva's Chinese translation by Karen C. Lang with chapter in English, *Buddhist Philosophy from 100 to 350 AD*, in *Encyclopedia of Indian Philosophies*, VIII, ed. Karl H. Potter. Delhi: Motilal Banarsidass, 1999.

Nāgārjuna, *Vigrahavyāvartinī*, edited from Sanskrit text with Introduction, Verse to Verse translation and explanation in Sanskrit and English by E.H. Johnston, Kamaleswar Bhattacharya, and Arnold Kunst. Delhi: Motilal Banarsidass, 1978.

—, *Mūlamādhyamikakārikā*, edited from Sanskrit text as a treatise and Verse to Verse translation and Notes by David J. Kalupahana. Delhi: Motilal Banarsidass, 1995.

—, *Yuktiṣaṣṭikārikā*, edited from Sanskrit and Tibetan texts with Introduction and Translation by Fernando Tola and Carmen Dragonetti, in *On Voidness*, Buddhist Traditional Series. Delhi: Motila' Banarsidass, 1995.

—, *Śūnyatāsaptatikārikā*, edited from Sanskrit and Tibetan sources with Introduction, Explanation, and Notes by Tola Fernando and Carmen Dragonetti, in *On Voidness*, Buddhist Traditional Series. Delhi: Motilal Banarsidass, 1995.

—, *Ratnāvalī*, edited from Sanskrit and Tibetan sources with Introduction and Explanation by Christian Lindtner and Karl H. Potter, *Buddhist Philosophy from 100 to 350 AD*, in *Encyclopedia of Indian Philosophies,* VIII. Delhi: Motilal Banarsidass, 1999.

2. *Translations and Modern Works*

Banerjee, Anukul Chandra, *Studies in Chinese Buddhism*. Calcutta: Firma KLM, 1977.

Barrow, D. John, *Impossibility, the Limits of Science and the Science of Limits*. London: Oxford University Press, 1988; New York: Vintage, 1999.

Bedi, Rajesh, *Sadhus—The Holy Men of India*. New Delhi: Brijbhashi Printers and Publishers,1991.

Benard, Elisabeth Anne, *Chinnamasta, the Awful Buddhist and Hindu Tāntric Goddess*, Buddhist Traditional Series. Delhi: Motilal Banarsidass, 1994.

Bharati, Agehananda, *Tantric Traditions*. Delhi: Hindustan Publishing Corporation, 1993.

Bhattacharya, B.K., *Logic, Value, and Reality*. Calcutta: Calcutta University, 1961.

Bhattacharya, N.N., *The History of Tantric Religion*. New Delhi: Manohar Publishers, 1982.

Bhikṣu, Thich Minh Chau, *The Chinese Madhyama Agama and the Pāli Majjhima Nikāya*: A Comparative Study, Buddhist Traditional Series. Delhi: Motilal Banarsidass, 1991.

Blake, Randolph and Robert Sekuler, *Perception*. New York: Alfred A Knopf Publishers, 1985.

Briggs, Weston George, *Gorakhnāth and the Kānphaṭa Yogis*. Delhi: Motilal Banarsidass, 1938.

Bu-ston, *History of Buddhism*, trans. E. Suzuki. Research Foundation Reprint Series, 5. Heidelberg, 1931.

The Cambridge Dictionary of Philosophy, ed. Robert Audi. London: Cambridge University Press, 1995.

Croucher, Michael, *The Way of the Warrior*. London, Bandom: 1986.

Dasgupta, Surendranath, *A History of Indian Philosophy*, 5 vols. Delhi: Motilal Banarsidass,1975.

Dasgupta, S.B., *An Introduction to Tantric Buddhist*. Berkeley & London: Shambhala, 1974.

Deshimaru, Taisen, *The Zen Way to the Martial Arts*. trans. Nancy Amphoux. New York: E.P. Dutton, 1982.

Dialogues of Plato, ed. Justin Kaplan. New York: Washington Square Press, 1950.

Eckel Devid, Malcolm,*Jñānagarbha's Commentary on the Distinction between the Two Truths*. New York: State University of New York Press, 1987.

Edgerton, Franklin,*Buddhist Hybrid Sanskrit Grammar and Dictionary*, vols. I and II. New Delhi: Munshiram Manoharlal Publishers, 2004.

Eliade, Mircea, *Yoga: Immortality and Freedom*, trans. Willard R. Trask. New York: Pantheon Books, 1958.

Fatone, Vincente, *The Philosophy of Nāgārjuna*. Delhi: Motilal Bnarsidass, 1981.

Ginsberg, Mitchell, *The Far Shore, Vipāsanā: The Practice of Insight*. Delhi: Motilal Banarsidass, 1991.

Goldman, Jonathan, *Healing Sounds—The Power of Harmonics*. Cambridge, Mass.: Element Books, 1992.

Goswami, Amit and Maggie Goswami, *Science and Spirituality—A Quantum Integration*. New Delhi: Munshiram Manoharlal Publishers, 1997.

Gribbin, John R., *Watching the Universe*. Hyderabad: University Press, 1998.

—, *In Search of the Big Bang: Quantum Physics and Cosmology*. Toronto and New York: Bantam Books, 1986.

Guenther, Herbert V., *Life and Teaching of Naropa*. London: Oxford University Press, 1963.

—, *Matrix of Mystery, Scientific and Humanistic Aspects of rDzogs-chen Thought*. London: Shambhala, 1984.

—, *Philosophy and Psychology of Abhidharma*. Delhi: Motilal Banarsidass, 1974.

—, *Yuganaddha—The Tāntric View of Life*. Banaras: Chaukhamba Sanskrit Series Office, 1952.

— and Chogyam Trungpa, *The Dawn of Tantra*, ed. Michael Kohn. London: Shambhala, 1988.

Haṭhayoga-pradīpikā of Swātmārāma, Practical Commentary by Viṣṇu Devānanda. Delhi: Motilal Banarsidass, 1987.

Hawking, W. Stephen, *A Life in Science*. New York: Penguin Books, 1992.

—, *A Brief History of Time—From the Big Bang to Black Holes*. London: Bantam Book, 1998.

— and Roger Penrose. *The Nature of Space and Time*. Delhi: Oxford University Press, 1997.

Highfield, Roger and Peter Convey, *The Arrow of Time*. London: Flamingo, 1991.

Hiriyanna, M., *Outlines of Indian Philosophy*. Delhi: Motilal Banarsidass, 1993.

Hoffman, J. Frank, *Rationality and Mind in Early Buddhism*. Delhi: Motilal Banarsidass, 1995.

Honderich, Ted, *The Philosophers*. New York: Oxford University Press, 1995.

Huxley, Aldus, *The Perennial Philosophy*. New York: Harper & Row Publishers, 1944.

Jayathilake, K.N., *Early Buddhist Theory of Knowledge*, first edn., London: George Allen & Unwin, 1963; reprint, Delhi: Motilal Banarsidass, 1998.

Johnston, E.H., *Early Sāṅkhya*, first edn. London: Royal Asiatic Society, 1937; reprint, Delhi: Motilal Banarsidass, 1974.

—, Kamaleswar Bhattacharya, and Arnold Kunst, *The Dialectical Method of Nāgārjuna—Vigrahavyāvartinī*. Delhi: Motilal Banarsidass, 1978.

Junjiro, Takakusu, *The Essentials of Buddhist Philosophy*, first edn., Honolulu: University of Hawaii, 1947; reprint, New Delhi: Munshiram Manoharlal Publishers, 2001.

Kalupahana, David J., *A History of Buddhist Philosophy*. Delhi: Motilal Banarsidass, 1994.

—, *Buddhist Philosophy*—A Historical Analysis. Honolulu: University of Hawaii Press, 1976.

—, trans., *Mūlamādhyamikakārikā* of Nāgārjuna (*The Philosophy of the Middle Way*). Delhi: Motilal Banarsidass, 1995.

Kashyap, Bhikkhu J., *The Abhidhamma Philosophy—The Psycho-Ethical Philosophy of Early Buddhism*. Delhi: Bharatiya Vidya Prakashan, 1982.

Keith, A.B., *Buddhist Philosophy in India and Ceylon*. Oxford, 1923; reprint, New Delhi: Munshiram Manoharlal Publishers, 1979.

Kloetzli, W. Randolph, *Buddhist Cosmology*. Delhi: Motilal Banarsidass, 1983.

Kochumuttom, A.Thomas, *Buddhist Doctrine of Experience*. Delhi: Motilal Banarsidass, 1999.

Lad, Vasant, *Ayurveda: The Science of Healing*. Santa Fe: Lotus Press, 1984.

Lama, Anagarika Govinda, *The Psychological Attitude of Early Buddhist Philosophy*, first edn., Britain, 1961; reprint, Delhi: Motilal Banarsidass,1991.

Lang, Karen C., *Aryadeva's Catuḥśataka*. Copenhagen: Akademisk Forlag, 1986.

Lopez, S. Donald, *Buddhist Hermeneutics*. Delhi: Motilal Banarsidass, 1993.

Max Müller, F., ed., *The Sacred Books of the East*, vol. XLIX, first edn., London: Oxford University Press, 1894; reprint, Delhi: Motilal Banarsidass, 1965.

Matilal, Krishna Bimal, *Logic Language & Reality*. Delhi: Motilal Banarsidass, 1985.

Misra, Rajnish Kumar, *Buddhist Theory of Meaning and Literary Analysis:* Emerging Perceptions in Buddhist Studies. New Delhi: D.K. Printworld, 1995.

Mohanty, J.N., *Essays on Indian Philosophy—Traditional and Modern*, ed. Purushottama Bilimoria. New Delhi: Oxford University Press, 1993.

Murti, T.R.V., *The Central Philosophy of Buddhism*: A Study of Mādhyamika System, first edn., London: George Allen & Unwin, 1955; reprint, New Delhi: Munshiram Manoharlal Publishers, 2003.

Nakamura, Hajime, *Ways of Thinking of Eastern Peoples, India, China, Tibet, Japan*, rev. edn. by Philip P. Wiener. Osaka: KUFS Publication, 1980.

Nārada, Thera, *The Buddha-Dharma or the Life and Teachings of the Buddha*, first edn., 1942; reprint, New Delhi: AES, 1991.

Narain, Harish, *The Mādhyamika Mind*. Delhi: Motilal Banarsidass, 1997.

Nishimura, Eshin Unsui, *A Diary of Zen Monastic Life Drawing*. Honolulu: University of Hawaii Press, 1974.

Pandit, M.P., *Thoughts of a Śākta*. Madras: Ganesh & Co., 1977.

—, *Studies in the Tantras and the Veda*. Madras: Ganesh & Co., 1973.

Park, Bae Sung, *Buddhist Faith and Sudden Enlightenment*, Bibliotheca Indo-Buddhica Series, no. 90, first edn., New York: State University of New York, 1983; reprint, Delhi: Sri Satguru Publications, 1991.

Patañjali Yogasūtras, ed. Prabhananda Swamy. Madras: Sri Ramakrishna Math, 1953.

Pritchard, W. Edgar, *The New Dialectics in Theory and Practice*. Perth: Pritchard, 1952.

Radhakrishnan, S., *Hindu View of Life*, first edn., 1927; reprint, New Delhi: HarperCollins India, 2000.

—, *The Basic Writings*, ed. Robert A. McDermott. Bombay: Jaico Publishing House, 1972.

—, ed., *The Dhammapada*. New Delhi: Oxford University Press, 1950.

Raju, P.T., *Introduction to Comparative Philosophy*. Delhi: Motilal Banarsidass, 1992.

Ramanan, K. Venkata, *Nāgārjuna's Philosophy as presented in the Māhāprajñāpāramitāśāstra*. Delhi: Motilal Banarsidass, 1975.

Rizzi, Cesare, *Candrakīrti*. Delhi: Motilal Banarsidass, 1988.

Russell, Bertrand, *History of Western Philosophy*. London: Routledge, 1946.

Śāntideva's Bodhicaryāvatāra, trans. Andrew Skilton and Kate Crosby. Oxford and New York: Oxford University Press, 1996.

Santina, Peter Della, *Mādhyamika Schools in India*. Delhi: Motilal Banarsidass, 1986.

Seal, Brajendranath, *The Positive Sciences of the Ancient Hindus*. Delhi: Motilal Banarsidass, 1985.

Singh, Sarva Daman, *Ancient Indian Warfare*. Delhi: Motilal Banarsidass,1965.

Speake, Jennifer, ed., *A Dictionary of Philosophy*. London: Pan Books,1978.

Stcherbatsky, Theodore, *The Conception of Buddhist Nirvāṇa*, first edn., Varanasi, 1968; reprint, New Delhi: Motilal Banarsidass, 1999.

Subramanian, V.K., ed., *Saundaryalaharī of Śaṅkarācārya*. Delhi: Motilal Banarsidass, 1977.

Suzuki, D.T., *Studies in the Laṅkāvatārasūtra*, first edn., London, 1930; reprint, New Delhi: Munshiram Manoharlal Publishers, 2007.

Tārānātha's History of Buddhism in India, ed. Debiprasad Chattopadhyaya. Delhi: Motilal Banarsidass, 1970.

Tillemans, Tom J.F., *Materials for the Study of Āryadeva, Dharmapāla and Candrakīrti*. Wien: Arbetiskreis für Tibetische und Buddhistische Studien Universitat Wien, 1990.

Tirukkural, ed. Rev. W.H. Drew and Rev. John Lazarus. New Delhi: Asian Educational Society, 1989.

Tola, Fernando and C. Dragonetti, *On Voidness*—A Study on Buddhist Nihilism, Buddhist Traditional Series. Delhi: Motilal Banarsidass, 1995.

—, eds. and trans., *Nāgārjuna's Refutation of Logic (Nyāya) Vaidalyaprakaraṇa*. Delhi: Motilal Banarsidass, 1995.

Tomio, Nagaboshi Shifu, *The Bodhisattva Warriors*. Delhi: Motilal Banarsidass, 2000.

Tuck, P. Andrew, *Comparative Philosophy and the Philosophy of Scholarship—On the Western Interpretation of Nāgārjuna*. New York and Oxford: Oxford University Press, 1990.

Watanabe, Fumimaro, *Philosophy and Its Development in the Nikāyas and Abhidharma*. Delhi: Motilal Banarsidass, 1953.

Wayman, Alex and F.D. Lessing, *Introduction to the Buddhist Tantric Systems*. Delhi: Motilal Banarsidass, 1968.

Weinberg, Steven, *Dreams of Final Theory*. London: Vintage, 1993.

Wood, E. Thomas, *Nāgārjunian Disputations—A Philosophical Journey through an Indian Looking Glass*. Delhi: Sri Satguru Publications, 1994.

Woodroffe, Sir John, *The Principles of Tantra*, pts. I and II. Madras: Ganesh & Co. 1990.

—, *Introduction to Tantra Śāstra*. Madras: Ganesh & Co., 1990.

— and M.P. Pandit, *Kulārṇava Tantra*, first edn., 1965; reprint, Delhi: Motilal Banarsidass, 1984.

3. *Journals and Other Publications*

Baggini, Julian, "Michael Dummett Interviewed," *The Philosopher's Magazine on the Internet*. Source: http://www. philisophers.co.uk.

Burri, Jean-Pierre, "The Moral Consequences of the Big Bang Philosophy." Source: http://www. BigBang.org / September 1999.

Chalmers, J. David, "The Content and Epistemology of Phenomenal Belief," *New Scientist*, February 26, 1994.

Cooper, David, "What is Existentialism," *The Philosopher's Magazine on the Internet*. Source: http://www.philosophers.co.uk.

The Encyclopaedia of Philosophy on Internet, "Ancient Greek Scepticism." Source: http://www.paradox.ucsc.edu.

Frank, Edler, "Reductio ad absurdum (reduction to absurdity)," *Metropolitan Community College*, Omaha, Nebraska. Source: http://www.metropo.-mccneb.edu.

Guy, Bugault, "On Śūnyatā," *Journal of Indian Philosophy*, Amsterdam.

Hawking, W. Stephen, "Quantum Cosmology, M-theory and the Anthropic principle ," Lecture at the University of Cambridge, copy published, http://www.damtp. cam.ac.uk/user/hawking.

—, "Does God Play Dice?" Source: http://www.damtp.cam.ac.uk/user/hawking.

Heisenberg, Werner, "Physics and Philosophy, the History of Quantum Theory," *Journal of the Royal Institute of Philosophy*, 1958. Source: http://www.royalinstitutephilosophy.org

Hoversten, Paul, "Relics of Universe's Birth Found," *USA Today*, April 24, 1992.

Ian, C. Johnston, "An Exploration of the Constitution and the Mechanical Origin of the Entire Structure of the Universe Based on Newtonian Principles." Source: http://www. philosophers.co.uk.

Kelly, L. Ross, "Immanuel Kant on Space and Time," *Journal of the School of Advanced Study—Philosophy Program*, University of London. Source: http://www.sas.ac.uk/philosophy.

Kuhn, S. Thomas, "The Structure of Scientific Revolutions," synopsis by Frank Pajares. Source: http://www.philosophers.co.uk.

Maffei, Paolo, "The Universe in Time," Cambridge, The MIT Press, 1989.

Mary, Klages, "Structuralism/ Post-structuralism Source," *The Philosopher's Magazine on the Internet*. Source: http: www.forum-philosophy.org.

Misra, Godabarisha. "Dissolution of Mind and Erosion of Impressions," *The Voice of Śaṅkara*, vol. 25, nos. 1 & 2, 2000.

Noble, John Wilford, "Big Bang Ripples Observed," *New York Times*, February 1, 1994, col. 6: 4.

Peebles, James P., "The Evolution of the Universe," *Scientific American*, October 1994, p. 52(6).

Yang, Jiou Lee, "Soren Kierkegaard," *The Philosopher's Magazine on the Internet*. Source: http://www.philosophers.co.uk.

Index